Joe R. and Teresa Lozano Long Series
in Latin American and Latino Art and Culture

Kitchenspace

Women, Fiestas, and Everyday Life in Central Mexico

Maria Elisa Christie   *Foreword by Mary Weismantel*

University of Texas Press ♦ Austin

Copyright © 2008 by the University of Texas Press
All rights reserved
Printed in the United States of America
First edition, 2008

Requests for permission to reproduce material from this work
should be sent to:
    Permissions
    University of Texas Press
    P.O. Box 7819
    Austin, TX 78713-7819
    www.utexas.edu/utpress/about/bpermission.html

∞ The paper used in this book meets the minimum requirements
of ANSI/NISO Z39.48-1992 (R1997) (Permanence of Paper).

Library of Congress Cataloging-in-Publication Data
Christie, Maria Elisa.
   Kitchenspace : women, fiestas, and everyday life in central
Mexico / Maria Elisa Christie. — 1st ed.
      p.   cm.   (Joe R. and Teresa Lozano Long series in Latin
American and Latino art and culture)
   Includes bibliographical references and index.
   ISBN 978-0-292-71794-7 (alk. paper)
   1. Fasts and feasts—Mexico. 2. Kitchens—Mexico. 3. Mexico—
Social life and customs. 4. Social networks—Mexico. 5. Women—
Mexico—Social conditions. I. Title.
   GT4814.A2C47   2008
   394.1'20972—dc22   2007038703

Para mi madre, Maruja Terremoto

Contents

Foreword

At the Kitchen Table   Mary Weismantel

"As I interview her from my seat at the kitchen table . . ." So begins a typical paragraph in Maria Elisa Christie's warm and engaging ethnography, *Kitchenspace: Women, Fiestas, and Everyday Life in Central Mexico*. That conjuncture of "interview" and "kitchen table" in the same sentence captures this book's dual qualities: it is one of those rare works that manages to be both serious social science, and a warm and intimate look at everyday life in a very particular place and time.

Dr. Christie did indeed spend many hours sitting at kitchen tables, and she invites us to do the same. But not just so that we can learn how to make bean tamales "with a navel"—one of the many wonderful glimpses of central Mexican cuisine that she provides. In addition to being an enjoyable read, this is an academic study, not a cookbook, nor a memoir of a year spent in an exotic locale. It is the result of serious anthropological research on a serious topic: kitchenspace, a neglected but critically important "site of gendered social and cultural reproduction."

Much of the book's appeal comes from the author's deft and comfortable placement of herself in the text. Her approach is personal and reflexive, in keeping with recent trends in ethnographic writing, especially among women of color—but not obsessively so. She is not anguished about her role, as some authors have been; she does not share her racial or class-based guilt with us, or write long paragraphs about the inherent power inequalities in the researcher's role. Instead, she speaks frankly and easily about her difficulties conducting this study as a single mother, and about her own background as a Spaniard in Mexico—a background that gave her the linguistic tools to do her work, but also marked her as a racial and ethnic outsider.

"Güera," "güerita" they called her at first, especially the men—"blondie," a Mexican slang word that can have unpleasant racial connotations, though sometimes it is also used fondly. In response, she referred to the women and men she worked with politely and appropriately. In the text, she calls the older women "doña" and the younger ones by their first names; and when she talks about overcoming the initial reserve and even hostility of the women she worked with, her sensitivity, common sense, and simple good manners make it easy to see why she eventually found her seat at the kitchen table. Rather than writing about the power imbalance that can cripple good ethnography, she pragmatically sets out to overcome it, presenting herself to the reader and to her informants as the appreciative student, rather than the intimidating social scientist with a clipboard.

This attitude is illustrated by my favorite quote, describing one of the many times she showed up in a woman's kitchen to administer a questionnaire:

> When I arrive for her interview, I am treated to an affectionate reception as she insists on braiding my hair before we start. Apparently I strike her as in need of care.

There are many ways we might imagine interactions between an uneducated Mexican woman and a Spanish researcher who is pursuing doctoral research at an American university, but few are as disarming as this picture of the older woman seating her young visitor firmly in a chair, comb in hand. And the authors' wry final comment, "Apparently I strike her as in need of care," strikes an amused and self-deprecating note that I like a great deal.

There is a similarly deceptive simplicity at work in the question of what this book is about. Just as the tangled and potentially fraught questions that arise when doing research across national, ethnic, and class lines find their resolution in a freshly braided head of hair, the kitchen tables at which Maria Elisa Christie conducted her research provide access to the much larger, more complex and difficult social worlds of contemporary Mexico. The notion that food and women's cooking are key symbols of culture is one that many of my students, especially those of Latino, African American, and Jewish descent, affirm with great conviction—but they have a difficult time articulating exactly how and why this is so. Social theorists have not always done much better, although historical studies such as Sidney Mintz's magisterial book on sugar, and archaeological research that establishes the deep roots of Mexico's connection to corn go far to explain the ways that food links us to our collective past. At the same time, studies of the rapid and often deleterious transformation of our food habits brought on by changes in the economics of food production, distribution, and consumption, such as Eric Schlosser's *Fast Food Nation* or Marion Nestle's *Food Politics*, document processes that are unmaking that history in seemingly irrevocable ways. This book builds bridges between several of these perspectives on food. It links the inarticulate but keenly felt personal assertions that kitchens are at the heart of culture, and the more systematic views of scholars, researchers, and journalists. And it explores the real-life juxtapositions that lie behind our contrasting images of Mexican food: the indigenous woman on her knees, grinding corn with a *mano y metate* as women have done in Mexico for thousands of years, and ubiquitous and now-iconic fast food items such as "nachos" that reduce the proud food tradition of Mexico to a pile of greasy chips drenched with garish neon-orange cheese.

The three communities where Maria Elisa Christie did her work are themselves poised between those two extremes, and this book provides a memorable snapshot of that conflicted position between tradition and modernity. (In fact, the women themselves speak in precisely these terms in describing their kitchens.) The three communities of Ocotepec, Tetecala, and Xochimilco (the site of the famous floating gardens, a remnant of the vast *chinampa* hydroponic farming system that once provisioned the Aztec city of Tenochtitlan), are close to major urban areas, and far from the more indigenous regions that often capture the imaginations of tourists and anthropologists alike—Oaxaca, Chiapas. The lives, dilemmas, and kitchenspaces documented here will resonate more with the memories and experiences of most U.S. Latinos and most Mexicans than those more exotic locales. Although the scale is much smaller, geographically, and the perspective more intimate, I was reminded of Eric Wolf's tender portrait of Mexico, *Sons of the Shaking Earth*, which likewise pays close and loving attention to the central zone.

Like that classic text, this book, too, in its own way provides a broad and dynamic panorama of the Mexican experience. Through her focus on cooking, the author opens a window onto multiple cultural and social domains. The first half of the book documents life at the community level through a look at festivals. Here, we see how despite constant and relentless change, some things are still important—not only the festivals themselves, but also the ferocious political battles over prestige long ago documented by anthropologists as the "ritual-political hierarchies" of festival sponsors. These still rage—and will continue to do so, if the thirty-year-long list of future sponsors for one celebration, the Niñopa, is any gauge.

Just as significantly, her book chronicles social life within households: in the first part of the book, and more so in the second, we catch glimpses of the problems caused by men's drinking and domestic violence, as well as of intergenerational conflict. And we gain insights into kinship patterns that Americans might find surprising. We all know that Mexicans value family—but we forget that "family" is not always and everywhere the same. Relations between women in the kitchen highlight the sometimes forgotten fact that Mexican families such as these are *not* the kind of nuclear families often assumed to be universal by Anglo-Americans, but something larger, more dynamic, and more complex. Christie provides a good summary statement about this in the last chapter, but some of her comments along the way are just as informative, as when she points out how common it is for an unmarried sister, rather than a wife, to be the woman running the kitchen in a household.

There are also insightful and evocative discussions of gender, such as Christie's comment that "given the combination of sensual pleasure and motherly nurturing in kitchenspace, the bonds between mother and son sometimes take on an almost incestuous quality at the table." The strength of mother-son bonds, and their preeminence over those between husband and wife, are aspects of Mexican and Mexican American culture (and other cultures as well) that have been commented upon elsewhere; here, we see their origins within kitchenspace. I like to tell my students that before they rush to judge Mexican culture as "more sexist" than Anglo American culture, they need to consider *all* the relationships between women and men, not just dating and marriage—and relations between women as well. It is worth noting that in the kitchen, youth and beauty are not the criteria of femininity that matter: as Christie points out, this is a place where wives lose out to mothers every time.

This study of central Mexican kitchens illuminates social, economic, and ecological processes that originate far outside the household, not by moving beyond or outside of kitchenspace, but precisely by retaining a close focus on it. Her study demonstrates a point I made long ago, that cooking is a powerful—and powerfully gendered—nexus that connects the household to the larger world in all its material and symbolic dimensions, including both the social and the ecological worlds that lie beyond four (or three!) walls.

In the beginning, the author describes how she initially planned to study environmental change, but turned to kitchens because of her desire to work with women. Sometimes the path away from one's goal ends up leading back to it: by focusing on the day-to-day cooking practices of women in semi-urban environments, she ends up providing a detailed picture of exactly how urban sprawl, the loss of farmland, polluted waterways, new work patterns, and changing cultural mores impact local ecologies and human health. In the end, we know an enormous amount about these changes—and, by looking at them from the space of the kitchen, we see them from the inside out, as everyday experiences and intimately familiar, inescapable processes.

Rather than the loss of wilderness, here we see the loss of backyard pigs, who previously functioned as living recycling units, consuming stale tortillas and leftover food that now add to the mounds of garbage that municipalities struggle to handle. Rather than the dramatic dietary changes experienced by migrants, here we see the steady inroads that meat and store-bought tortillas are making on a diet that is still far more home-cooked and healthy than what many of us eat, but that is far less so than it was within living memory. (It is noteworthy that male physicians and female patients alike accept the notion that "traditional" dishes are to blame for a diet that has become too "greasy," rather than the enormous increase in red meats at the expense of vegetables, and the replacement of stone-ground with store-bought carbohydrates.) In focusing on these semi-urban areas, and on small-scale transformations that nonetheless have large environmental and biocultural impacts, this book provides an important dimension to our understanding of the totality of ecological transformations underway in Mexico and across the continent.

Although this study has an elegiac tone at times, mourning lifeways, ecologies, and kitchenspaces increasingly endangered by dubious forms of progress, it keeps close enough to its informants' point of view to stay honest. Modernity is liberating as well as destructive, and there is nowhere better to see its contradictory effects than in the kitchen. In the same breath, these Mexican women decry the loss of traditional values and the "laziness" of a younger generation unwilling to spend hours on kitchen drudgery—and yet extol the labor-saving products available to them today, and complain bitterly about the unremitting servitude of a life spent in the kitchen. Furthermore, like contemporary people elsewhere, they are keenly aware of these acute contradictions—contradictions that also show up in the attitudes of their new, wealthy neighbors, who complain about unpleasant aspects of rural life such as smelly pigs in backyards, but are the most fervent participants in festivals that celebrate rural culture and regional cuisine.

One of the most significant contributions this book makes to the study of food and cooking, and to our understanding of Mexican culture and society, is in the use of handmade maps drawn by the women themselves of their kitchenspaces. The maps, and perhaps more importantly that process of making them and the conversations that accompanied their making, are rich and telling. This technique elicited lovely, detailed information about the kitchens, and drew information out from the women that they otherwise found difficult to articulate. The questions they asked before making their drawings call attention to the multiple ambiguous but meaningful boundaries that exist between inside and outside, public and private, yard and house, gardening and cooking, male and female realms, modern and traditional, everyday and festival practices. The kitchenspaces they inhabit are open and closed, big and small, in ways that the urban and suburban middle-class U.S. kitchens portrayed in television and the movies are not.

Ultimately, *Kitchenspace: Women, Fiestas, and Everyday Life in Central Mexico* is a book-length reflection on one further dichotomy, one as ambiguous and provocative as any of the others. This is the question of female power and powerlessness. The kitchen, as Christie portrays it, represents both. It is the source of women's pride, and the locus of a rich and treasured cultural tradition expressed in beliefs about the living souls of tamales and the unique *sazón* of individual women or of women from particular families. At the same time, it is a prison that traps women into endless drudgery, and forces them into work perceived as lacking prestige or value.

The women themselves are eloquent on this topic. But so, too, are several of the most memorable images and themes that emerge in descriptions of kitchenspace. One is the behavior of men while they are there:

> Men came, waited to be served, ate, and left . . . They spoke little, never interrupted the woman of the kitchen, and left their dishes on the table.

The ambiguity of this behavior is striking: the men appear simultaneously as dismissive of the life of the kitchen and the woman who runs it as they are intimidated into silence by it.

Perhaps most expressive of the difficulty in reading any single meaning into the kitchenspaces of Ocotepec, Tetecala, and Xochimilco is the central concept that cooking must be performed with devotion and with joy. The image of women dancing to keep the food happy is a delightful one; and the notion that the same woman who begins stirring a demanding dish must stay with it until it is finished speaks to the significance that is accorded to the cook. But these ideas have their oppressive side. It is funny when an older man comments that the young cook must have been angry to have made such a spicy dish—but it is also a warning that female emotions must be contained. Women spoke repeatedly of the need to prevent discord from entering the kitchen lest it spoil the food—and by extension, of their own need to remain—or at least act—contented despite sometimes stultifying situations, in order to maintain harmonious family life. The desire for a good meal, and a happy family, and the conviction that only a knowledge-able and devoted woman at work in the kitchen can provide those two most valuable and pleasurable of things, is both the source of these women's greatest power and joy—and a force that keeps them from seeking those qualities elsewhere. It speaks to the author's talents as a writer that she is able to portray this dilemma so clearly and eloquently here. And it is a tes-tament to her honesty that, although she makes a compelling case for the value of the central Mexican kitchenspace for the women who cook there (and their fortunate families, who eat such delicious fare on a daily basis), she also lets us see that like a great mole, the ingredients that make up this rich and fragrant space are both bitter and sweet.

Preface

In the spring of 1986 I wandered into an alley in one of the traditional barrios of Xochimilco looking for a place to live. The acute housing shortage that followed the September 1985 earthquake in Mexico City—and the birth of my first son two months earlier—had made it difficult to find a reasonably priced rental, and I had been searching for months just outside the city. That day several women had congregated around a makeshift kitchen full of enormous clay and aluminum pots over firewood hearths on the side of the street or, more precisely, at the end of the main alley. They were enjoying the camaraderie, talking and laughing as they waited for the tamales to finish cooking, stirring the pots as needed. The celebration, which they called *un ocho días* (an eight days), marked the one-year anniversary of a man's death. Like the year before—and many to come—it involved neighbors, family, and extended kin sharing food and drink over an entire week. Moments after I arrived, a teenaged girl plucked my baby from my arms and I was welcomed into the barrio with a plate of tamales and a cup of *atole* (a hot corn drink).

Little did I know then how frequent ritual celebrations were in Xochimilco, always involving food. A relative newcomer to Mexico, I had been in the country for nearly a year; but my Spanish origin and years in Central America and the Caribbean did little to prepare me for the food and fiestas that I would find there. In my years of residence in the barrio, the sight of women cooking together outdoors—and the sound of fireworks announcing a parade or fiesta—formed part of the texture of everyday life. If not for the massive quantities and mouth-watering quality of the food, and the otherwise closed nature of the neighborhood, I might have come to take Xochimilco's elaborate fiestas for granted. Instead I thoroughly enjoyed the pleasure of joining in as a guest at the consumption stage of fiesta after fiesta for the next six years and on many recurring visits after that. When I returned in 2000 as a graduate student intent on carrying out a year of ethnographic fieldwork for my dissertation, I was committed to participating in earlier stages of the fiesta. I hoped to join the women preparing the food, something that proved much more difficult to achieve yet infinitely more rewarding.

Living in Xochimilco may have provided me with an exaggerated appreciation for the importance of food and women's role in community celebrations; but later, when my dissertation committee encouraged a comparative approach including two other sites, the focus on food preparation spaces proved to be a unique and fertile approach to exploring nature and society relations in central Mexico. It also allowed me to explore gendered spaces too often left out of such studies.

Despite the key role of women and food in community celebrations, however, it would be misleading to portray these as the only essential factors. For this reason, this book includes many "ingredients" that fall outside the parameters of kitchenspace. As with cuisine, each element is important in combination but irrelevant alone. I also present individuals and events as interrelated with others: I hope to make clear that women are members of households and communities, special events are part of the fabric of everyday life, and particular activities combine with others that give the ensemble meaning within their social and spatial contexts. When one family hosts a celebration, extended social networks in the community are activated to provide the necessary labor and resources for success and are strengthened in the process.

Acknowledgments

While I alone am responsible for the shortcomings of this book, many people contributed to its production and deserve recognition. First and foremost, I thank the women in Xochimilco, Ocotepec, and Tetecala who hosted and befriended me and whose stories and spaces I share with readers here; without their generosity there would be nothing more to say. The work of many scholars who came before me made this a valid dissertation project before it became a book manuscript. Some of them are cited here, and others go unmentioned: I am grateful to them all.

While it is the people of Xochimilco who drew my attention to the cultural and social significance of food and fiestas in their community, my earliest intellectual debts are to the professors associated with Women's Studies at the University of Oregon, who first exposed me to feminist research frameworks and women's histories and writings. Had it not been for Mavis Mate's undergraduate history courses on Women in Social Movements and Barbara May's focus on Spanish women authors, I might never have proposed to my doctoral committee at the University of Texas at Austin a study of gendered spaces and narratives associated with food preparation. Their encouragement and their willingness to allow me the flexibility to consider "whatever goes into the pot" are a tribute to their openness to new ideas and the scholarship of Latin Americanist, feminist, and cultural geographers who have preceded me. I would like to thank my chair, Greg Knapp, and the other members of my committee: Karl Butzer, Bill Doolittle, and Steve Hoelscher at the University of Texas and David Stea at Texas State University. I also wish to acknowledge Julie Tuason, who, though only on my committee for a short time, provided invaluable guidance during my literature review of feminist geography and research methods.

I am eternally grateful to my mentor, Clarissa Kimber, professor emeritus of geography at Texas A & M University, for encouraging me to "call a fork a fork and a spoon a spoon." I appreciate her friendship, scholarly example, wit, and encouragement. Miles Richardson at Louisiana State University and Sidney Mintz at Johns Hopkins University inspired me with their work and were gracious enough to meet with me and discuss my ideas.

I owe special thanks to three advisors in Mexico who guided me during my fieldwork: Cathy Good Eshelman at the Escuela Nacional de Antropología e Historia, Margarita Velázquez Gutiérrez at the Centro Regional de Investigaciones Multidisciplinarias of the Universidad Nacional Autónoma de México (UNAM), and Juan Carlos Gómez Rojas of the Departamento de Postgrado en Geografía at UNAM. I am also grateful to my research assistants: Yazmín Flores Romero in Ocotepec, Martha Domínguez Nájera in Tetecala, and José Torres Medina in Xochimilco.

Preliminary research for this project was funded by the Tinker Foundation through the Teresa Lozano Long Institute of Latin American Studies (LLILAS) at the University of Texas. A Florence Terry Griswold Scholarship from the Pan American Roundtables of Texas and a FIPSE (Fund for the Improvement of Postsecondary Education) Trilateral Fellowship from the U.S. Department of Education partially supported my dissertation fieldwork. Funding sources from UT Austin were critical at various stages, including an International Education Fee Scholarship, the Liberal Arts Thematic Fellowship, a Veselka Travel Grant, and a Bruton Fellowship. A doctoral fellowship from the Austin branch of the American Association of University Women (AAUW) provided funds for the writing stage of my dissertation.

I thank my editors at the University of Texas Press for their patience and support and the anonymous reviewers for their helpful and critical comments. I am also very thankful for the excellent copyeditor who scrutinized the final text, made infinite corrections, and helped make it more readable.

Every single parent knows that a strong support network is essential to maintaining productivity, not to mention sanity. Many generous people in Austin and Mexico helped care for my children during my doctoral studies, sharing the challenges and joys of parenting and offering their time, friendship, and moral support. They are too numerous to name here, but I could not have done it without them.

Finally, but foremost, I thank *los tres* Navarrete Christie—Carlos Manuel, Juan Francisco, and Mario Antonio—for their humor, wisdom, and love; for keeping the link with Mexico alive; and for putting up with the sacrifices required of graduate students' children, particularly when they live in several worlds at once.

A Taste of Three Places

Xochimilco, Distrito Federal

Seven *comadres* (co-godmothers) sit in a circle, talking as they slit guajillo chiles open with iron nails and deseed them. Two huge *costales* (sacks) sit in the center. "Do we leave the veins in?" they ask. The hostess—Doña Consuelo—decides. Later we use Coca-Cola to wash our fingers—it works best, they all agree. But be careful who you touch, they joke. *Chalitos* (gooey pork rinds) from the freshly killed pig sit in a clay pot by the fire. We will be served *tacos de chales* on hot tortillas as well as pico de gallo. The host family's name is printed in gold letters on a basket covered with a hand-embroidered napkin. Over the fire is another huge clay pot: *la abuelita* (the grandmother) stirs the pasta in fried tomato sauce before adding chicken broth. This *sopa de pasta* will be served with the fried pork (*carnitas*) to those coming today for the house blessing. The new house was built for the Niñopa, a revered baby Jesus figurine, who will move in with his many trunks of clothes and toys.

Se vende chinampa (*Chinampa* for sale)

A priest will come to bless the house and costumes of the dancers (*chinelos*) and to warn against drunkenness. He is a real priest—not a chocolate priest (*cura chocolate*), as church officials call the impostors who sell their services for events outside church control, in people's houses and yards. The breeze changes and brings the smell of the pigs. Seventeen of them are left, to be slaughtered the coming week when *las tías* (the aunties) continue preparing the big feast for February 2, Día de la Candelaria—the day the new *mayordomos* (sponsors) receive the Niñopa for the year and people take their Niño Dios (Christ Child), children, and corn to be blessed at the church. Looking up from my work, I see flowers and cauliflowers on the *chinampa* (floating garden) across the canal. The water is barely visible under the scum on the surface. At the nearby Plaza de la Asunción, a sign announces: *Se vende chinampa* (*Chinampa* for sale).

Ocotepec, Morelos

Walking through town, I hear the loudspeaker blasting from the roof of a car, announcing another meeting to organize against the theft of Ocotepec's communal lands for the construction of a supermarket. We arrive at the house of Doña Dolores, where she makes tortillas by hand outside over her firewood stove. She has done so since she was eight, half a century ago, and sells them like many other women in this town, often to the city people from nearby Cuernavaca. Doña Dolores stands by her metate or grinding stone, using it to knead the dough by hand if no longer to grind it. She still boils her own corn with lime, but now she takes it to grind at the mill. The *comal* (griddle) is aluminum, though many in this town use clay, even if it is easily broken by children. Doña Dolores was born in Ocotepec, her grandparents as well, she stresses: she can tell me about the place. Her friend who brought me, Doña Isidra, is not from here ("no es de aquí"). Born in Puebla, she came as a child more than fifty years ago. We help with the tamales. As usual, the *vaporera* (steaming pot) has ears (corn husks tied on the handles), so that the tamales will not hear fighting or disagreement. Otherwise "se enojan" (they get angry) and won't cook right. We talk through the din of the hammers, as men build a house for younger family members, pouring cement beside the sleeping dogs. The land was all milpa (cornfield), Dolores tells me. Now there are houses. Soon her last cornstalks will disappear. "¡Qué triste!" (How sad), she says. "How will I live?"

Este terreno es propiedad comunal (This is communal property)

Tetecala, Morelos

This is *tierra caliente* (hot land), a place where people cross the street to walk in the shade on the other side. "Tetecala la hermosa, pura gente buena" (Tetecala the beautiful, only good people), people tell me. The fertile fields are covered with food. Anyone with a mango orchard here used to be rich. Things have changed. This year they tried using growth hormones to beat the flood of mangos from the southern state of Guerrerro to market—every day counts. Tomatoes have given way to flowers for export. Two weeks ago tomatoes sold at twenty pesos per kilo (about US$1.00 a pound) in Mexico City; today they sell for three. No one laments the days when they grew cucumbers and tomatoes, the seasons when they would let the townspeople take the harvest rather than lose money getting produce to market in Cuernavaca. Now flowers go to la Central de Abastos in Mexico City, Brazil, and other places far away, while U.S. and Japanese companies pay folks to grow okra for export. An *apantle* (irrigation ditch) brings water from the river to the fields. Pesticides flow back in, polluting the river—along with the dead dogs that people dump, angering some.

We walk through the fields full of black sapote (*Diospyros digyna* sensu lato), mangos, bananas, nopales (prickly pear), papayas, corn, beans, squash,

Squatter with a tractor-tire hearth in Tetecala

peanuts, and nardos (*Polianthes tuberosa*). On the edge of town lands, we find a woman outside a shack and children sitting with her around the stove. "From Yautepec," she answers our inquiry about her origin. Doña Eustoquia warns her against buying *tierras ejidales* (communal land). Firewood burns on the cement-filled tractor tire, with tortillas on the *comal*. Chickens cackle near her chile and epazote plants. Kind words notwithstanding, Doña Eustoquia is certain that the woman is up to no good, living on the outskirts like that. Good people live in the center. Why do the newcomers leave their communities in Guerrero and Morelos? No good reason, certainly.

Kitchenspace

INTRODUCTION

Kitchenspace

This book offers glimpses of women's lives and community celebrations in Xochimilco, Ocotepec, and Tetecala from the perspective of kitchenspace, a term I coined to describe my research site. For the purpose of this book, I define kitchenspace as the place where food is prepared, whether indoors or outdoors—usually a combination of the two. Kitchenspace is a privileged and gendered site of social and cultural reproduction, where society's relationship with nature is inscribed in the patterns of everyday life and ritual celebrations.

It became clear soon after initiating my fieldwork that "kitchen" or *cocina*—as used in Mexico as well as in the United States—was too narrow a term. The word "kitchen," defined as a "place with cooking facilities" (*Webster's Ninth Collegiate Dictionary*) or a "room or part of a room or building in which food is prepared and cooked" (Microsoft Word dictionary), and its contemporary connotations fail to incorporate the complexity and nature of the multiple spaces in which I found women preparing and cooking food. Describing the kitchen in an Andean village, Mary Weismantel (1998: 3) says that it is "the warmest and most central place in the Zumbaguan household, the heart of daily life." She puts "kitchen" in quotation marks to point out the inadequacy of the term in her study site.[1]

When I asked women to draw maps of their kitchens, they sketched an "everyday" kitchen (*la cocina de diario*) and a fiesta, firewood, or "smoke" kitchen (*la cocina de humo*), one usually overlapping the other. Several referred to the partially indoor, everyday kitchen as the "heart of the home," while the fiesta kitchen—usually outdoors in the house-lot garden—was periodically transformed into a center for community participation when they hosted a special meal. With the only water source and the firewood hearth usually located outdoors, everyday cooking activities for the family spill over into the house-lot garden, just as during fiestas the community spills over into the otherwise private space of the home (Christie 2004).

Kitchenspace is vital to maintaining traditional forms of women's organization. Gendered and embodied knowledge, including when and how to prepare certain foods, is selectively transmitted from one generation to the next along with the grandmother's mole (traditional sauce) recipe and many beliefs and rituals unique to kitchenspace.

For me, coming from a Western European tradition, the word *cocina* or "kitchen" brought to mind an indoor space with four walls and a roof. Yet the food preparation sites that I explored often had no walls at all; and even if they did, some of the kitchen work was nonetheless performed outdoors in the house-lot garden. I chuckled when Esmeralda, a young woman in Tetecala, complained aloud about not wanting to spend her life "dentro de estas cuatro paredes" (within these four walls) as she felt her family wanted her to do, because the space in which she prepared food all day long, day after day, had three walls and not four. While she clearly felt trapped by the social expectations that restricted her movement and options in life, the physical structure of her kitchen did not match her mental image and the social reality of a closed space.

The boundaries of kitchenspace are evidently defined by social activity and gendered relationships rather than by physical structures. Kitchenspace is to kitchen as gender is to sex—both are social constructions. My definition of kitchenspace is not dependent on any structure or cooking facility per se. Kitchenspace is created and maintained by the food preparation activity carried out by gendered subjects. In this sense, it provides a framework for the exploration of what Judith Butler (1990: 25) calls the "performative" nature of gender. At the same time, the shifting boundaries and temporal nature of kitchenspace indicate that it too, like gender, is constituted by performances (see Peake and Valentine 2003: 107–108). I consider various aspects of the interaction with nature in this gendered space, where changing cultural identities are negotiated, re-created, and celebrated as "tradition" is continuously redefined.

Kitchenspaces are women's domain. Men sit down to be fed, eat, leave their dishes on the table, and go out to the street to drink and talk. Inside the home, kitchens are not community spaces. It is there that individual women assert control over their world. The kitchen is one of the few places where men listen to women. And so women tell their stories over and over, to each other, to their children, perhaps to themselves. Kitchenspace,

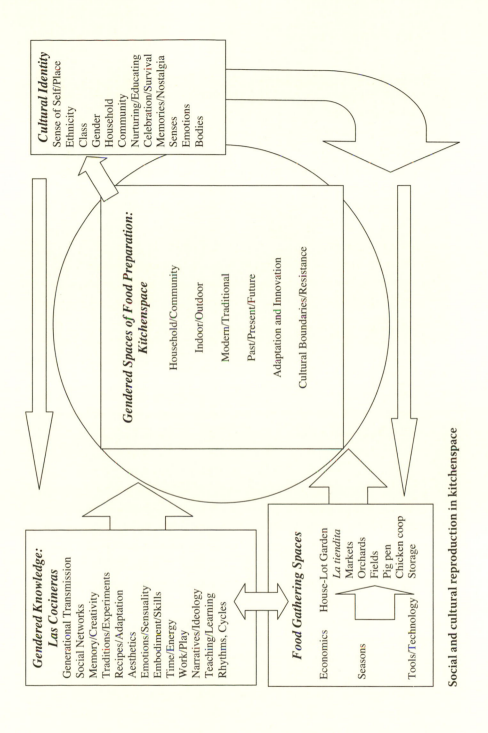

Cultural Identity
Sense of Self/Place
Ethnicity
Class
Gender
Household
Community
Nurturing/Educating
Celebration/Survival
Memories/Nostalgia
Senses
Emotions
Bodies

**Gendered Spaces of Food Preparation:
Kitchenspace**

Household/Community

Indoor/Outdoor

Modern/Traditional

Past/Present/Future

Adaptation and Innovation

Cultural Boundaries/Resistance

**Gendered Knowledge:
Las Cocineras**
Generational Transmission
Social Networks
Memory/Creativity
Traditions/Experiments
Recipes/Adaptation
Aesthetics
Emotions/Sensuality
Embodiment/Skills
Time/Energy
Work/Play
Narratives/Ideology
Teaching/Learning
Rhythms, Cycles

Food Gathering Spaces

Economics   House-Lot Garden
                      La tiendita
                      Markets
                      Orchards
Seasons   Fields
                      Pig pen
                      Chicken coop
                      Storage
Tools/Technology

Social and cultural reproduction in kitchenspace

Kitchenspace

including the spillover into the house-lot garden, is women's space or, more specifically, women's territory.

Nature

The initial question guiding my research was "How is nature in the everyday lives of ordinary women?" By this I mean how the natural environment plays a role in their lives in a larger sense, including a particular cosmovision and its celebration through ritual fiestas: the tamales that women make to celebrate the first ears of sweet corn at harvest time; the herbs, ornamentals, chickens, and pigs in women's courtyards; polluted rivers, canals, and fish; domesticated vegetables and "volunteer" plants that sprout in kitchen dump heaps. It encompasses anything that the women I worked with contemplated when they referred to "la naturaleza," including changes that they often experienced and lamented in kitchenspace.

In their book on cosmovision and the ritual identity of indigenous peoples in Mexico, Johanna Broda and Félix Báez-Jorge (2001: 16; my translation) define cosmovision as "the structured vision in which members of a community combine in a coherent manner their notions about the natural environment in which they live and the cosmos in which they situate human life." In my research communities, the symbolic reaffirmation of human dependency on nature is expressed in celebrations based on the agricultural calendar and careful observation of nature for centuries. Society's relationship with nature is mediated in part by the saints and other dead, who help bring rain to the fields for a bountiful harvest. Ritual foods are offered to the spirits on multiple occasions, including the extensive celebration for Días de los Muertos (Days of the Dead) in November,[2] to help ensure their intercession with the forces of nature on behalf of the living.

The Place: Three Communities in Central Mexico

The focus of my inquiry is the perspectives and practices of ordinary women in Xochimilco, Ocotepec, and Tetecala, all semiurban communities with roots in prehispanic Nahuatl culture. Reflecting the diversity that characterizes Middle America in general and Mexico in particular (West, Augelli, et al. 1989), each of these sites is unique in terms of ethnicity, physical geography, and cultural traditions, while sharing many cultural traits characteristic of Mesoamerica. Located along the Neovolcanic axis in the Mesa Central of the Mexican Plateau, they share a once-fertile lacustrine environment. Xochimilco, the northernmost of my three sites, lies just south of Mexico City. Tetecala, the farthest south, is located in the adjoining state of Morelos near its borders with the states of Guerrero and Mexico. Ocotepec, just outside of Cuernavaca, the capital of Morelos, is located adjacent to the Chichinautzin nature reserve, approximately sixty kilometers from both Xochimilco and Tetecala. Traveling at least part of the distance on the Autopista del Sol (the toll road that connects the nation's capital with Acapulco), it takes approximately two hours to drive from one end of my sites to the other. An extensive network of buses, *rutas,* and *colectivos* (collective taxis or minivans) connects the three as well—with Cuernavaca and Mexico City as obligatory transfer points—and is the most common form of public transportation for residents of the region.

Given the changing and heterogeneous nature of Xochimilco, Ocotepec, and Tetecala, my references to them as "communities" throughout this work by no means imply a homogenous unit of people with identical interests or behaviors (Agrawal 1997; Gujit and Shah 1998). To the contrary: gender, generation, ethnicity, class, and other differences are important and are reflected in food preparation practices and spaces, among others. I have not found a better word than "community" to use here. I would prefer the word *pueblo* (village) to community and also use it on occasion, but it does not have an appropriate counterpart in English and indeed can have negative connotations in Spanish: *gente de pueblo* (village people) implies something like "hicks" in American English, reflecting the antirural bias existing in the United States as well as in Mexico. In addition, "village" brings up the specter of the anthropologists' idea of poor, "primitive" people with quaint customs that have not changed for centuries and the classic studies of Tepoztlán, Morelos, by Robert Redfield (1930) and Oscar Lewis (1960, 1963). My research communities are bound together by shared practices and history, including centuries of *mestizaje* (mixing of Spanish and indig-

Map of research sites.

enous elements) and the discrimination of rural and indigenous elements that has long characterized Mexico.

Despite the pervasive economic hardship in my region of work, I do not like to use the term "poverty" or "poor" to describe the communities or people who live there. Such a term seems to deny the resourcefulness that I observed. In the context of central Mexico, poverty is often defined by urban standards and carries an implicit condemnation of traditional culture as well as an assumption that anybody with sense should aspire to new technologies, rampant consumerism, and other components of "progress." By U.S. standards most of the people with whom I worked would be considered "poor," and indeed many of them considered themselves *pobres* (poor people), *gente humilde* (humble people), or simply *trabajadores* (workers). But they differed considerably in terms of resources (income or otherwise), which was always evident in kitchenspace. Significantly, however, all of them drew on rich extended family and community networks for support and had unshakable faith in their ability to survive in the future.

My sites are more representative of Latin America's increasingly urban society than are the tropical rainforests often targeted for environmental research and conservation by the international scientific community. Tropical biodiversity is concentrated in northern and southern Mexico, but the majority of the population historically has been concentrated in the central highland. Together with industrial and agricultural activities, this puts tremendous pressure on the natural environment. Research about people's relationship with nature in this region can provide insights into comparable Latin American contexts where indigenous and mestizo peoples face new challenges upon migrating to urban centers in search of a living. The growth of nearby cities—aptly called *la mancha urbana* (the urban stain) in Mexico—transforms their communities into suburbs, bedroom communities, or periurban areas (Ávila Sánchez 1997, 2005; Canabal Cristiani 2000; Losada et al. 1998; Rueda Hurtado 2001; Torres Lima 2000). In a world now over 50 percent urban—with Latin America in particular an overwhelmingly and increasingly urban society (Doolittle et al. 2002)—scholars and policymakers alike will have to grapple with new dimensions of human interaction with the natural environment. "Urban" populations in developing countries often retain many aspects and spaces of nonurban culture (WinklerPrins 2002), creating what scholars in Latin America have called *la nueva ruralidad* (the new rurality) (Ávila Sánchez 2005; Giarracca 2001).

Perhaps no category is as important in Xochimilco, Ocotepec, and Tetecala as whether a person is *de aquí* (from here). "Belonging" or not is a matter of significant tension and reflects some of the complexities and contradictions inherent in any notion of collective identity. In all three sites, belonging is defined to a great extent by the relationship to the land. In Xochimilco and Ocotepec it is reaffirmed through participation in community fiestas. People whose ancestors worked the land for generations under traditional land tenure systems (communal, *ejido, chinampera*) consider themselves and are considered by others to be members of the community.[3] Whenever I interviewed people who were not born in Xochimilco, Ocotepec, or Tetecala, they would immediately clarify that they were not legitimate spokespersons. "No soy de aquí" (I am not from here), I heard many times over from people who had spent most of their life in the community in question. People who are "from here" make it clear to people who are not that their voices are not representative of local interests.

Particularly in relation to decisions over local land—exacerbated by the 1992 amendment to Article 27 of Mexico's Constitution that allowed for the sale of previously inalienable *ejido* (collective) land (Nuijten 2003)—locals deny "newcomers" the right to participate in community forums, regardless of how many years they may have lived in the town.[4] Xochimilco and Ocotepec share a history of organized resistance to changes in land and water use resulting from the growth of the city—Mexico City or Cuernavaca, the capital of the state of Morelos (Canabal Cristiani et al. 1992; Rueda Hurtado 1998, 2001). The struggles of Tetecala, far from urban centers and surrounded by ex-haciendas and large expanses of private land devoted to agriculture, have been different. Producers large and small have suffered from economic restructuring and deteriorating market conditions. One person there said to me that mangos used to be like gold, whereas returns are so low now that most townspeople have had to abandon their orchards and fields.

Nonetheless, the three communities share an agricultural tradition with a diversity of expression. People in Xochimilco have been producing flowers, vegetables, and corn in raised-bed agriculture for over five hundred years; the *chinampas* are still the basis of the region's intensive agriculture (Crossley 1999; Ezcurra 1990; Rojas 1990) as well as cultural identity (Canabal Cristiani 1997). In contrast, Morelos, and especially the agricultural region surrounding Tetecala, has been known for its rice and sugarcane plantations since shortly after the arrival of the Spaniards in the sixteenth century. Its smallholder agriculture and campesino (agrarian) tradition gave rise to the national agrarian hero of the Mexican Revolution, Emiliano Zapata (Sarmiento Silva 1997; Warman 1976). Tetecala is considered to have had significant agriculture as early as 1594, and it was a market for the sale of locally grown sugarcane, banana, jicama, Mexican plum, watermelon, *mamey* (*Pouteria sapota*), corn, and beans by the late nineteenth century (Rangel Montoya 2000).

In each of my sites, multiple economic crises and disastrous agricultural policies of the type that have crippled much of the Mexican countryside have forced many people to abandon their land. The population pressure and urbanization in the first two sites have led to tremendous land speculation, from which many locals have been able to profit. Few people in Tetecala today can afford to make a living from the land unless they rent it out to foreign companies or plant cane for the nearby Bacardi plant in Zacatepec—an economic activity that is less common than before. Because of the rise in the price of land as well as the distance from large markets (*centrales de abasto*) and the collapse in agricultural prices, many people there have been reduced to hiring themselves out for low wages on their own land alongside cheaper labor from the south of Mexico. Surprisingly (and probably due to its history as a political center), Tetecala has a more urban character and identity, even though 80 percent of the economically active population in the municipality is involved in agriculture and animal husbandry, according to an internal report by the municipal government in 2001.

The geographic location of Xochimilco and Ocotepec, on the periphery of large urban centers, is important here. People's discourse in these two communities upholds the values of their rural and indigenous roots even as they prefer to downplay such roots in order to benefit from their relationship to the city and modernity. Townspeople's historical and ongoing resistance to the "theft" of their water and land by the neighboring city as well as, paradoxically, the benefits that they receive from its proximity help sustain their fiestas, which they view as a clear expression of who they are and who they are not. They complain that the city "is swallowing" them— and indeed housing is undoubtedly replacing agricultural lands and urban values are infiltrating their communities. Most people in Xochimilco and Ocotepec are able to stay there, however, thanks in part to the employment (however marginal) and markets provided by Mexico City and Cuernavaca.

Meanwhile Tetecala, though still the commercial and political center of its region and historically at the trade crossroads for merchants from the states of Morelos, Mexico, and Guerrero, is increasingly off the beaten path. It has lost most outside visitors to the Acapulco toll road, which bypasses the town and thus discourages people from visiting the springs and a historic resting place for the Empress Carlota, Tetecala's main tourist attractions. More importantly, now people rarely pass through on their way to the Grutas de Cacahuamilma and the popular silver-mining town of Taxco in nearby Guerrero, which were once reached by the old highway that goes through Tetecala.

The antiurban discourses of Xochimilco and Ocotepec reflect their location at the periphery of urban centers that have historically encroached on their lands and water. In contrast, Tetecala finds itself in the paradoxical position of being at the center of a region that is increasingly weakened by its peripheral relationship to important economic and demographic centers. Unlike the other two communities in my study, its agrarian identity is not buttressed by a contradictory relationship to a city that offers painful but patently beneficial economic alternatives to living off the land.

One woman from Tetecala called it a sad town (*un pueblo triste*). Indeed, unlike my other sites, which have increased opportunities despite the chaos of rapid growth, Tetecala seems to be a town in decline. Construction of a new university campus there was halted soon after it began, leaving a scar on the landscape, emblematic of the lack of options for young people; most of them leave town to seek opportunities elsewhere. In many ways, my research communities reflect the urban bias characteristic of national policies and the painful transition that Mexico is attempting in its aim to be a "modern" nation able to compete with others in an era of free trade.

Residents in each of my sites purchase the majority of their food. In all three, however, some people—primarily older men—still plant subsistence corn and beans and a little produce. A man in Ocotepec told me that planting your own corn today has more sentimental value than economic value. People grow corn for ritual use as well (as we will see in the harvest for the Niñopa in Xochimilco) and attach tremendous symbolic and emotional significance to their cornfield or milpa. Many people—women in particular—raise animals for food, primarily as an economic strategy in prepara-

tion for a particular celebration. In all three sites, most people recognize
and appreciate the taste of truly fresh food.

The changing nature of the population, particularly with rural to urban migration and migration to the United States, constantly redefines the
boundaries of each of my communities. Sometimes, as in the case of Don
Miguelito in Chapter One, rural migrants come to the city (Mexico City,
Cuernavaca, or Tetecala) in search of work but end up as agricultural laborers in the semiurban periphery. The collective identity in each of my sites—
to the extent that they have one—is based in part on marking the boundaries not only in relation to relative newcomers but in contrast to neighboring
towns such as Tepepan in the case of Xochimilco, Ahuatepec in the case of
Ocotepec, and Coatetelco in the case of Tetecala. In all three, this contrast
with the "other" nearby community is often described in terms of culinary
traditions, though it is based in part on historical conflicts over territory
and natural resources.

For the purpose of my work and in relation to collective identity, the
barrio (neighborhood) is more important than the town or pueblo. All of
the collective food preparation activities for community celebrations that
we explore in this book are linked to a particular barrio, not a town. Traditional barrios have their roots in the prehispanic *calpulli* (land of the clan),
in which residents held land in common. These barrio-like units formed
the basis for territorial organization and the extraction of tribute (*tequitl*).
More importantly, the *calpulli* were of sacred origin and linked to the "gods
called *calpulteteo,* whose intervention guaranteed the fertility of the land"
(Rueda Hurtado 1998: 17). Not all of these barrios are traditional or based
on a *calpulli,* but the *mayordomos* in barrios that are not (for the Santa
Cruz celebration in Ocotepec and the Candelaria celebration in Tetecala)
nonetheless use traditional forms of barrio organization in order to host the
meal.

All three of my sites are prehispanic in origin, with names derived from
Nahuatl. Xochimilco means "where flowers are sown" (from *xochitl,* "flower"; *mil-li,* "cultivated earth"; and *co,* "place"). Ocotepec means "hill of the
pine tree" (*cerro del ocote,* from *ocotl/ocote* and *tepetl/cerro*), as illustrated
by its prehispanic glyph. Tetecala means "place with many houses with
stone vaults" (*tete,* "stone"; *tecali,* "house with vaults"; *la* or *tla* refers to a
large quantity; or Tetekalla, from *tete,* plural of "stone"; *kalli,* "house"; *tlan,*
a contraction meaning "abundant place").

Prehispanic glyph
of Ocotepec

The historical record shows that the Xochimilcas, one of the eight original Nahuatl groups to migrate from the mythical Aztlán to the Valley of Mexico, settled on the edges of Lake Tenochtitlan just after the collapse of the Toltec Empire in 1156 AD (Carlos Martínez Marín, cited in Maldonado Jiménez 2000: 244). From there, they spread to parts of Morelos beginning in 1300 and were one of three groups to settle in what is now Ocotepec. According to several accounts, the Tlahuicas—another of the eight groups from Aztlán—founded the first barrio in Ocotepec, which existed prior to the arrival of the Spaniards in the sixteenth century and is still known by its original name, Tlalnihuic,[5] as well as its official Spanish name, La Candelaria (Maldonado Jiménez 2000; von Mentz de Boege 1995). A sixteenth-century map of the parish of Cuernavaca shows Ocotepec to be one league outside of the city.

First founded by the Xochimilcas during the Aztec Empire in the last five hundred years before the arrival of the Spaniards (Hernández Cortés 1999), Tetecala first appears on a 1583 map referring to the pueblos that compose part of the *alcaldía mayor* (district) of Cuernavaca (Oriak Villegas 1997). Vestiges of prehispanic human settlement from the Olmec, Chichimec, and Tlahuica period have been found in the region. Years after an earthquake destroyed the town, the current settlement of Tetecala was founded in 1680 by mestizo and mulatto immigrants from Guerrero, fleeing abuses at the hands of the Spaniards. Becoming a municipality in 1821, it was officially declared a city by the government and acquired its current name of Tetecala de la Reforma in 1873.

The populations of the three sites differ in size, among other things. Xochimilco is much larger than Ocotepec and Tetecala put together. For this reason, and due to the prior relationships that facilitated my research, I chose to focus on only one of its seventeen traditional barrios (though I follow its inhabitants' networks where they lead me). It is a barrio considered particularly traditional by locals, a place where people maintain their customs ("ahí guardan las costumbres"). I have kept the name of the barrio out of this book, just as I have changed people's names to respect confidentiality. All three communities show an increase in population in recent years, even as they lose local population to outmigration. Xochimilco's population of 369,787 in 2000 (INEGI 2000a) had risen from 332,314 five years earlier and 116,493 in 1970 (Secretaría de Industria y Comercio 1971). Those numbers refer to the population of the Xochimilco *delegación* (including the town proper and the smaller villages). Tetecala's official population count in 2000 was 6,917 (INEGI 2000b), up from 4,514 in 1970 (Secretaría de Industria y Comercio 1971).

Cuernavaca (whose numbers include Ocotepec) went from 160,804 in 1970 (Secretaría de Industria y Comercio 1971) to 338,706 in 2000 (INEGI 2000b). Ocotepec's official population count stood at 8,451 in 1995 (INEGI 1995). While city authorities today consider it to be a *poblado* (small community) and subunit of Cuernavaca, Ocotepec is a community on the outskirts of the city known for its elaborate Days of the Dead celebrations and other traditional fiestas. A sign on the outskirts of town indicates that Cuernavaca is two kilometers away by road, though the city has recently grown to the edge of Santa Cruz (Holy Cross), one of the barrios explored here.

Common elements in all three places include changes in land use and livelihoods, markets replacing fields as a source of food, and changing gender roles, particularly as more young men and women obtain higher education or take jobs away from home. Yet many food traditions persist, even when the details of their preparation have evolved over time. Older women play an essential role and take pride in preparing food for their families and communities. Corn and beans remain fundamental staples in these once rural towns, and firewood is still used in cooking, if only for tortillas and fiestas.

Xochimilco, Ocotepec, and Tetecala all have been urbanized to different degrees. Their relationship to city life has changed over time, with an increasing insertion of the population into the urban labor market, the arrival of wave after wave of migrants from poorer regions in Mexico and refugees from the smog and pace of Mexico City, and heightened crime related to drugs, poverty, and government corruption. Despite the differences among the three sites, stemming in part from their proximity to Mexico City and relationship to the land, population growth and urbanization combined with inheritance patterns have had visible impacts on the traditional kitchen in all three. Nevertheless, each retains many rural traditions and attitudes that are in part maintained and revitalized through the constant arrival of campesinos from other regions.

"¡Aquí Es el Mole!"

Sense of place in Xochimilco, Ocotepec, and Tetecala—as in much of Mexico and indeed many parts of the world—is rooted in the flavors of culinary traditions that people associate with home—both pueblo and family. "¡Aquí es el mole!" (Mole is the thing here!) people would inevitably respond with gusto when I asked that they "tell me about this place" (*cuénteme de este lugar*). Regardless of the multiple variations, including *mole negro* (black mole) from Oaxaca, *mole poblano* (from the state of Puebla), or the many red and green moles in my research communities, mole is believed to have originated in a convent in Puebla during the colonial era. It is traditionally served with *guajolote* (turkey) and tamales for weddings and other important celebrations, including key agricultural fiestas and rituals. It may also be served with chicken or pork.

Mole (from the Nahuatl word *molli*, meaning concoction) is a thick, rich sauce made from various chiles (usually including pasilla, ancho, and mulato but sometimes even guajillo chiles); bread and tortillas; chocolate or cacao beans; almonds, sesame, and other seeds; raisins; cloves, pepper, cumin, cinnamon; and many other ingredients. (See the mole recipes in Chapters Two and Six and others in Hernández Cortés 1999; ISSSTE 1985; and Kennedy 1986.)

Mole is considered the quintessential Mexican fiesta dish throughout the central and southern part of the country. Yet several young women told me that they do not know how to make mole, because their *abuelita* (grandmother) always managed to send them away from the hearth on some errand at a crucial point during the elaborate process. Often the elderly guardians of the family recipe only relinquish it when they are ready to give up their strategic position in kitchenspace. Despite some young women's complaints about being kept out of the kitchen, plenty of others groaned at the excessive amount of work that mole requires and swore they would never stir the huge mole pot again. Preparing traditional fiesta food in central Mexico is unquestionably an arduous task that many women today are not inclined to take on, although some consider it an honor.

Fiestas, Reciprocity Networks, and Ritual Kinship

Food is at the heart of ritual celebrations marking life-cycle and seasonal transitions in Mexico. Women prepare special dishes for community fiestas revolving around representations of religious figures, *quinceañeras* (celebrations of a girl's fifteenth birthday; see Chapter Three),[6] family and community celebrations marking planting and harvest time, and more. Such celebrations depend on women's reciprocity networks for the various meals at their center and play a significant role in integrating different sectors of the population and forging or maintaining critical alliances within and beyond the community. They serve a social redistributive role; enhance the reputation of the host family, barrio, and community; and help maintain regional reciprocity networks. While the majority of people in each of my communities are Catholic, one of the relatively recent changes causing tension is the rise of evangelical groups, whose converts cease to participate in traditional celebrations. While this situation has led to violence in some rural communities in Mexico, in this region it has not done so, though some of the women I met expressed animosity, suspicion, fear, and sadness regarding the ensuing loss of traditions and changing alliances.[7]

Hosting a fiesta is a serious commitment requiring extensive social networks for support. Both the ritual fiestas of folk Catholicism which dominate the countryside and the life-cycle fiestas allow hosts to expand their support network and alliances through the system of ritual kinship or *compadrazgo* (godparenting). Besides blood relatives, women's networks include *comadres* (co-godmothers). Initially associated with sharing the responsibility for raising a child, the system of *compadrazgo* is an institution adopted from Spain and the Catholic church in the sixteenth century. It has evolved into a system of long-lasting reciprocity upon which people draw for support for a variety of things, including the preparation and costs of a special meal.

The fiesta is the result of months or years of accumulating necessary resources. This can be done by planting crops or raising animals, stockpiling ingredients, saving money, and obtaining formal commitments from others to share in the labor and expense. The final period of intensive work extends over several days or even weeks and involves various tiers of meals in addition to the principal *comida* (meal) around which women's organization revolves. Women gather in the house-lot garden, sitting in a circle around a table or a sack of dried chiles, tamarind, or hibiscus flowers, exchanging stories, strategies, and jokes as they work. The *mayordoma* (hostess in charge) supervises all tasks carried out by the women, who come together to volunteer services through formal arrangements. Each one fulfills her *comisión* (prearranged task) with a solemn sense of duty; I was never allowed to join in just because extra hands were needed. Instead I was always directed to the *mayordoma* so that she could use me as she saw fit. The *mayordoma* has the final word when questions arise and is responsible for the meal that will bring honor or shame onto her household and community, depending on its success. At the same time, she may personally cook a less expensive and simpler meal for the women who have come to help prepare the fiesta food; indeed she is required by tradition to feed them—and any accompanying children—for as long as they are providing what must be seen as community service.

In Xochimilco, where not a day goes by without a collective celebration, fiestas clearly form part of everyday life. Yet even in places that do not have such a hectic rhythm of celebrations, fiestas mark the communal social life and require extensive organization and preparation throughout the year. In his book on public celebrations and popular culture in Mexico, William H. Beezley cites a 1977 survey reporting "5,083 civil and religious occasions throughout the year in which no more than nine days go by without a fiesta somewhere in Mexico" (Beezley et al. 1994: xiv). In a scene typical of the region, the members of a neighborhood council meet on the day after a celebration in Ocotepec to make plans for the following year, writing down specific commitments and names and reading aloud the names of those who contributed to the fiesta that has just concluded (Chapter Two). A meal called the *recalentado* (reheated), made of the previous day's leftovers, is

Women of the circle: cleaning chiles for the mole

a key component of the event in this town. Among other things, the list compiled that day notes who will be responsible for cooking meals for the musicians and other special guests the next year.

Food preparation for fiestas forms part of an elaborate and traditional cargo system. The cargo system in indigenous communities in Mexico and its relation with traditional fiestas and cosmovision have been amply studied, though scholars tend to focus on men's role in political and religious cargos (Aguirre Beltrán 1991; Broda 1971, 1982, 1988, 1991a, 1991b, 1993; Broda and Báez-Jorge 2001; Cancián 1976; Korsbaek 1996; Medina 1987; Neurath 2000; Padilla Pineda 2000; Sepúlveda y Herrera 1974; Villa Rojas 1947). Those undertaking women-centered research in traditional communities, however, bring attention to women's roles as cargo holders, as in Lynn Stephen's *Zapotec Women* (1991) and Christine Eber's study of women in highland Chiapas (1995). Catharine Good Eshelman's paper on ritual food in an indigenous community (2001b) in the state of Guerrero, Mexico, also looks at the key role that women play.

Beverly Chiñas (1973, 1993) focuses on the Isthmus Zapotec region in southern Mexico, which has important differences from my region of study, including the relatively egalitarian relationship between the sexes there and the lack of steady income from wages or salary in most households at the time of her research. Her discussion of ritual contributions to fiestas as a form of mutual aid and means of gaining status is similar to what I found in Xochimilco and Ocotepec, however, though less so in Tetecala:

> Every ritual contribution, voluntary or otherwise, represents either the payment of ritual obligations or the prepayment toward ritual obligations the household anticipates at some future date, an on-going system in which a balance is never struck. But it is more than simple economic expediency which motivates people to make voluntary ritual contributions. Perhaps more importantly, contributions are a means of maintaining the household's status in the community. People who cooperate, who contribute as often as possible, even the poorest, will be spoken of as *buena gente* while households who refuse to participate or participate with reluctance will be ostracized. *"No corresponde,"* Juanecos say of such persons. "When he dies, there will be no one to carry him to the cemetery." To Isthmus Zapotecs who value so highly the security of kinsmen and neighbors a worse fate would be difficult to imagine. (Chiñas 1973: 77)

Chiñas concludes that despite attacks on the fiesta system by members of the mestizo culture who saw it as "wasteful and senseless,"[8] hosting what she refers to as "public fiestas" (for the saints) was still an important means of gaining the highest respect in the community. Later (Chiñas 1987: 10) she went so far as to call women "the heart of Isthmus Zapotec ceremonial exchange" and noted that the wife was the major initiator and instigator of fiesta sponsorship in all but one case known to her, even though the cargo was held in the husband's name. Chiñas (1987) reported that women's contributions in money and labor were much greater than men's and had increased in recent decades while men's had decreased. In part because of men's waning enthusiasm and participation, Chiñas (1973: 79) predicted that the reciprocal relationships behind the fiesta system "would probably decline," which she thought would be "especially tragic for the women."

Sponsorship of religious fiestas is the result of a *promesa* (vow) by the hosts to the religious figure. When the celebration is for the neighborhood patron saint or other key figure such as the Niñopa in Xochimilco (Chapter One), however, such commitments are formalized in writing in community forums. Individuals often make their vow in a time of crisis when praying for a holy figure to intercede on behalf of a family member or in thanks for what they consider a miracle or special gift resulting from divine intervention. The fulfillment of the vow brings prestige to the fiesta hosts and provides opportunities for other community members to contribute regardless of their wealth (with labor in kitchenspace, for example) and gain favor as well. Such *promesas* and further reciprocal aspects of the fiestas link Xochimilco, Ocotepec, and Tetecala with other communities in their region as they exchange commitments in support of celebrations. While some *mayordomos* agree to prepare food for a large number of guests or even to host a religious figure for an entire year, others make smaller commitments and may receive a group of pilgrims from another community with food or provide tortillas, fireworks, or candles for an event. In Tetecala, for instance, a neighboring community traditionally contributes the giant papier-mâché statues called *gigantonas* for an annual parade (Chapter Three).

A family's prestige is on the line when it hosts a fiesta for a popular religious icon; the entire barrio is judged by the decorations, fireworks, and food. The men organize to clean the streets, hang colored lights and streamers, and sometimes even paint the outside of the neighborhood houses in preparation. The women from the host barrio and the social networks of the hostess come together to prepare the food. Given the importance of food in the ceremonial cycle and collective identity and the gendered nature of ritual space, it is important to study women's role in fiesta food preparation, including not only the *mayordomas* who take on formal responsibilities in this area but the gendered networks that provide support. As stated in different words by many of the women whose voices I present here, without women's knowledge, networks, and hard work, collective celebrations—both sacred fiestas centered on religious figures and life-cycle celebrations such as baptisms, weddings, and ceremonies for the dead—would not have the meaning or form that we encounter today and an important community space would be lost.

Relationships

It is difficult to access either the semipublic space of the fiesta kitchen or the private space of the everyday kitchen on the more intimate terms required for ethnographic work. One senior researcher at the Morelos Institute of Culture warned me that it would be impossible, telling me that the "kitchen is the most reserved place of the home."[9] Personal connections, recommendations, and introductions were critical to my success, as were my patience and persistence, though I certainly did not always get what I wanted. Throughout my fieldwork, I was plagued by the contradictory sense of powerlessness on one hand, given the obstacles I sometimes encountered, and disproportionate power on the other. I was acutely aware of my option to leave behind the difficult circumstances of so many of the women I met and return to the material comforts and relative security that they would never know.

Spending so much time with people in the trenches, so to speak, and writing a doctoral dissertation on the food preparation activity that took so much of their time and energy was a way of validating women's work and experience. Some women remarked to others with pride that our conversations were to become part of a university *tesis*. Nonetheless, the bottom line is that the women's lives became fodder for my work, while I only contributed my friendship, a pair of hands, a few photographs, and answers to their questions about myself and about other towns' fiestas. Out of a desire to "give back," I wrote my first article on this work in Spanish (Christie 2002) and shared it with them so they could see and show others that their stories were in print, a testament to the importance of their contributions.

With many women, I earned their confidence in part through my participation in laborious kitchenwork activities during fiesta preparations. Building relationships took time, even in Xochimilco, where some never forgave me for having moved out of the neighborhood years before to go to the United States; they were further upset after my return that I left frequently to visit other communities. In fact, the greatest difficulty about working in three different sites was not the logistics of travel—further complicated by my childcare needs—but people's jealousy and desire to claim me as their own. This situation reproduced itself within each community as well, where a close relationship with one woman or household sometimes precluded a relationship with another. Not being fully immersed in one site was a constant reminder of my power to leave and avoid fully committing to any one group.

Gender roles weighed heavily in my research and my relationship with the women in this study. Sharing time and spaces with them included balancing different roles and joining their families with my own for recreational activities. Having children facilitated my relationships in the field, although my responsibilities as a single parent impeded the immersion I wanted. Parenting duties were fully acceptable and understandable to my hosts, much more so than my intellectual aspirations. My sons were present even when they did not accompany me, because of their importance as an organizing principle and common cultural denominator. When I could not stay to eat after spending the day preparing food in one household, my inappropriate and untimely departure was acceptable only because I was leaving to pick my kids up from school and because women were able to send food along for them. Not having children in the cultural context of my research sites would have made my work more difficult. Not having a husband was not so uncommon, though on occasion it created suspicion that I sought to prevent early in my fieldwork by wearing a wedding ring bought at a pawnshop before I left Austin.

My fluency in Spanish together with my own ethnic and religious identity helped me to overcome barriers as well. Born in Seville, Spain, I speak Spanish as my native language, though my accent long ago blended into something closer to Mexican than anything else as a product of having lived in Mexico for years. In the communities where I worked—and indeed throughout Mexico—I was usually called *la güera*—the Mexican term for light-skinned or blonde. While my father is American and I spent most of my school years in the United States, people identified me as Spanish and insisted on calling me *la españolita* (the diminutive makes this a term of endearment for a Spanish woman). Raised Catholic, I was comfortable with the expressions of faith that formed the context for most of the fiestas I was involved with. My experience in saying the rosary in Spanish—a practice I found painfully tedious as a child—turned out to be especially helpful.

Finally, I believe my willingness to learn from the women in my research communities as I blundered through tasks that fully revealed my incompetence helped people gain confidence in me or at least amuse themselves with my efforts. I laughed with them when they teased me about my lopsided tortillas and poorly wrapped tamales. When I helped make bean tamales for Palm Sunday in Ocotepec, the women giggled gleefully and told me that I was earning a degree in soaking corn husks.

My enthusiasm and interest in people's food customs and the pleasure with which I ate what they cooked facilitated friendly relations with both men and women. They were pleased and usually surprised that a person they identified as urban, educated, and of higher social status appreciated their food, including the blood sausage made from a freshly slaughtered pig. My early years in Mexico spent overcoming my vegetarianism at the hands of a carnivorous father-in-law from Michoacán—a state known for its excellent *carnitas*—paid off. Without a doubt, sharing a part of our lives and especially kitchenspace allowed us to get to know each other and overcome some of the distance separating us.

Writing This Book

Little did I know as I made the long drive back to Texas following my year of intensive fieldwork that the greatest challenges lay ahead. Indeed, they seemed to multiply as I attempted to organize my findings into a coherent text. I wanted to transmit the richness, complexity, and vibrancy of kitchenspace without contributing to essentialized notions of "the Third World Woman" (Mohanty 1984) with my own language of power and claims to knowledge. Over and over again I turned to feminist ethnographers such as Lila Abu-Lughod (1991, 1993) for ideas on how to "write women's lives" and write "against culture." My intent is to portray partial perspectives and situated knowledges grounded in women's embodied experiences in kitchenspace (see further discussion in the next chapter).

Like Abu-Lughod, Laura McClusky (2001), Ruth Behar (1993), and others, I settled on women's narratives and edited versions of my fieldnotes to tell women's stories, presenting them in a nonlinear fashion, offering fragments of time and space. I aim to communicate "the ethnographic present" (Hastrup 1990) while inviting my reader to question my interpretations and conclusions. Drawing on Carter Wilson, author of *Crazy February: Death and Life in the Mayan Highlands of Mexico* (1966), McClusky (2001: 14) says that "spirit, missing in traditional ethnographies, . . . is narrative ethnography's strength." This form of writing, which does not break a work into chapters with thematic titles such as "Religion" or "Kinship," she says, "can allow ethnographers greater room to describe the holistic nature of social systems by demonstrating how culture works" (2001: 19). Despite criticism to the contrary, McClusky (2001: 15) notes that "authors of ethnographic novels process and analyze their raw data, or field notes"; they "choose to include certain things, in certain ways, and they choose to exclude other things altogether."

The complete contents of my box of ethnographic notebooks, reflective journals, and typed transcripts of interviews and analysis of my participant-observation experience are certainly not included here. In addition to choosing which things to leave out, I did not observe or understand many elements, such as aspects of their lives that the people I interviewed chose not to share and occurrences that took place before and after my study. When I replayed the tapes of my interviews while writing this book, I was surprised to hear how much I missed the first time around and did not include in my neatly typed transcript: I focused on respondents' answers to my questions—however irrelevant these may have been—and ignored interesting "side comments" and sounds such as roosters crowing, trucks roaring by, or children yelling.

I would betray the honesty and vulnerability with which women shared their stories with me if I processed and reprocessed them to suit my ever-changing ideas. This narrative ethnography documents a moment of rapid social and environmental change, "frozen in time" but I hope alive, capable of transforming my reader and generating new interpretations in the future.

To avoid rendering people's expressions and experiences sterile despite taking them out of their sociocultural contexts and placing them in a two-dimensional treatise, this book includes key words, phrases, and even some monologues in the first person and in Spanish. I believe that this makes it more useful to Spanish speakers and Latin Americanists, while the accompanying English translations render it accessible to others. In addition to the geographically specific style and vocabulary of the Spanish used in my three sites—which readers from Spain and from other regions in Latin America or even Mexico may find foreign or grammatically incorrect—the language of kitchenspace includes many terms in *mexicano* (Nahuatl). My translations are not always literal but seek to communicate the sense of what was said. The Glossary clarifies commonly used words and terms.

Reading This Book

The following chapter describes various academic literatures that form the intellectual context for this book, including contributions from feminist scholarship that provide the conceptual framework. It introduces the three methodologies that I employed and my research questions. It also explains how preliminary fieldwork led to my focus on the gendered spaces of food preparation. Students, academics, and others interested in "the construction of knowledge" and the nuts and bolts of research within the parameters of university scholarship may find that chapter indispensable. Others with a more general interest in Latin America, Mexican cuisine, and kitchenspaces or women's lives and narratives may prefer to skip it entirely. Many of the methodological issues raised there are woven throughout the remainder of the book and addressed in the conclusions.

The nested scales of my inquiry begin with embodied and gendered subjects that are embedded in both household and community relations. The food preparation activity at the heart of household and community spaces is supported by, and in turn supports, extended social networks. The social and cultural aspects of production and reproduction in these social and physical spaces are geographically specific to the culture region of central Mexico. If we begin with the activity of food preparation, the order of these spaces starts at the center with the gendered subjects, then moves to the household, the community, and finally the region. Access (for outsiders such as the author and readers of this book), however, is exactly the reverse. For this reason, I introduce the reader to the semipublic spaces of the fiesta kitchen before entering the more intimate space of women's kitchen narratives.

The core of this book is divided into two main parts: one describes collective food preparation for particular celebrations; the other provides glimpses of everyday life and kitchenspace from the perspective of individual women. Both parts include a chapter for each of my three sites. The chapters in Part One are organized chronologically to reflect different stages of food preparation; I attempt to communicate their extended timeframe by using several entries for each celebration.

Food preparation activity may occur in the present, but fiestas are linked to the past through the long-term planning and preparation they require. They also represent the future: the celebrations often mark a new beginning and display people's faith in what the future will bring. The narratives in Part Two include much reminiscing about the past, an activity that seems inherent in the experience of kitchenspace in my region, where the ghosts or memories of people long gone crowd the tables they once shared with those still living. Together, Parts One and Two transmit a sense of place from women's perspectives and spaces.

A key difference between Part One and Part Two is methodological. The first part is drawn from my participant-observation experience, from the ethnographic journals that I took with me into the field every day, and from the typed or handwritten reflective essays that I wrote up every night. The second is based on unstructured and structured interviews (women's responses to my questionnaire), some of them recorded on tape. Part Two also includes descriptions of kitchenspaces based on my observations and some women's hand-drawn maps. The two parts share recurring characters: some of the women in Part One appear again in Part Two. The final chapter discusses some of the issues raised in Parts One and Two, including the dual and gendered nature of kitchenspace.

Portions of this book (including some of my photographs) have been published before in slightly different forms in the *Journal of Latin American Geography* (2002), the *Geographical Review* (2004), and *Gender, Place and Culture* (2006). I thank the editors of these journals for granting me permission to reproduce them here.[10] I have chosen not to provide date and place references every time I cite one of the women in my study, which would distract the reader and unnecessarily clutter the pages. Every quotation in Part One occurred on the date listed in the subhead of the section in question. Because each chapter in both parts is dedicated to one of my three sites, it is unnecessary to name the place. Women's narratives and monologues in the first person in Part Two are a compilation based partly on structured interviews and responses to my questionnaires but also on unstructured interviews and conversations that took place on repeated visits to women's homes between September 2000 and August 2001.

Some readers may prefer to focus on one community at a time, learning about Xochimilco's fiestas in Part One, for instance, and then immediately reading the Xochimilco section in Part Two to hear more from the women who live there. People particularly interested in folk traditions or fiestas might choose to read only Part One, while those exclusively interested in women's narratives and everyday lives may choose to read only Part Two; I suggest, however, that Parts One and Two complement and provide the context for each other.

My hope is that this book will bring attention to the contributions of women whose work and ingenuity in kitchenspace are generally taken for granted and thus rendered invisible. I think it is important to stress that they tend to be as overlooked in Mexico as in most other countries and certainly in the academic literature. During my fieldwork I was invited to present my research on several occasions at the national university (UNAM) and the Universidad Autónoma del Estado de Morelos (UAEM). Discussions following each presentation revealed that students from Mexico City and Cuernavaca were for the most part oblivious to the magnitude of the fiestas in their neighboring communities (Xochimilco and Ocotepec, respectively). Those who were aware of the fiestas, including students from the communities in question, sometimes confessed that they had not given a second thought to the women preparing the food. One professor told me that he originally thought I was attracted to "the exotic" in Mexico but came to realize that I was shining a light on an important aspect of Mexican culture that people take for granted and scholars ignore. While my focus is certainly geographically specific, I would venture to suggest that a study of kitchenspaces anywhere—including our own homes and communities— would also reveal significant but understudied aspects of culture, gender, and nature/society relations.

During my fieldwork I often marveled at the absurdity of my attempt to capture the essence of place and experience in a little spiral notebook or my microcassette recorder. Despite my inadequacies in this sense, I hope that the following pages provide readers with some idea of the flavors, smells, sounds, and images of kitchenspace in Xochimilco, Ocotepec, and Tetecala. If readers find the text a bit chaotic but full of life, it will begin to approximate the experience of being there.

POINTS OF DEPARTURE

Feminist Frameworks, Women-Centered Studies

This work is explicitly feminist in its aim to bring attention to the significant contributions that women in kitchenspace make to social and cultural reproduction. Feminist methodologies inform my recognition of the privileged standpoint and power imbalance that I bring to the relationship with my research subjects. I employ participatory methods and a "strong reflexivity" (Naples with Sachs 2000; Wasserfall 1997), which I am convinced are necessary if scholars are to stop re/producing false certainties that necessarily erase important wrinkles of reality—disproportionately women's realities.

As a geographer, I found the conceptual framework offered by feminist political ecology (FPE) particularly useful, given its focus on gendered knowledge and everyday life in relationship to natural resources and the environment (Rocheleau, Thomas-Slayter, and Wangari 1996). FPE starts with the assumption that "there are *real*, not imagined, gender differences in experiences of, responsibilities for, and interests in 'nature' and environments, but that these differences are not rooted in biology *per se*. Rather, they derive from the social interpretation of biology and social constructs of gender, which vary by culture, class, race, and place and are subject to individual and social change" (1996: 3). One of three critical themes, gendered knowledge, is explored as "reflected in an emerging 'science of survival' that encompasses the creation, maintenance, and protection of healthy environments at home, at work and in regional ecosystems" (1996: 4). The other two themes that FPE considers are gendered environmental rights and responsibilities and gendered environmental politics and grassroots activism. FPE "addresses the convergence of gender, science and environment in academic and political discourse as well as in everyday life" (1996: 9).

While feminist political ecology is the point of departure for my inquiry, I focus more on the survival or reproduction of culture than on the physical survival of humans or the environment, though certainly the three are tightly linked in food preparation spaces. I chose to work with ordinary women whose social participation and relationship with the environment revolve primarily around their responsibility for food preparation at home and in their communities, rather than women who organize politically around environmental issues. Nonetheless, changes in the environment—including pollution, erosion, and the use of agrochemicals and genetically modified seeds—have had impacts on people's livelihoods and are reflected in women's adaptive strategies and discourses.

Transparency and self-reflection are central to my goal of revealing the untidy process of research and showing that the process is critical and at least as significant as the findings. I use these as tools to call attention to the dilemmas of ethnographic fieldwork and to subvert my authority to tell women's stories. I avoid a metanarrative that would create the illusion that this book presents an objective and totalizing Truth. Obscuring the power of the researcher to define the research project and its results is precisely what has permitted scholars to ignore women, kitchenspaces, and other less powerful, attractive, or currently in-vogue topics. While I aim to keep the focus on the subjects, places, and spaces in question, this book also tells the story of the year-long journey of a graduate student learning and un-learning how to do research. My class privilege, race, ethnicity, education, language, and circumstances all affected the interactions and experiences that I share here.

My research responds to feminist critiques of the exclusion of ordinary people and everyday life in Western science that argue for the validity of knowledge gained from the lived experience (Bordo 1986; Harding 1986, 1991) and to calls from feminist geographers to put women on the map (Monk and Hanson 1982; Seager 1992). It draws on literature from the social sciences concerning social reproduction (Merchant 1990). The Cartesian dichotomies—particularly the mind/body and nature/culture splits—that serve as the basis for the dominant methodologies in the production of Western knowledge (Bordo 1986; Butler 1990, 1993; Merchant 1980; Rose 1996) exclude the majority of women's contributions throughout history and those knowledges which do not fit into a positivist approach to reality. True to the definition cited for "feminist geographies" in *The Dictionary of Human Geography,* I "draw on feminist politics and theories to explore how gender relations and geographies are mutually constructed and transformed" (Pratt 2000: 259).

I borrowed the dynamic and existential concept of embodiment from medical anthropology (Csordas 1994) to incorporate people's experiences of dwelling (Heidegger 1971) in particular environments into my inquiry—including the emotions, beliefs, and knowledges associated with kitchenspace. Despite the longtime interest in the body shown by feminists and anthropologists, geographers were slow to take interest (Longhurst 1995, 1997; Massey 1995; Nast 1994; Rose 1995, 1996, 1997). Significantly, it is the body and not embodiment that became the focus initially, perhaps because of geographers' place-based approach (but see, for instance, Kwan 2007). Nonetheless, the body is increasingly recognized as an important site of social and political interactions.[1]

My approach to embodiment resonates with Deidré Matthee's work in the Western Cape province of South Africa. I too found that in my research communities, food preparation rituals "involve embodied knowing, which enhances women's sense of their capacities as transforming agents," "opening up spaces in which to reshape women's familial and societal position" (Matthee 2004: 438). Embodied knowing is crucial in food preparation, beginning—in my sites—with the selection of fresh ingredients (primarily at the market): women carefully assess meats and produce by touching and smelling. Cooking itself requires technical abilities, nimble fingers, strong backs, and more; indeed women told me that a *cocinera* (cook) must have *ingenio* (creative ability), the right touch, and experience. Keeping embodied experience and knowledge central to my inquiry helps me approach the women who shared their kitchenspaces with me as powerful subjects rather than as passive objects of investigation. I present them as agents rather than as victims of change.

Donna Haraway's (1988) notion of situated knowledges and positionality strongly informs my work and serves as a theoretical bridge to embodied experience as well as place. It explains why I choose to make my presence in the research process explicit and my role in the construction of knowledge transparent. Haraway argues for the recognition of location in the production of situated knowledges grounded in a particular embodied standpoint and place; she suggests that there is a need to recognize and combine situated knowledges and the "power of partial perspective" (as opposed to a disembodied view from everywhere and nowhere: Rose 1996) as a pathway toward greater objectivity.

Making women visible has long been a feminist objective; my goal is to create space for the stories of ordinary women in the developing world and to help us better understand their lives. I would be honored for this book to complement a series of other women-centered studies published by the University of Texas Press, including Christine Eber, *Women and Alcohol in a Highland Maya Town* (1995); Tracy Bachrach Ehlers, *Silent Looms: Women and Production in a Guatemalan Town* (2000); Laura McClusky, *"Here, Our Culture is Hard": Stories of Domestic Violence from a Mayan Community in Belize* (2001); Brenda Rosenbaum, *With Our Heads Bowed: The Dynamics of Gender in a Maya Community* (1993); and Lynn Stephen, *Zapotec Women* (1991).

Food, Cuisine, and Cultural Identity

Food and cuisine can be approached from many different perspectives. This book takes cuisine as an expression of cultural identity (Counihan and Esterik 1997; Simoons 1994) and cooking practices and everyday living as spaces where ordinary people express desires and tastes and resist the powerful forces that rework the social environment (Curtin and Heldke 1992; de Certeau and Mayol 1998). Since the 1980s anthropologists have shown that the subject of food presents opportunities to investigate social and cultural transformations (Mintz 1985, 1996, 1999; Weismantel 1989a, 1989b, 1991, 1998, 1999). In the face of increasing poverty and dramatic changes in the social and physical environment, women's ingenuity in keeping families and traditions alive from kitchenspace can be seen as an act of cultural resistance (Christie 2002).

Kathleen Schroeder's work (1990) represents the first extensive study on the kitchen by a geographer. In her chapter on "kitchen life" Weismantel (1998) includes many topics echoed in this publication: the recycling of waste products through the family pig, women's power related to the distribution of food, and reciprocity and redistribution through the ritualized exchange of food and drink. Exploring the symbolic use of cuisine in discourse relating to ethnicity, she says that "cuisine features among the most important markers of ethnicity" because of the "function of cooking and eating as a means of asserting cultural identity." "The act of cooking food, and thus transforming it, is a means of expressing what people think of themselves, who they are, where they live, and what their place is in the natural and social world and in the political and economic systems of the nation" (Weismantel 1998: 194).

There is no shortage of books on Mexican food, including Salvador Novo's classic *Cocina mexicana* (1883), Diana Kennedy's many cookbooks and studies, including *The Cuisines of Mexico* (1986), and Laura Esquivel's popular book (turned film) *Como agua para chocolate* (1989). At the turn of the century the Mexican National Council for Culture and the Arts published an impressive series of cookbooks that include extensive ethnographic data and celebrate the cultural importance of Mexico's regional foods (Echeverría and Arroyo 2000; Hernández Cortés 1999; Pérez San Vicente 2000; Torres Cerdán 2000).

Many scholars have undertaken studies on the culture of corn in Mexico, on its persistence in the face of the culture of wheat brought from the Old World by the Spaniards, and on misguided national agricultural and food policies (Bonfil Batalla 1982; Mier Merelo 2000; Warman 1976). In his book *¡Que Vivan los Tamales!* Jeffrey Pilcher (1998: 5) claims that "the study of cuisine illustrates the significance of women and domestic culture in the formation of national identities." But for the most part little attention has been paid to the kitchen or the role of women, in whose hands the preparation of culinary dishes usually lies.

In *Many Mexicos* (1967; first published in 1941), Lesley Byrd Simpson referred to corn as an "exacting" and "demanding" "tyrant" that is the common heritage of Mexico. "From one end of Mexico to the other the grinding of the masa and the patting of tortillas is the morning song of life" and is "so thoroughly a part of the immutable *costumbre*," reflected Simpson (1967: 12–13), that "the vendors of the labor-saving gadgets and those kindly people who would emancipate the Indian woman from her ancient drudgery will not completely interrupt the rhythm of the *tortilleras*." Despite many changes—including modern technologies embraced by women—it is still true that the rhythm of life is to a great extent in the hands of Indian or mestizo women in the kitchen and that corn is still the common denominator in the diet of central and southern Mexico.

Domestic Spaces: Home

This study concerns itself with what some might call "domestic" or "private" space.[2] Besides the space inside the home and the family unit usually associated with it, kitchenspace includes the house-lot garden and community relations. Feminist scholars in recent decades have played an important role in deconstructing biases and public/private binaries, establishing gendered spaces in the household as subjects worthy of academic inquiry (for instance, Ahrentzen 1997; Hayden 1981; Oberhauser 1995, 1997; Seager 1987; Spain 1992). Research has also shown that women's role in gendered household space is vital for the transmission of culture (Friedmann 1992), particularly in the case of indigenous women (Arizpe 1989). Geographers, economists, sociologists, and others have studied the importance of the household unit for economic survival and the well-being of the family and of women (Almeida Salles 1988; Barbieri 1984; Dwyer and Bruce 1988; Friedmann 1992; González de la Rocha 1986; Kimber 1966; Loyd 1975, 1981; McC. Netting 1993; Oberhauser 1995, 1997; Reinhardt 1988; Schroeder 1990; Velázquez Gutiérrez 2000).

Considering the diverse and multivalent nature of women's experiences of home in a North American context, Sherry Ahrentzen (1997: 77) says that the narrow spectrum we see in popular media and academic research "is framed by an ideology that supports dichotomy rather than diversity—of a division of 'home life' from 'work life,' of a private from public sphere." Thus, she says, studies on the home tend to portray it either nostalgically or as "the major site of women's oppression." The same ideology that upholds a sexually separatist system of public and private spheres identifies women with the private sphere, "best exemplified by the domicile and domesticity, and men with the public sphere of labor and politics" (Ahrentzen 1997: 79). Challenging the conventional ideal of the privatized home, she presents a "cacophony of voices and experiences . . . and demonstrates a greater variety in women's experiences and meanings of home than the research literature often suggests" (Ahrentzen 1997: 87).

Here I present a diversity of voices and experiences from so-called domestic spaces. I show that the kitchenspaces where my research takes place are key to the establishment and maintenance of vital social reciprocity networks; they have little to do with the notion of domesticity and social

isolation often associated with the suburban housewife or what is generally considered private space. The homes I visited in Xochimilco, Ocotepec, and Tetecala tended to be multigenerational, with more than one person involved in food preparation. Given women's continued success in sustaining and reproducing the labor force from the kitchen despite precarious and deteriorating economic conditions, even cooking for the family can hardly be seen as "private" (see Folbre 1988). In the case of community celebrations, the kitchen or house-lot garden becomes the center of community activity and a vital space from which women establish and maintain social reciprocity networks. The home, or the house-lot garden in any case, is transformed into semipublic space by women's networks.

Mona Domosh (1998: 277) considers various studies on kitchens (Buckley 1996; Lupton 1992; Sparke 1995) and the significance of the kitchen "as a site confirming gender and sexual identities in various distinct cultural contexts." Suggesting that geographers long avoided the home "because these spaces are so meaningful, so complex and so close that we tend to keep our distance from them in our research," she concludes that feminist geography has shown the home to be "rich territory . . . for understanding the social and the spatial" (Domosh 1998: 281). Despite its significance, the particularly intimate space of the kitchen presents formidable challenges to researchers (Christie 2003; Schroeder 1990). In addition to the difficult access—and mainstream geographers' persistent lack of interest in gendered spaces—the bias against the kitchen evident in much feminist research may discourage work in this area. The limited diversity in existing studies—primarily based on the experiences of white, Anglo, urban, middle-class women—restricts our understanding of the relationship between space and society around the world. The recent set of papers on kitchens in *Gender, Place and Culture* 13 (5 and 6) is an exciting and welcome development.

The House-Lot Garden

Since the mid-twentieth century cultural geographers have shown interest in gardens and yards, including their food-related aspects (Sauer 1952).[3] While a "masculinist bias" in geography (Sundberg 2003)—and a bias toward "field" research and agriculture over domestic spaces and gardens—may have discouraged further consideration of spaces close to the home,

geographers have increasingly remarked on their cultural and social significance. Clarissa Kimber (1966: 116) was a pioneer in this sense, with her early studies in the West Indies showing dooryard gardens to be "an intimate form of land use . . . particularly revealing of cultural habits and inheritances." Hinting at the emotional and social importance of gardens, Kimber said that their general purpose "seems to be for consumption and exchange with neighbors and for the use and pleasure of the gardener"; she found it "a matter of status to be able to give presents from the garden" (Kimber 1966: 106–107).

Kimber noted that the exchange of garden products supported reciprocity networks. More recently, Antoinette WinklerPrins (2002) has stressed the importance of garden products for critical social networks in the case of rural-to-urban migrants in Brazil. I found that a different sort of garden product—food prepared in the house-lot garden—confers status (on the cook, the household, and the barrio receiving guests) and helps sustain critical social networks. In this way house-lot gardens play an indirect role in subsistence when their functions as an extension of the kitchen for household chores as well as for entertainment, recreation, and display—functions that Richard Westmacott (1992) identified in his study of African-American gardens and yards in the rural South—combine to strengthen social networks that provide a safety net and material support.

In his feminist political ecology study of urban kitchen gardens in highland Guatemala, Eric Keys (1999) reports that Mayan women not only supplement household needs in the house-lot garden but have a primary role in educating children—transmitting knowledge and values—regarding the natural environment. Stressing that the garden is the location of "important non-material elements of Mayan lifeways," Keys (1999: 98) says that the educational role of women in this space "surpasses that of material production, gender empowerment, and horticulture architecture of the garden, those elements that have received the most attention from cultural and political ecology geographers."

In her study of ethnicity and change among Yucatec immigrants in Quintana Roo, Laurie Greenberg (1996) links the house-lot garden with the maintenance of cultural identity. She found that species native to Yucatán or long used in typical Yucatec dishes were the most common plants in the house lots and concludes that "house lots are an important space for eth-

nic continuity because they offer families a site for ethnic and individual expression, autonomy in continued subsistence practices, and control over diet" (Greenberg 1996: 355). I found that while these gardens provide space for women to raise small animals on food scraps, nonmaterial elements of culture in the house-lot garden are most significant.

Cultural inheritances in the house-lot garden go beyond the embodied knowledge or reciprocity networks required to prepare community feasts or the recipes themselves. Women transform raw food ingredients into sufficient calories to support human existence—quite a feat, considering the precarious economic circumstances of many in the study region—and into culturally appropriate dishes that satisfy the palate and prejudices of those who eat them. Given the importance of food and fiestas in the house-lot garden in maintaining a sense of cultural continuity and critical social networks, changes in this intimate form of land use should become a greater priority for cultural and political ecologists as well as feminist and cultural geographers.

Preliminary Research

Studying kitchenspace was not my initial plan, though few things link humans to the earth as concretely as food or reflect cultural traditions as clearly as food preparation. Living in Xochimilco had left me no doubt about the central role of food in community celebrations, but my decision to study food preparation spaces was also strategic. A preliminary research project exploring nature in people's everyday lives which I undertook to test my research methodology led me to realize that I would have to make adjustments if I wanted to incorporate women's perspectives and spaces.

From the start I was committed to ensuring that women were not excluded from my study of nature and society relations, as I had found to be the case in most of the cultural and political ecology literature I had read until that point, with the exception of feminist political ecology. Soon after initiating work with several households of recent Mexican immigrants in Texas to explore their relationship with the environment and natural resources, I found that I had to readjust my parameters and keep women at the center of my focus. This was in part because the women were not accustomed to representing themselves as experts or being spokespersons for their household or community but also because questions about "environ-ment" or "ecology" led people to contemplate spaces beyond the home and house-lot garden.

Although I had known most of the families in my study for three years and had shared many conversations, evenings, and weekends with the women during our kids' soccer games, they repeatedly referred me to their husbands for answers to my questions.[4] This was particularly frustrating, because I knew the women were the ones who had planted the fruit trees, herbs, and other plants in their gardens—often obtaining the seeds from Mexico through their kinship networks and sometimes planting before the house was even completed. They were also in charge of raising the goats, rabbits, or chickens in the immediate vicinity of their house.

I chose to reorient my questions to focus on the specific area of expertise that women recognized as their domain: cooking spaces and activities. This allowed me to hone in on a gendered and neglected view of the environment, concluding the preliminary study with a "nature in the kitchen" approach. Later I found this focus to be effective in legitimizing my introduction to women in semirural communities outside Mexico City and in Morelos and initiating conversations about nature in more domestic terms.

Qualitative Methodologies and Research Questions

This book is based on eleven months of qualitative field research in 2000–2001, building on fifteen years of prior experience and relationships in cen-tral Mexico. My methodology was inspired by Miles Richardson's creative and multidisciplinary approach to place in "Being-in-the-Market versus Being-in-the-Plaza" (1982) and his unique mixture of anthropology and cultural geography. I sought to understand the experience of "being in the kitchen" by accompanying women in their food gathering and preparation tasks. I employed participant-observation and ethnographic interviews, both structured and unstructured (Richardson 1982, 1984, 1990; Spradley 1979). Finally, I adapted the technique of gendered resource mapping from feminist political ecology and asked women to make hand-drawn maps of their kitchens (Rocheleau, Thomas-Slayter, and Edmunds 1995). All three methodologies represented significant challenges; they were effective only in part and with varying combinations of determination and humility.

As a participant-observant, I helped with extensive food preparation weeks prior to celebrations, cleaning rice, chopping kilos of carrots for rice, peeling sacks of tamarind, and removing the veins and seeds from chiles for mole until I had blisters on my hands. I said many rosaries, ate enough lard and fresh cream to hurt my gall bladder, and drank my share of *atole*, pulque, tequila, and beer.

As the women with whom I worked became accustomed to my presence, I was increasingly transparent about my camera and my notebook. Some women were suspicious of note taking. For the most part I sought privacy to write down even short quotations, systematically typing up an extensive ethnographic record and hand-writing reflective entries in my hardback composition notebooks at the end of each day. Other women insisted on watching me write down exactly what they said, remarking that they were afraid I would forget something and wanted to make sure their words would be remembered. While I always introduced my research project and obtained women's permission to document their activities, it was clear that even when women were comfortable with my presence they took on more of a public or official stance and tended to ham it up around my notebook and camera.

Particularly in group settings, participant-observation rather than interviews brought me closer to everyday behavior and conversation. Working with the "women of the circle"—as I came to think of the collective work parties, usually in the shape of a circle—meant that I could keep my hands busy with the same task that occupied theirs and concentrate on listening rather than talking. In this way my presence interfered little with the group's activities and conversation. Elizabeth Fernea (1969) reported a similar experience when she joined women's sewing circles in her ethnography of an Iraqi village. Participant-observation raised many questions and sometimes provided information that people contradicted in interviews—creating further opportunities for discussion with the women who were *de confianza* (on more intimate terms).

In addition to endless unstructured interviews and nearly three hundred days of participant-observation, I completed several lengthy formal interviews in each of my sites, including a few recorded on tape.

After several months of progressive contextualization (Vayda 1983), allowing the actions, words, and emotions of my research subjects to point

The author cleaning rice for Palm Sunday in Ocotepec

me toward what was important and relevant to them, I developed the following research questions to organize my inquiry:

1. "What are the gendered spaces in the landscape associated with food
gathering and preparation and how have women adapted to changes in
these spaces during their lifetime?"

2. "What do women know about their environment from the context of
food gathering and preparation in their everyday lives and how do they
interact with nature in this context?"

3. "What can women's narratives about food in their specific geographic
contexts tell us about their culture and identity?"

Nearly five months into my year of fieldwork, I developed a four-part
questionnaire based on these three questions, which I modified after a few
trial runs. With help from local research assistants in Ocotepec and Tetecala, I applied a total of seventeen structured interviews in the last month
of fieldwork, twelve of these recorded on tape. One of the unexpected findings and lessons I learned from that process was that the interviews carried out by young male assistants yielded completely different results from
those by the young female assistants. This appeared to be due in part to
their different knowledges of food preparation and women's spaces and to
the women interviewers' ability to recognize and willingness to pursue potentially useful tidbits of information that came up in the process. Another
important factor was the very different ways in which the women that they
were interviewing treated the students: in a performance of gender roles
and reflective of the normative nature of kitchenspace, the women insisted
on sitting the male students down and feeding them.

The first part of my questionnaire introduced the research subject, their
community, and the research theme and was useful in defining my sites
from the perspective of their inhabitants.

A second part focused on spaces supplying food and other ingredients
needed for cooking, such as fuel and dishes. It sought to determine women's
access to and perspectives on environmental and market conditions and
the relevance of these spaces to their food gathering and preparation. These
data provide a frame of reference for my focus on kitchenspace.

A third part looked at culture and technology, delving into the knowledge required to obtain and prepare certain foods, where that knowledge
was gained, and how it was transmitted (or not) to younger generations.

Here I paid special attention to gender roles and came across a few surprises. In Xochimilco, for instance, when most households farmed and sold their vegetables for a living a few decades ago, grandfathers commonly prepared meals for the children and taught girls to cook while the grandmothers were at the market selling and the parents were working in the city.

Part four of the questionnaire touched on social relations, including spaces of reciprocity and power. It explored the social importance of food preparation and strategies from the kitchen, such as what women prepared when time was short or food was scarce. Perhaps more interesting from a cultural perspective were the substitutions that were or were not acceptable in the kitchen and under what circumstances.

Toward the end of my year of fieldwork, I asked several women to draw maps of their kitchen and include the things that were most important to them. While participative mapping was especially effective in revealing perceptions and uses of space and repeatedly brought attention to the social and dual nature of kitchenspace, it was even more difficult and intrusive to apply than structured interviews and, like these interviews, was often counterproductive. The older, illiterate women, who were often the best sources, were especially reticent to take a pencil in hand and usually asked me to make the sketch in their stead, which defeated my purpose. In the end, however, this methodology was critical to my findings.

In addition to these methods, and as an effort to document the extensive and complex material culture of the kitchen, I made detailed inventories of the containers, tools, food supplies, and other items in several kitchens. This took place during the final weeks of fieldwork and only in the homes of women with whom I had developed particularly close relationships. I also took over forty rolls of slides during the year, including most of the images in this book. Paying close attention to detail, I tried to observe and listen with my heart as well as with my eyes and ears.

Throughout my research I struggled to understand the stories and spaces that women shared with me. Again and again my assumptions and ideas about nature and society interfered, as did the many luxuries I take for granted. My understanding of people, places, and events was limited by the preconceived notions that filtered my interpretation of the participant-observation and predisposed me to observe and hear certain things while ignoring others. As I became more and more familiar with my research subjects, details that I previously found insignificant came to the foreground.

Attention to detail

Fortunately, I developed friendships and ongoing dialogues with several generous and intelligent women in each of my sites who called my attention to things that they felt I should consider, introduced me to people, took me places, and helped me put some of the pieces together.

I have found no single answer to the overarching question that guided my research: "How do ordinary women in central Mexico experience nature in their everyday lives?" While each of my methodologies had shortcomings and even produced conflicting data, I believe that the combination of multiple sites and approaches gave me access to different perspectives. These, together with my flexibility and willingness to follow my intuition, provide a less clear but more faithful depiction of people and place and nature and society relations. While this makes it difficult to generalize and form definitive conclusions, which I know will bother some readers, it brings me closer to my goal of understanding how different women in one part of the world experience nature and participate in their communities.

PART ONE
Women of the Circle

Part One introduces each of my three research communities
by exploring several celebrations in each. In Chapter One
on Xochimilco I present key ingredients in the folk Catholicism celebrations that are also relevant for the following two
chapters. These include the gender lines in kitchenspace,
fireworks (unquestionably a male domain), and the musicians and dancers who are usually present. Other elements
include the barrio as a key geographical unit, the sense of
time, young people's participation in the fiestas, and the tension between tradition and modernity. In all three chapters
the date of the journal entry indicates when the activity being described (usually in the present tense) takes place.

Fiesta hosts in Ocotepec and Xochimilco display their
wealth by burning as many fireworks as they can afford in
order to impress members of the community and especially
members of other barrios. People in these two towns say
that the fiestas have gotten bigger and better with time and
will continue to do so. The woman in Tetecala who hosts
the meal for the Virgen de la Candelaria reports that she is
afraid the tradition will soon die out because of the increasing number of people who expect to be fed and the reluctance of the neighbors to contribute to the expenses.

Why is it that traditional fiestas have been growing in
Xochimilco and Ocotepec—even as the agricultural basis for
their celebration has shrunk—while they have been disappearing from Tetecala? I did not systematically compare
fiestas or kitchenspaces in Xochimilco, Ocotepec, and Tetecala, but a few factors seem to be obvious, beginning with
ethnic identity. Significantly, and in contrast to my other two
sites, none of the people in Tetecala reported speaking an
indigenous language in the recent census (INEGI 2000b).[1]

Some of the migrants who have settled on the outskirts of town, however, undoubtedly come from indigenous communities in Guerrero, and some of the older women I met spoke Nahuatl. The first two towns also share a similar (and linked) indigenous history and an ancient barrio structure populated continuously by the same ethnic groups—and indeed the ancestors of many of the current residents (still fed by women in rituals for the dead) for hundreds of years.

Tetecala, in contrast, has suffered several resettlements over the centuries and is inhabited primarily by a more recently arrived mestizo population. Tetecala's lack of traditional barrios and changes in people's religious affiliation are fundamental to its social organization. The population is not settled into well-recognized barrios based on prehispanic *calpulli,* each with its own chapel. In Xochimilco and Ocotepec these provide a strong sense of place and form the basis for the fiesta system. The neighborhood that hosts the fiesta in Tetecala on February 1 does not even have a name; people referred to it as "the barrio by the clinic."

In Chapter Two on Ocotepec we find that, as in Xochimilco, the Catholic faith of the majority plays a key role in the traditional fiestas. In contrast to Xochimilco, where many barrio fiestas are organized outside the control of the church, in this case barrio and community organizations responsible for the fiestas are directly linked to the church, often meeting in the barrio chapel to conduct business. Finally, unlike Xochimilco and Ocotepec, Tetecala has a strong presence of evangelical Protestants, specifically Jehovah's Witnesses, whose members are forbidden to drink—an essential element of participation in traditional fiestas.

Other differences between the three sites become evident in their fiestas. In contrast to the barrio that I investigate in Xochimilco, which is very closed and generally hostile to newcomers from the city participating in its traditional fiestas, Ocotepec opens its doors—literally—to the growing population spilling over from Mexico City and Cuernavaca. In the celebrations surrounding the Day of the Dead festivities for which it is well known, for example, strangers as well as friends go from house to house visiting the *ofrendas* (offerings to the dead) and are served something to eat and drink in each one. Without a doubt, the food tourism benefiting vendors with permanent and temporary kitchens is a key economic activity in Ocotepec (as it no doubt is in Xochimilco), but not enough to help the majority or prevent the massive outmigration that Xochimilco—unlike my other two sites—appears to have been spared.

Chapter Three on fiestas in Tetecala is shorter than the first two chapters because, with the possible exception of a meal for the Virgen de la Candelaria on February 1, I did not find in Tetecala the type of complex and semipublic kitchenspaces that I found in Xochimilco and Ocotepec. That does not mean that Tetecala has a shortage of celebrations, only that they tend to be more private and less religious in nature. As far as I was able to discern, celebrations in Tetecala are not based on the elaborate community networks and organizing committees that I found in my other two sites. Thus the activities in kitchenspaces there contrast with those in Chapters One and Two. I believe that this provides a useful comparison and, together with the multiple narratives in the next three chapters, can help us avoid making assumptions about women, kitchenspaces, or communities in central Mexico.

1 Xochimilco

"Short on Days to Celebrate Our Fiestas"

Xochimilco's fiestas, traditional foods, plants, and canals attract tourists and shoppers from the adjacent capital city and the interior of Mexico. Its canals and *trajineras* (traditional vessels like gondolas), made famous in part by their depiction in classic Mexican movies and contemporary soap operas, are both an attraction and an environmental disaster. People use the *trajineras* and smaller flat-bottomed "canoes" to navigate the canals that weave throughout Xochimilco, in particular to reach the *chinampas* to work the land and to transport the produce home. Larger versions are also used for tourism. Xochimilco has two large covered markets (including the *mercado de plantas*, where people buy cut flowers and live plants) and an adjoining open-air market; all three markets offer fresh and cooked food. The local tourist bureau promotes the city's many civic and religious celebrations. As one young woman told me, "Aquí en Xochimilco nos faltan días para celebrar nuestras fiestas" (Here in Xochimilco we are short on days to celebrate our fiestas). While the street parades and fireworks—with lots of food for sale—are open to anyone, the celebrations and meals in people's homes and house-lot gardens are not accessible to outsiders.

In this chapter I concentrate particularly on the celebrations surrounding the Niñopa, a local baby Jesus figure with prehispanic roots that attracts crowds every day of the year. I narrate events including a Posada (traditional Christmas procession and party) on December 16, 2000; a house-blessing on January 21, 2001; and the actual day of the Niñopa on February 2, 2001.

Many of Xochimilco's celebrations involve walking the streets with *imágenes peregrinas* (pilgrim images) and gathering outside somebody's house to eat and drink—usually in the center or at the back of the property. It would be difficult to overstate their magnitude. In the change of the *mayordomía* (sponsorship) for the Niñopa on February 2, 2001, the main meal of the day was served to over five thousand followers—most of them in the street. At one point a woman was sent to pick up over two hundred pounds of tortillas preordered at the neighborhood *tortillería* (tortilla factory); later somebody had to go buy more.

Adoration of the Niño Dios (child Jesus) in Xochimilco began prior to 1588; documents from 1650 refer to several Niños Dios and the indigenous leaders who founded their chapels and became their *mayordomos*, with the people (as opposed to church authorities) in charge of the care of these religious objects (Canabal Cristiani 1997: 43). While the Niñopa is a particularly cherished child Jesus, the festivities surrounding his image are but one example of the integration of daily life and fiesta in Xochimilco as well as of the syncretism of indigenous agricultural celebrations with Catholic images. Most people in the community and visitors from outside the community experience these celebrations from the table.

Without a doubt, the Niñopa is the most venerated figure in Xochimilco, but almost as popular is el Niño de Belén (the Child from Bethlehem). He is a particular favorite in the barrio that shares his name and is loved by Xochimilcas throughout the town. As evidence of the lack of animosity between the two figures and their followers, several people proudly pointed out to me that a neighbor recently had held a party for the two of them together. I often found in Xochimilco that fiestas featured twin deities—symbols of fertility and reminiscent of the emphasis on duality in the prehispanic cosmovision. I never observed this in my other two sites, where the fiestas were more closely tied to the church itself.

Besides the Niñopa and the Niño de Belén, another key image in Xochimilco that draws immense and devoted crowds is a representation of the Virgen de los Dolores (Virgin of Dolores), known as the Virgen de Xaltocán for the barrio where she resides. A special food preparation event on February 26, 2001, where I found that men were the primary cooks, provided an interesting opportunity to explore gender roles in kitchenspace.[1]

The Virgen de Xaltocán's sanctuary dates to 1524, when the first Franciscan monks called it "the Holy Name of Jesus." Associated with agriculture and one particular barrio, she is venerated throughout the community and celebrated every day for an entire month. This is in addition to several celebrations before and after that period as part of the preparations for that and the following year's fiestas and her visits to other barrios during June, July, and August. Legend has it that in the eighteenth century an elderly woman with a statue of the Virgen de los Dolores found the sanctuary rebuilt and her house converted into a church, in which the little Virgin "wanted to stay" (Canabal Cristiani 1997: 43). She is also said to have appeared to a campesino returning from the *chinampa* in his canoe.

The chapter closes with a glimpse of the day of the Holy Cross in Xochimilco, which is also the day on which people celebrate construction workers (who are of course fed and given that afternoon off) throughout Mexico.

El Niñopa

An exhibit at the Museum of Popular Cultures, Coyoacán, in Mexico City on November 24, 2000, described the role of El Niñopa:

> The Niñopa . . . holy infant, syncretized 500 years ago with the child version of Huitzilopochtli.[2] His name has two meanings: Child Father or Child of the Place. The cult to the Niñopa, made by indigenous hands out of *colorín* wood, originally began in a Xochimilco chapel founded by an Indian cacique called Martín Cortés Alvarado, known as the Old Man. Since then, he has continued to be adored as a very miraculous baby Jesus, whose principal fiesta is February 2, day of the Candelaria, when he changes *mayordomos* or hosts, who must take care of him in their house for an entire year.

Nothing represents Xochimilco more than the Niñopa (the "child of the place") or brings as many people together to share a meal. A central figure that permeates the everyday lives of many Xochimilcas, the Niñopa is the most venerated and miraculous of several baby Jesus figures in the community, often referred to simply as *la sagrada imagen* (the sacred image).[3] The Niñopa, a hand-carved wooden statue, is treated like a live child, hearkening back to prehispanic religious beliefs despite the devout Catholicism of his followers. Stories of his mischief as well as his legendary miracles abound, and his appearance produces intense emotion among his followers. The Niñopa is received with love, devotion, fireworks, flowers, and food throughout Xochimilco. People say that his image brings good fortune to those who visit him, pray to him, bring him gifts, or simply carry a photograph of his likeness. On the Niñopa's daily processions, the figure is always shielded from the sun and the rain.

The oral tradition surrounding the Niñopa reflects Xochimilco's history of resistance to religious and political authorities, which dates back to the precolonial era, when the Xochimilcas were forced to produce food and flowers for the Aztec Empire. Spanish tax collectors later complained

Taking the Niñopa home

about locals who contributed little to their coffers but nonetheless exhib-
ited great wealth in their lavish fiestas. The Niñopa is said to have survived
the years of repression of religious activity during the War of the Cristeros
in the period following the Mexican Revolution because the people hid and
protected him. A legal struggle with the Catholic church in the mid-1970s
concluded with the Niñopa obtaining the status of Mexican citizen. He
was provided with a lawyer and bank account. Celebrations in Xochimilco
grew, with people protecting him from the threat of the church by guarding
and venerating him in their homes.

The Niñopa is the most loved religious figure of Xochimilco; nearly every
family claims association with him. Everyone seems to recall stories told by
an aunt, uncle, or grandparent who once hosted him in their home and tells
them eagerly, as someone might relate an anecdote about the distant childhood of a favorite grandson. Indeed, in many ways the Niñopa is treated
like family, though revered like a god. The celebrations in his name weave
further ties of reciprocity among his worshippers.

The list of people waiting to host the Niñopa (future *mayordomos*) extends over thirty years into the future. Serving as the Niñopa's godparents
for the year or even for a day or a morning, while extremely costly, brings

great honor to the family and the barrio. The Niñopa's fiestas are celebrated by surrounding barrios as well as by devout followers, some of whom come from as far as the southern state of Oaxaca to venerate him. His worshippers often bring gifts and are traditionally received with something to eat and drink.

The celebration of the Niñopa and the responsibility that the *mayordomos* take for ensuring the appropriate veneration for the year require the support of an extensive network of *comadres, compadres,* and neighbors to support the host family. The *mayordomos*—generally a couple with the support of a family and barrio—keep the small figure in their home for a year. They enjoy a position of status among neighbors and religious and lay officials that comes with the responsibility of assuring that the baby is safe and worshiped according to tradition. The hosts must welcome admirers who visit the *sagrado infante* (holy child) and must hold a rosary (prayer open to the community) every night.

The rosary is always followed by a small but symbolic snack in a ritual that resembles the Holy Communion of the Catholic church, though corn tamales, wheat cookies, or bread replace the thin wafer blessed by a priest. "Lo que uno pueda dar" (Whatever you can give), people say, meaning that anyone is welcome to worship the Niñopa—and host a rosary in his or her own home for an evening, for instance—regardless of economic means. In fact, what the host serves at the various Niñopa ceremonies throughout the 365 days of the year is always the subject of public scrutiny, as are the other components of the highly ritualized celebrations that Xochimilcas have come to expect. They have grown in size and lavishness, becoming increasingly expensive over the years.

Besides guaranteeing the Niñopa's safety and offering a nightly rosary, the *mayordomos'* responsibilities involve hosting a special Mass at least once a month, including February 2 and Christmas; securing hosts or *posaderos* to celebrate the Posadas that occur nightly from December 16 through 24; maintaining the belongings of the *imagen* (image) in good shape and turning them over to the following *mayordomos* when the time comes; and relinquishing the Niñopa to the new *mayordomos* "without any opposition" (Orta Hernández 1991: 118).

After the annual change of *mayordomos* on February 2, with the help of a committee composed of past and future *mayordomos,* the Niñopa's legal representative must make sure that the Niñopa's extensive and ever-growing inventory of belongings—clothes, toys, furniture, jewelry—is passed on to the new *mayordomos*. After future *mayordomos* are put on a waiting list, they and their families begin the preparations and accumulations required to receive the Niñopa, sometimes building a new house as well as raising animals and planting corn for the special meal with which he is received in his new home.

While the *mayordomos* have a great and costly responsibility and enhance their status because of this role, the work, cost, joy, and honor are shared throughout the year to some extent by the family and community members who contribute to the care and celebration of the *santo niño* (holy child). Food is a necessary accompaniment to his veneration, and families often contribute part of the food or drink that is prepared and distributed at Niñopa events. Many women work with the *mayordoma* to prepare and distribute meals for given celebrations.

At the principal annual event on February 2 the current *mayordomos* relinquish the Niñopa to the next hosts, who announce the *posaderos* and barrios that will offer the traditional Posadas during the Christmas celebrations. The *mayordomos* must agree upon their *posaderos* at least ten years in advance. While the hosts offer the general public a delicious traditional meal on the Día de la Candelaria (February 2), the *posaderos* are treated as special guests and often served a slightly different menu. In 2001 the *posaderos* were given a basket with additional food to take home after the collective meal—including a special batch of mole prepared for the occasion.

Not surprisingly, given the weight of the hosts' responsibility and the importance of the Niñopa to the community, the committee that determines whether to allow a potential host onto the list investigates the possibility of family support in case of unexpected setbacks. In one recent case, two unmarried sisters who petitioned to be *mayordomas* were denied on the basis of not having family to fall back on if they had trouble fulfilling the commitment. I was told that the *mayordomos* had never failed in the past. The unexpected death of a couple scheduled to be future hosts, whose children were underage at the time of their death, led to a switch between families on the list. This gave the orphans more years to prepare to carry out their parents' promise, rendered even more important in light of the tragedy.

In addition to the key celebrations on February 2 and the Posadas preceding Christmas, the Niñopa is hosted by a different family from a barrio of Xochimilco nearly every day of the year. On rare occasions—and with special permission and protection—a family from a nearby town outside of Xochimilco may borrow him for a day. Regardless of who hosts him for the day, taking him home to a private celebration with family, friends, and neighbors after the daily morning Mass, he must be back in time for the evening rosary at his (that is, the *mayordomos'*) house. Wherever he is, admirers are welcome to visit, bring him gifts, and pray. They may kiss the hem of his dress, though they are not permitted to touch his body. The sick are allowed to take home the cotton that is used to wipe the baby's face in the morning toilette routine, which is said to have curative powers.

The participants in the nightly rosary are invited to eat and drink after saying the rosary and singing the *arrullada* (nursery song). People line up to kiss the baby's holy garment as he is held in the arms of his host and then file outdoors to form another line for the *atole* and tamales or bread and coffee. Participation in this final closing ceremony while the baby is being put to bed is important; often people who are not hungry or thirsty still go through the line and take the special offering home to eat and drink later or to share with someone who is not able to attend or is ill and believes in the Niñopa's healing powers. All or part of the *merienda* (snack) may be offered by a special *mayordomo* who takes responsibility for the tamales or the milk or the rosary on a given night—often the family who borrowed him for the day. This provides the opportunity for others to share the honor, the expense, and—presumably—the protection that the miraculous child bestows.

People bring flowers or other gifts for the sacred infant. "La imagen recompensa" (The image rewards you), everyone tells me. Among the legendary stories told of the Niñopa, many credit him with saving the life of someone who was involved in a potentially fatal accident on the way to visit him or when carrying a photograph or other relic: one man was thrown from his car on the road to Xochimilco but emerged without a scratch, thanks to the Niñopa's divine intervention. Another man whose *chinampas* were kept safe from the thieves that plague many farmers in Xochimilco attributed this to his prayers to the Niñopa.

After the rosary, the group sings a lullaby as the Niñopa is dressed for bed and retired to his crib. In the morning, when the *mayordoma* goes to his crib to wash his face and dress him for the day, she often reports finding his toys and marbles strewn around on the ground. Legend has it that the Niñopa likes to play with his toys in the night and that he particularly enjoys going out on the canals in his own little *trajinera* to see the flowers traditionally cultivated on the *chinampas*.

November 24, 2000: El Niñopa Has His Own Fireworks

"Here if the roosters don't wake you the fireworks will," says Señora Rosa, as she listens to me complain about the blasts that woke me up at 7 a.m. Between the amplified dance music that often drifts across the canals as late as three in the morning and the fireworks and church bells before morning Mass, sleeping in this town takes some getting used to.

I am sitting at the table in my neighbor's kitchen; she stands over her stove preparing my eggs with nopales (cactus paddles). Hot tortillas wrapped in an embroidered napkin are piled high in a basket in front of me, with a jar of salt and one of canned jalapeños beside it. She apologizes for not having fresh salsa.

The sound of fireworks this morning was immediately followed by the familiar notes of a traditional brass band. Half asleep, I ran up on top of my flat roof to watch the procession slowly make its way out of the *callejón* (alley) toward the local chapel that marks the entrance to my neighborhood. Looking down, I saw the swirling capes of the *chinelos* (masked dancers) that accompany most religious processions in Xochimilco, spinning and hopping in energetic yet drunkenlike movement. They were taking the Niñopa to Mass. The rear was brought up by the *cohetero* (fireworks expert), who was using his cigarette to light one long bottle rocket after another, sending them whistling up toward the heavens. Fireworks are part of the celebration in every fiesta in Xochimilco. This morning Señora Rosa informs me that the Niñopa's fireworks have a particular softer sound that differentiates them from all others and alerts his followers to his passing.

Chinelos

The *chinelos* are a key ingredient in Xochimilco celebrations. Some say the tradition of *chinelos* came to Xochimilco from Tlayacapan in the early part of the twentieth century, when the *movimiento indigenista* (indigenist movement) brought representatives from that nearby community to Milpa Alta, just outside of Xochimilco, for political meetings. Others are adamant that the dancers diffused from Tepoztlán, a place more often frequented by Xochimilcas today and well known for a tradition of fiestas very similar to Xochimilco's, including *chinelos*, fireworks, and mole. Perhaps both are correct. Slightly different styles of dress may reflect a difference in temperature or in wealth between the two villages: one made of cool cotton weave and one (adopted in Xochimilco) of thick, rich velvet. In any case, everyone agrees that the *chinelos* came from Morelos and that they are here to stay.

The *chinelos*, like the fireworks, entice young people to participate in community traditions. Each year little boys and girls are anxious to wear their striking velvet *chinelo* outfit for the first time. Hopping up and down on the street alongside the older dancers, they become exhausted and are collected by their mothers after a relatively short distances.

According to the local museum in Tlayacapan,[4] the peculiar costume is said to have been designed by hacienda laborers from Morelos to poke fun at the extravagant nightgowns worn by the wives of the wealthy landowners, mocking them with awkward movements, sounds, ridiculous elbow-length gloves, and plumed hats. The mask includes an exaggeratedly pointed beard made of horsetail and green or blue eyes, both non-Indian traits associated with the stereotypical Spaniard. Historically the masks concealed the mestizos' identity, allowing them to ridicule the ruling class and protest

Chinelitos

labor abuses during the three-day Carnaval prior to Ash Wednesday that marked the onset of Lent. The hacienda owners—fearing rebellion—gave their workers these days to blow off steam without fear of punishment before entering the relative fasting and elimination of meat that preceded the feasting on Easter Sunday according to Catholic tradition. The mask and Carnaval (reminiscent of ancient Venetian carnivals) created a measure of temporary political space for the local population: the mask wearers would shout or sing insults aimed at the *patrón* (landowner) in high, falsetto tones and pin offensive statements to the back of his robe.

The three-day carnival is still celebrated in Tlayacapan, and the extensive popular fiestas in Mexico arguably serve as a social safety valve for the poor to eat, drink, and dance their woes away. The *chinelo* dance is not generally considered a ritual of resistance by participants in Xochimilco, however, but one of faith. Rather than offering insults to authorities, the *chinelos* today bear images and sometimes words expressing religious sentiment and showcasing fancy handiwork on their backs. Contemporary designs on the robes reflect the interests and commitments of the wearer and have changed over time. In a fascinating blend of traditional and popular culture, icons on the Xochimilcas' backs this year include imagery of plumed serpents and other Aztec gods, though the favorite Mexican symbol—la Virgen de Guadalupe—holds her ground.

Some people purchase a *chinelo* robe at an exorbitant price; most sew their own or at least bead and embroider the design on the back. This includes the teenaged boys, who often participate in community festivities by joining a *comparza de chinelos* (an organized unit that makes a commitment for a specific period, often to a particular religious icon). A group affiliated with the new *mayordomo*, composed primarily of family and neighborhood teens (male and female), formed a *comparza de chinelos* to accompany the Niñopa throughout the year when the barrio was hosting.

With *chinelo* robes, *quinceañera* dresses, baptism gowns, and the tortilla napkins and aprons regularly required for different fiestas, Señora Rosa and her sister, Señora Josefina (who has been sewing for money since she was eight), are kept busy year round. Xochimilco's party tradition provides Señora Rosa's family and many others with important income-generating opportunities: sewing, knitting, and making all sorts of *manualidades* (handicrafts), including candles and confetti-filled eggs with the shells that are perpetually being saved in the kitchen. Having apprenticed with a hairdresser from Xochimilco living in Mexico City as a child, Señora Rosa maintains a modest hairdressing business on the side, working from a little wooden room in the back of her house, not only cutting and dying hair but often creating fancy hairdos for women attending parties. She also combines hairdressing and sewing skills to create hairpieces for religious statues with the cuttings she saves from her clients' hair. This year she made one for a *virgencita* (statuette of the Virgin) that a neighbor wanted to take on his annual pilgrimage to a site in the far-away state of Oaxaca. On other occasions her hairpieces were taken to pilgrimage sites in Puebla and Tlaxcala. Most of her hairpieces, however, are worn by miniature Virgin Marys in Xochimilco homes.

The Barrio

This morning Señora Rosa tells me the name of the barrio that will host the Niñopa for the day, surprising me once again with how quickly she is aware of information on community life from her place in the kitchen. Of course she also collects the latest gossip when standing on her front step by the blue wooden door leading into the *callejón.* Everyone leaving the neighborhood must pass in front of her, and those with whom she is on speaking terms stop to say hello and good-bye. The women put their bags down and wipe their hands on their aprons before shaking her hand.

The barrio you are from is one of the most important identity markers here and is the geographic unit to which people belong. The town has seventeen traditional barrios. Each has its own fiestas and specific traditions, though they all celebrate Xochimilco-wide fiestas with other barrios. Xochimilcas identify each other by last name, which they often associate with a particular barrio. People may participate in celebrations all over town or marry into a new barrio but still consider themselves to be from the barrio where their grandparents were born. Some of the women I interviewed who had lived in my barrio for over thirty years surprised me by clarifying that they were actually from another barrio ("soy de San Juan," for instance) but had married into the one in which they now resided. When I interviewed a person outside of the *callejón,* Señora Rosa would ask for the person's name and then tell me which barrio that family was from, insisting on the original barrio associated with the family name even if the individual no longer lived there.

Being from one barrio is considered altogether different than being from the one across the street. The *sacristán* (priest's assistant), who in this case is responsible for community relations in the chapel, was from the next barrio over. He lived in a house that had been in his family forever, across the plaza and directly facing the chapel. The neighbors were very suspicious about him being involved in their church and community activities instead of his own.

It does not help the sacristan's popularity that his role is in part to try to enforce church policy on controlling the proliferation of sacred images and the degree of eating and drinking, despite his participation as an eating guest at these very celebrations. He failed in his attempt to put an end to the barrio tradition of serving tamales and coffee inside the chapel on Holy Easter Friday and told me of his futile attempts to convince people in the neighborhood to bring their Holy Crosses, Virgin Mary, and Jesus figures to the chapel for a blessing on their feast day.

The visiting priest from *la parroquia* (the parish)—as people call the main church in Xochimilco's central plaza a few blocks away—wanted to bless all the figures in a single service on their days of celebration, which created a logistical as well as doctrinal problem. Instead, the *sacristán* lamented, people insist on having a fiesta in their homes so that they can invite guests, serve food and drinks, and hire a *cura chocolate* (fake priest) to say a few words in a brief and unofficial ceremony.[5] With the increasingly large number of images,[6] and the many feast days on which Xochimilcas celebrate them, it is logistically impossible for the local parish to meet the demand for a priest's service. At the same time, the Catholic church is under pressure from criticism by Protestant churches that its flock is engaged in idolatry. Despite the proliferation of reliclike images, the people I interviewed were acutely aware of such criticism and always quick to point out to me that the Niñopa and the *virgencita* were only representations of the one and only true Jesus Christ and Virgin Mary.

According to several daughters of the barrio who had married and moved out, young women there had a reputation for having little education. What was most striking to me in all the years that I lived there, however, was how many young people married within the barrio. Señora Rosa's house was perhaps an extreme case: her elder son and her sister's only daughter were married to a pair of siblings from one end of the *callejón*, while another son and daughter were married to a pair of siblings from the other end. In each case the young couples had purchased land on the outskirts of Xochimilco. One of the couples had been building a modest home for over ten years and continued to live in Señora Rosa's house, sharing the bedroom with two daughters who were now teenagers, much to the father's frustration and despite his efforts to save the money he earned as a chauffeur in Mexico City.

November 3, 2000: *El Cohetero*

Fireworks are a key ingredient in community celebrations in Xochimilco. I took the opportunity provided by the close relationship between Señora Rosa's son-in-law Antonio and Don Agustín, one of the most important *coheteros* in town. I visited him in his workshop past Milpa Alta. "No smoking" signs are painted on the shop's exterior. From Xochimilco, Popocatepetl is only visible towering behind the cathedral downtown on the few clear days of the year, but here the volcano is undeniably the most dramatic part of the landscape. Antonio used to be one of Don Agustín's assistants and still helps out on occasion. Members of his family will be heavily dependent on Don Agustín for fireworks throughout their year at the head of the Niñopa *mayordomía*.

"No sé lo que es pedir un trabajo" (I do not know what it is to look for work), Don Agustín tells me right off the bat. Descended from generations of *coheteros*, he is proud to say that in thirty-five years of making fireworks he has never had to look for a job. Instead people come all the way out to his workshop to contract with him for their parties or call his house in Santa Úrsula, Coyoacán, at 2 a.m. to reach him at home. His workshop used to be in Coyoacán as well (inside Mexico City and not far from Xochimilco) until an accident blew it up, killing his wife and several relatives. Authorities then forced his shop out of the crowded city area.

Known for his quality fireworks and for their spectacular purples and oranges—which he says are hard to produce due to a scarcity of the necessary materials—Don Agustín benefits from having a daughter who is a chemical engineer and provides him with access to many of the chemicals he needs. He is a kind and gentle man, whose neck shows burn scars; his hands are peeling from constant exposure to gunpowder. His knowledge includes the periodic table, which he manipulates to produce the colors in his displays and to which he refers frequently during our conversation. In addition, he knows how to create all kinds of *castillos* (castles), *toros* (bulls), and other structures that require artistic creativity as well as engineering knowledge. The transportable parts are often assembled in the barrio's public plaza in front of the chapel or other open area by lifting the wooden components with a pulley and connecting them with ropes.

Don Agustín's crew includes young men and women who work around the clock as deadlines approach, packing seemingly endless amounts of gunpowder into little tubes. They throw their entire bodies into the assembly process on-site, sometimes wrapping the ropes around themselves and leaning into them to stop the wind from blowing the *castillo* over before it is lit. Don Agustín tells me that fathers allow their daughters to work with him because they entrust them to his care but that sometimes he has to send the young women home when they start wanting too much freedom.

Don Agustín is proud of his sons, three of whom took his profession. Two are on their own and specialize in different kinds of *bombas* (bombs), while his youngest—a teenager—works with him packing the small *cohetes* (fireworks) that are wired together to form larger structures. This son, as well as one of the older ones, is an excellent illustrator, drawing the figures that they then sculpt out of wire and gunpowder. While his creations have been featured all over the world, including the Panoramic Studios in Los Angeles, the Olympic Games in Barcelona, and Carnaval in Rio de Janeiro, Don Agustín claims that he always turns down invitations to travel. He says that he is usually too busy preparing fireworks for traditional Mexican communities such as Xochimilco.

"Why do people like *cohetes* so much in Mexico?" I ask him. "Es un complemento que si no lo llevan a la fiesta, no es fiesta—como una posada sin cacahuates o la Feria del Mole sin mole" (It is a component that if you do not take it to the party, it is not a party—like a Posada without peanuts or the Mole Fair without the mole), he says with a laugh, his eyes twinkling.

La Feria del Mole is an annual fair celebrated in the town of San Pedro, in the adjoining county (*delegación*) of Milpa Alta. It draws merchants who sell mole of many different varieties that visitors can sample and purchase and traditional clay pots and dishes that are commonly used in the region for fiestas as well as for everyday cooking and eating. San Pedro is famous for its own high-quality mole that many local families prepare year round to sell as powder or paste or prepare in their own local restaurants, which generally offer exquisite *tamales de frijol* (bean tamales). As in several other villages in this region, San Pedro's economy is boosted by promoting and commercializing a specific food product for which it is known. Other examples in this immediate region include the Feria del Amaranto and the Feria del Nopal, which promote and celebrate the traditional food crops amaranth and nopales, which both are prepared in a variety of popular ways.

Don Agustín takes the opportunity to invite me to several upcoming events in Xochimilco for which he is preparing fireworks (some for pay, others as a gift), including the annual pilgrimage to La Villa to pay homage to the Virgen de Guadalupe. Devotees come from all over Mexico, sometimes walking for weeks to arrive at her shrine north of the city. Aside from the pilgrimage culminating on December 12, the day of the Virgen de Guadalupe, different towns have an annual pilgrimage on specific days of the year. Catholics in Xochimilco, Ocotepec, and Tetecala share two principal pilgrimages which are traditionally very important to their communities: the annual visit to the Virgen de Guadalupe in La Villa on December 12 and an annual visit to Chalma on different dates for each community.

Don Agustín and Antonio laugh heartily, recalling the failed attempts of a recent local head of government (*la delegada*) to apply a 25 percent tax on the money that Xochimilcas paid for fireworks three years ago. When the people refused, the delegate retaliated by withholding police support for the processions. The party went on without them, with *mayordomos* organizing their own crews to control traffic and keep order among the large number of people who join in the street processions en route to the house hosting the fiesta. I laughed too, telling them about a similar situation that I found described in colonial documents I was perusing in the Archivo de Indias in Seville. Spanish authorities in the 1600s complained about the large and expensive fiestas that the Xochimilcas were regularly hosting and the difficulty that the tax collectors had in extracting even a portion of that wealth.

"What kind of money and quantities are we talking about?" I want to know, to get an idea of the proportions of Xochimilco's festivities. "En una buena fiesta se queman cuarenta gruesas de cohetes" (In a good fiesta forty *gruesas* of fireworks are burned), Don Agustín tells me, and the host spends over 180,000 pesos. One *gruesa* equals twelve dozen, so the host of a good party provides 5,760 fireworks at an approximate cost of US$20,000 at the current exchange rate of 9 pesos to the dollar. The show is not only for the immediate guests, who are close enough to share a collective excitement as well as pleasure, but also for the Xochimilca community at large, which enjoys the lights in the skies regardless of their distance from the party.

At an upcoming Posada in the barrio of Tlacoapa, Don Agustín tells me, the hosts will spend 210,000 pesos (US$23,333) for fireworks to be burned in less than two hours. His costs for a finished *castillo* are about 10,000 pesos (US$1,111). A small bull costs 500 pesos (US$55) and a large bull twice that amount. The *toritos* (little bulls) are particularly exciting and even dangerous, resembling the running of the bulls in Pamplona, Spain, in some ways. Someone—always a man as far as I heard—carries the wire structure in the shape of a bull on his head. He runs around a crowded plaza as it shoots *buscapiés* (fireworks that whistle along the ground) near the feet of the participants. They certainly cannot be called spectators, given their full-bodied interaction with the bull—perhaps "involuntary participants" would be more appropriate.

"Why do they spend so much?" I ask, wide-eyed and incredulous. Don Agustín does not hesitate: "Por la crítica al posadero" (Because of the criticism of the host). He adds: "People inevitably say things like 'despite having so much money, they only made mole and not *carnitas.'*" Yet despite the close social scrutiny of appropriate food and fireworks for fiestas, Don Agustín laughs and says that he does not do all the fiestas in Xochimilco because most people pay poorly and purchase low-quality goods, which he does not provide. He says it amuses him to see the *cohetero* at the barrio fiestas making the sign of the cross and praying before lighting the *castillo*, unsure of his work. Perhaps food is more important than fireworks, but here people in charge also make the sign of the cross at several stages in the cooking process.

I ask Don Agustín if he thinks that these traditions can endure in the future. "These traditions—the food, the pulque, and the fiestas—will never cease. It is a custom people already have," he assures me. "My son sees me sign up to contribute a barrel of pulque for a local fiesta and later my son will grow up and do the same thing," he says, echoing the confidence that many Xochimilcas have expressed to me that local traditions will continue forever, though perhaps "improving" in the future.

Don Agustín refers to the formal *promesa* that people usually make at least a year in advance to contribute something to the fiesta of a particular holy figure. A *promesa* can also mean the vow to undertake a pilgrimage for a given number of years. For instance, a person who prayed to el Señor de Chalma (the Christ of Chalma) asking that his or her mother be saved from an illness might promise to walk from home to the holy site every year for twenty years. On the pilgrimage to Chalma that I undertook with a group from Ocotepec, I was passed on the difficult mountain trail by people of all ages, from the very young to the very old.

Don Agustín offers the following reflections, referring to Mexicans who have migrated to work in the United States:

> *De Tijuana pa'ya, ya no hay costumbres para los festivales y las fiestas—ya es puro pizza y Kentucky [Fried Chicken]. Pero esa misma gente manda muchos verdes con la lista de lo que quieren que se compre para la fiesta del barrio o del pueblo: el castillo, la música, las flores, la misa, y la comida.* (From Tijuana on up, there are no customs for festivals and parties anymore—it is all pizza and Kentucky Fried Chicken. But those same people send plenty of greens [dollars] back with a list of what they want to be purchased for the barrio or village fiesta: the castle, the music, the flowers, the Mass, and the food.)

Food is the measure of tradition. While Mexicans may lose some of their traditions in the United States, he assures me that many people send money home to purchase key ingredients for community celebrations in their barrio or pueblo. Despite men's primary responsibility for slaughtering pigs and cattle and preparing *carnitas* and *barbacoa* (meat steamed in oil drums), *la comida*—everything made in a *cazuela* (clay pot)—is in the hands of the women.

Time/Rhythms

Rereading Mariano Azuela's classic novel about the Mexican Revolution *Los de abajo,* from my room in *el callejón,* I reflect on the seasonal sense of time that is palpable in this community and that sets it apart from the huge neighboring metropolis. Azuela refers to the long and uneventful days of the Mexican countryside, interrupted only by news brought in by the *arrieros* (muleteers) on donkeys. This barrio is amazingly isolated and rooted in the past even though locals have been working for salaried jobs in Mexico City for nearly a century, especially after the city redirected the water from the local springs to provide for the increasing needs of the growing population. "The city stole the water," Xochimilcas say, rendering many canals dry and *chinampas* unproductive for a few years before the government began replacing the clean water that it took with wastewater that it pumped back. Even despite obvious changes in this town over the fifteen years since I first came here to live in 1986—more people, more cars, more pollution, and more crime—the rituals that bind everyday life with fiestas provide a sense of stability and predictability.

As in most small communities, people frequently get excited and gossip about events in the neighborhood, such as a man leaving his wife or somebody being robbed in the alley. By and large, however, events like the Popocatepetl volcano erupting are absorbed into cyclical patterns, making each year much like the one before. With so many fiestas and *mayordomías* on the calendar, people regularly plant corn or raise pigs, chickens, or cattle for a particular event. Even people who do not have animals are often linked to a family that does. They may save dried tortillas and food scraps for a neighbor who stops by every other day or so to collect them in a bucket or a wheelbarrow. Many women embroider napkins and baskets in which to serve the tortillas at the next celebration or save eggshells to fill with confetti for children to smash on the Day of the Child (April 1), the next birthday party, or a Posada.

When I see Señora Rosa saving crate after crate of eggshells as she did when I met her fifteen years ago and hear her expressing anxiety about a daughter's pending operation or a *comadre*'s deteriorating health, it seems like yesterday or fifty years ago, maybe more. The many intricate details of preparing for fiestas that pervade daily life in Xochimilco somehow keep the chaos of the city and of life in general at bay—most of the time anyway.

December 16, 2000: Primera Posada del Niñopa

Anyone who came near the barrios of Caltongo or Xaltocán in a vehicle tonight made a mistake. The Niñopa procession blocked the two main streets for over two hours. Antonio invited me to join his family to see the fireworks and collect my *colación* (consisting of peanuts and candy) at the first Posada. I cannot refuse the opportunity to speak with his mother, Doña Margarita, and his grandmother, Doña Consuelo, especially since they will be hosting the Niñopa this coming year and I have been trying for months to meet with them. I appreciate Antonio's intercession, because Señora

Rosa's attempts to assist my research with introductions have proved to be counterproductive. Not surprisingly, my close relationship with her has made it harder to speak with her in-law, Antonio's mother, and several others in the barrio as well.

The taxi driver we enlist for transportation leaves us halfway to the Posada, refusing to get too close and be trapped by the mob. By the end of the evening I am exhausted from walking from one end of Xochimilco to the other and back in the icy wind.

We begin in the barrio of the first *posadero* of the season. The family borrowed the Niñopa this morning and now hosts the Posada at the home of the *mayordomos* who are currently housing the sacred figure for the year. The crowd joins the procession and accompanies the baby Jesus figure across town in full fanfare.

The fireworks lighting up the sky are the first sign that we are getting close to our destination. The hosts have enlisted a team of well-dressed volunteers for crowd control. Very professional-looking young men and women with nametags and two-way radios keep the crowds at the sides of the streets so that the fireworks crew, *chinelos,* musicians, and the host family solemnly carrying the Niñopa can walk down the center and through the narrow alleys. Clearly the group has no need for police support from the local government.

Ahead of the procession some young men pull a little cart full of bottle rockets or *luces de Bengala* (long sparklers),[7] lighting them by the armful and distributing them to the crowds. We fall in step with the procession, stopping now and then to watch a spectacular fireworks display—including a mini-*castillo* with twirling figures that ends with the host family's name in lights. Antonio, whose allegiance is to Don Agustín, does not miss an opportunity to point out the poor quality of the display, noting the excessive smoke and lack of power, which results in people being showered with fire more than once. On one occasion a rocket is fired into the branches of a tree and comes down on the head of an elderly woman. As usual, I marvel at the level of risk that is accepted as a part of everyday life.

As we walk, I am impressed by the many booths of traditional candies and snacks that line the street. *Alegría* (literally, "joy") is a candy made of honey and amaranth seed. Amaranth (*Amaranthus cruentus* Linnaeus) or *huatli* was widely consumed in prehispanic Mexico but was practically eradicated in the colonial period because the Spaniards considered the amaranth figurines of Nahuatl gods that were eaten during special celebrations sacrilegious. Modern agronomists and nutritionists have recognized its high protein content (Warman 1976: 19).

The booths also sell pumpkin-seed candies, local fruits caramelized in sugar, quesadillas and *sopes* (corn patties like fat tortillas with pinched edges, with toppings such as beans and salsa) on huge *comales,* and more. What surprises me is the new addition: microwaved popcorn, which is fast becoming a standard in fairs and street processions as well as in the market. People tell me that this is not really new—they always loved popcorn, but used to eat it only at the circus. Women stand by their microwaves on the sidewalk, with long extension cords leading back inside their house in a unique connection between indoor and outdoor—as well as private and public—kitchenspaces. I wonder if microwave technology and the commercialization of microwavable popcorn (which now appears in the markets in individual packets alongside the ingredients for mole) have brought new traditions or simply allowed Mexicans to celebrate more easily with corn, the key ingredient in most of their celebrations. Like the electric blender that many use to make salsa, the microwave is one more element of modernity that facilitates and is swallowed up by Mexico's dynamic and resistant culture.

After the last fireworks display outside the gates of the host's house, the Niñopa is taken into the huge garden, which is opened to all who want to participate in the rosary. Hundreds pack into the yard, which is adorned with piñatas, little flags of *papel picado* (flags made of crepe paper with decorative and sometimes very intricate cutouts), and lights of every color—all strung overhead. After the rosary, all who have gathered and patiently waited out all the "Hail Marys" and "Our Fathers" of the final ceremony line up to gather the *colación:* little brown paper bags filled with toasted unshelled peanuts and the special Christmas candy that everyone expects at such an event. The bags are stamped with the name of the family that hosted this first Posada of the Christmas season. As we walk home, cracking open and eating our peanuts, we pass many smaller fiestas where people have pulled their tables and *cazuelas* or *comales* into the street to celebrate the aftermath of the Posada with friends and family.

December 17, 2000: Cows on *Chinampas*

I ask Doña Claudia if thievery is indeed a key reason why many people have stopped farming the *chinampas* these days, as many have told me. She says it is true: "Se dedican a eso . . . a ver cuando están maduros los elotes para pasar a robarlos" (There are people who devote themselves to that, just waiting for the corn to be ripe so they can come by [on a canoe] and steal it).

Doña Claudia retorts in anger when I mention the bulls that were stolen from Antonio's grandfather: "Well, why does he take his animals to the *chinampas?*" Don Miguelito had been raising and selling the cattle milk to help with his family's expenses for the upcoming Niñopa *mayordomía.* One morning when he went to feed them on the *chinampa* he found only the remains of two that had been slaughtered on the spot and taken away as meat on a canoe in the middle of the night. After that incident he moved into a little shack on the *chinampa,* where he sleeps every night, guarding the remaining cattle with a gun. Doña Claudia answers her own question, explaining that Don Miguelito had to move his animals onto one of the family *chinampas* a few years ago when they started building the house for the Niñopa in the house-lot garden where he was stabling them at the time.

Many families in the *callejón* raise their cows and pigs on the edge of the canal. Doña Claudia, like many other neighbors, criticizes the people who allow animal waste runoff into the canal. She appears to be in her sixties. As is usually the case when I speak with older women about how things have changed or stayed the same, she refers to the days when the canals were so clean that you could drink the water and see a spoon at the bottom. In her opinion, the people who raise animals on the edge of the canals are largely responsible for the water pollution in the community. I remember, however, that the neighborhood organized to oust a tire manufacturer whose industrial process at the mouth of the *callejón* was heavily contaminating the water. That effort was led by Doña Claudia's own husband, whose livelihood—like that of so many other Xochimilcas—depends on growing plants that he waters directly from the canal.

December 26, 2000: Don Goyo and the Mole

Over sixty thousand people from three states near Xochimilco (Mexico, Morelos, and Puebla) are in shelters tonight as a result of the government's emergency response to the eruption of Popocatepetl a few days ago. Referred to respectfully as "Don Gregorio" or more intimately as "Don Goyo" by the people in the largely indigenous communities that surround the volcano, "he" has been relatively quiet since then. Among the people interviewed by TV news crews today, a 107-year-old man says that Don Gregorio has been kind thanks to the regular offerings of mole that people have been making him for centuries and continue to make today. Neighbors later tell me that refugees in Cuernavaca's shelter—many of whom were forcibly evacuated—complained bitterly when they were served fried chicken on Christmas Eve. Mole would have been more appropriate but beyond the scope of the soldiers to prepare.

January 20, 2001: Making *Carnitas*

I arrive at the home of Antonio's family early in the evening. As it turns out, the uncle who will be coming to butcher the sow is late. He is still busy on a job that he began yesterday, butchering four pigs for another fiesta. With many newly arrived people wanting to maintain local traditions in which they have never participated, some do not know what they are getting into when they agree to host a celebratory meal. The uncle complains about folks not having the right pans or enough firewood for him to do his job correctly.

Things do not get started until 10 p.m. I feel like a soldier in the field now, so unappetizing is this particular participant-observation episode to me. I do not want to be here at all; but as this ritual is a core part of the fiesta's preparation, I feel it is my duty, and Antonio's family clearly expects my presence. I cheat, however, joining the squeamish young women in the outer circle, where we do not have a full view of the slaughter. They share in the excitement but stick together, separate from and behind the men, who seem eager to get as close as they can to the slaughter. As on other ritual occasions, the house-lot garden is clearly gendered space, with the men usually closest to the meat and the alcohol. But even though I cover my ears, the sow's prolonged, piercing squeals are impossible to keep out. One of Antonio's cousins tells me that my feeling sorry for her only prolongs her agony. I feel guilty about my cowardice until I learn that *la abuelita* is in her room crying her eyes out for her pig at the same time. Perhaps it is she who is prolonging the poor sow's suffering.

This pig is sacrificed for the formal ceremony tomorrow, the blessing. A priest will come to bless the Niñopa's newly constructed house as well as the *estudiantina* (musicians) and the *comparza de chinelos* who will accompany the Niñopa throughout the year-long *mayordomía.*[8] They are mostly young kids from the *callejón,* some of whom are learning to play a musical instrument in order to participate, though one of the most enthusiastic is a cousin who lives in downtown Mexico City. *Carnitas* and other dishes will be served. The sow's fourteen piglets—all pretty big themselves though not half her size—will be killed over the next twelve days throughout preparations for the big day on February 2. They will go in part to feed the *cocineras* who will be working every day to prepare the main meal.

The slaughter takes place right between the pigpens. I feel bad for the piglets in those pens that are so close to their mother's death. Tools include an axe to stun the sow, a knife to cut into her heart and kill her, and two pans to gather her blood for the *moronga* (blood sausage). A huge kettle of water boils over firewood, awaiting the hide, so that it can be scraped hairless and made into *chicharrón* (cracklings) and *chales* (thick, gooey pork rinds with a little meat on them). The uncle, his son, and his nephew Antonio work past 3 a.m. When they stop, they leave the meat hanging until morning, when they will continue preparing the food for the day's guests.

Señora Rosa has told me that Antonio's uncle makes the best *carnitas* in the barrio—quite a compliment, for this barrio in particular. "Son las únicas que no me caen mal" (They are the only ones that do not make me ill), she claims. I am never sure about Señora Rosa and her food tolerance: she proudly and stubbornly continued to eat mole throughout the years when she was saving money to have her gallbladder removed, despite a doctor's warnings that she had to stop eating anything heavy. The way older people insist on eating mole against doctors' orders seems to be more than a matter of pleasure and taste and suggests that they do not believe the doctors know what they are talking about. Another neighbor who is known as being *muy fiestera* (a real partier) shared a bag of green tea with me, saying that it was her protection against feeling ill after eating mole. She carried several bags in her purse at all times in case of an unexpected celebration.

The next day at the cooking site I tell Antonio's uncle that I have heard of his reputation and want to know what makes his *carnitas* so good. He responds by listing many of the ways in which people who do not know what they are doing often ruin *carnitas,* such as boiling the meat in water instead of frying it in its own lard. He soaks the meat in tequila, oranges, pineapples, milk, and herbs before frying it. No wonder they smell and taste so good, I think, recalling what a short time I lasted as a vegetarian when I first arrived in Mexico fifteen years ago.

I do not last long in the yard tonight. Early in the butchering process, when it becomes obvious that I am not going to come to the front, Antonio takes my camera away from me so that he can take pictures himself. Fine: it is his pig, after all, and I am feeling a little dizzy and weak in the knees. I find that I can at last make myself truly useful with the final cleaning efforts in the Niñopa's new house, using my nails to scrape the paint off the windows. My extra height proves a real bonus, and I work past midnight, happy to have the opportunity to contribute. Antonio's *abuelita,* silent and suspicious every time I have been around before, finally speaks to me when I leave: "Buenas noches, güerita" (Good night, blondie).

January 21, 2001: Women of the Circle

I arrive early in the morning. Two women are already here cleaning *jamaica* (hibiscus blossoms) in the yard. I ask the *abuelita*—as everybody calls her out of respect—for an apron.[9] Now I understand why many women in Xochimilco wear an apron over nice and not-so-nice clothes. Today most of them are wearing a sweater.

After years of making *agua de jamaica* for my children, today I learn that—according to these women—the best way is to select two types of *jamaica:* one for flavor and one for color.[10] Two large sacks have been purchased at the principal wholesale market in Mexico City (the Central de Abastos), along with 550 pounds of rice and 440 pounds of beans as well as crates of onions, chiles, tomatoes, and more.

With three of us in the circle, we soon finish cleaning the *jamaica* and move on to the huge sack of guajillo chiles for the *barbacoa.* It appears that the house blessing that will take place later today formally launches the work party, for soon the circle widens to include six women. Most are in their sixties or older, though a young woman from Puebla who married into the community is here with her mother-in-law and young daughter. The elderly women are clearly the guardians of tradition and respected as such. Some young women in the barrio have even told me that *las abuelitas* hide the mole recipe from the younger women, especially their daughters-in-law.

Antonio's mother, Doña Margarita, is an elementary school teacher who works morning and afternoon shifts. His grandmother, Doña Consuelo, and her husband, Don Miguelito, made the commitment to this *mayordomía* over two decades ago.[11] *La abuelita* works all day taking care of the animals in the house-lot garden, cooking for the family, and, recently, making final preparations for the Niñopa. She is in charge of organizing the work crew today and throughout the preparations, assigning each member a specific *comisión* (task). Doña Margarita and the *abuelita* are both preparing food themselves and supervising the crew of women volunteers.

Several circles of women form. The Olivares sisters—never absent from a barrio commitment or a church event—chop serrano chiles, onions, tomatoes, and cilantro to prepare pico de gallo (salsa made of chopped rather than ground ingredients) for the *carnitas*. At the end of the day the Olivares form their circle again, this time to wash dishes in a series of buckets.

Many people bring us food as we work throughout the day. First *la abuelita* passes us *tacos de chalecitos* (the most delicious part of the pig for my taste, but only when freshly cooked and still warm). Somebody else brings a basket of fresh white cheese cut into little cubes, another a basket of cookies. A man arrives with a basket carrying rum and Coca-Cola as well as tequila; after offering drinks to the men sitting around the yard talking or helping with the meat, he finally offers some to the women. Then another round of *chales*, pico de gallo, warm tortillas—not bad at all.

In the back corner of this makeshift outdoor kitchen, women in another circle stir pasta with a wooden spoon, sautéing it in a little oil in the largest clay pot I have ever observed—large enough to take a bath in. The *cazuela* permanently resides in that particular corner, but I have not seen it turned right side up until today. Earlier a woman took the tomatoes to grind at the *molino* (mill) in the plaza just outside the *callejón*. It is ready to pour over the fried pasta; then the women add fresh chicken broth. *Sopa de pasta* is a standard first dish for everyday meals in central Mexico. On this occasion it is being prepared for the workers—both the women cooking and the men cleaning up the neighborhood.

No one goes hungry in these circles. And no one is lonely. As the drinking continues, the men get more emotional. They hug and talk; some cry. The women talk, laugh, and keep working. The circle expands and contracts as some women join and others leave throughout the day, but the gender lines never vary.

The conversations surprise me. They are spicy like the chiles we are cleaning: jokes and complaints about men, gossip about women. This is definitely a powerful circle of female energy—womenspace. My questions and notebook have no place here, so small and finite in contrast to the overflowing reality. It is best to shut up and listen, so I do.

Señora Rosa says she does not like to go to fiestas because everyone is always criticizing everything and everybody else. Today I understand what she means. It is also a place where people notice your skills and willingness (or slowness) to participate in the collective tasks. She told a horror story of arriving early at a fiesta many years ago and being assigned to make a large amount of rice in one of the huge *cazuelas*—something she had never done before, which threw her into a panic. Luckily another person arrived shortly afterward who knew what to do. But, she complains, there is too much gossip in these circles and little to do with God in all the eating and drinking, despite the presumably religious nature of the celebrations. I think that she does not like fiestas in part because staying away from them creates distance from the neighbor women: they know too much about her already, and she knows too much about them as well. She leaves the fiestas to her sister Josefina, whose presence fulfills the need for the participation of her household. Josefina is such a permanent fixture at local fiestas that she has a reputation for getting around as much as the Niñopa.

Today on several occasions I observe the raised eyebrows. At one point the women of the circle question the way we are doing things. Several of us have been deveining the guajillo chiles for a while when a woman asks: "Do we leave the veins in or not?" The eldest woman is usually in charge; in this case the *mayordoma* is both the eldest and the boss, so Antonio's *abuelita* is called in to determine the course of action. The women of the circle glance sideways at each other when she says to leave the veins in. We proceed, leaving both the veins and seeds in now and removing only the stem of the chile, until Antonio's mother, the next-ranking authority after *la abuelita*, comes and says in protest: "What? You are leaving the seeds in?"

When somebody explains that we are doing what the *mayordoma* requested, her daughter, Doña Margarita, decides that there has been a misunderstanding. We are to leave the veins in for spiciness but definitely take the seeds out. They are saved to be taken to the *molino* the next day for another favorite Xochimilca dish, *pepitas de chile*. Made with onion and garlic and sometimes sesame seeds ground alongside the chile seeds, this poor person's mole is unbeatable served with nopales.

What most impresses me about this episode and several others is that nobody in the circle dares to question the *mayordoma* even when all the women know we are doing the wrong thing. I come up against similar boundaries and hierarchies that limit individual decisionmaking later when I try to jump in to help somebody with a specific task. My spontaneity and volunteerism are unwelcome in this setting. The women are not authorized to negotiate their preassigned responsibility. Their allegiance to the *mayor-doma* and to carrying out their commitment or *comisión* as agreed upon in advance supersedes any individual decision or variation on the theme. Each time I finish my chore I am sent back to Doña Consuelo for her to decide what I should do next.

Talk around the dining table is often sexual in Mexico, full of details related to bodies and desire, as might be expected in the sensual realm of food. But while plenty of jokes revolve around chiles in thinly veiled references to the male organ, more blunt talk is usually reserved for same-sex crowds. Within this social context, perhaps the following incident should not have come as a surprise to me.

Doña Margarita's husband approached us and tried to joke with me. "Cuidado no vaya a tocar a Don Panchito" (Be careful not to touch Don Panchito), he says with a chuckle. His sexual innuendo—feigning concern that I might touch my ex-husband's genitals with burning chile residue on my fingers—insinuated a close relationship with both my ex-husband and myself that he did not have. It was totally inappropriate and unexpected, particularly given the powerful gendered space on which he was treading, and I sat there wondering just how drunk he was. Perhaps made bolder by my silence, he made the mistake of following up with a direct insult to the older women of the circle: "¡Eso es para las señoras grandes, ellas ya no agarran nada!" (That is for old women, they do not touch anyone anymore!). The implication was that only older women should be working in the circle peeling chiles because they were too old for sex and would not be touching a penis for the rest of their lives anyway.

One of the old crones in the circle turned to him and fired back: "¿No que nos agarramos a nosotras mismas?" (But do we not touch ourselves?). The women of the circle burst into peals of laughter at this allusion to women's sexual self-sufficiency and masturbation. Doña Margarita's husband hastily retreated like a whipped pup with his tail between his legs. He was not the only one surprised.

Something about the collective, outdoor, and semipublic space of the cooking circle in the house-lot garden invites intimate conversation and hearty laughter. Over and over in my fieldwork I found that in the gendered and social environment of collective food preparation women tended to talk about personal details that are generally not appropriate in mixed company or in a more intimate setting, including the indoor kitchen.

I think of a parallel with the plaza in Mexico and other Latin American settings, where it is socially acceptable for unmarried couples (*novios*) to kiss and hold each other in public in ways they would not dare to in the more private setting of the home. I wonder, is the house-lot garden to the indoor kitchen as the park is to the bedroom? Both are central spaces where apparent transgressions of conduct take place, perhaps because members of the community are actively supervising the space and ultimately control the limits of the transgressions.

January 21, 2001: Don Miguelito

God brought Don Miguelito to Xochimilco. "Soy analfabeta, pero soy un hombre honrado y de mucha fe. Me gusta conocer" (I am illiterate, but I am an honest man with much faith. I like to learn/know). Work is what is important, he tells me. Who knows what will happen to us? Looking me straight in the eyes, he asks: "Do you know when you are going to die?" "Well, no," I reply. "You see?" he asks rhetorically, satisfied, though far from smug. He has made his point.

I am giving my fingers a break from peeling chiles in the women's circle and have joined the men in the back of the yard, where the *carnitas* are almost done. This breaks the unwritten rules of gendered space and is allowed only because of my outsider and temporary role. Every now and then another woman comes back with an empty platter that she loads with the hot *carnitas* coming out of the huge metal pot sizzling over the firewood.

Don Miguelito and his friends, many of whom speak Otomí like himself, are drinking pulque. I drink tequila; others drink Brandy Presidente and Coke. Brandy Presidente is a common and inexpensive brand of rum made from sugarcane in Mexico and should not be confused with the more expensive brandy. It is popular among the middle-class, the young, and those aspiring to climb the social ladder, who consider it superior to the indigenous pulque made from the century plant and now drunk mostly by older, traditional men in central Mexico.

"What do you think of our traditions?" Don Miguelito asks me. "Beautiful, aren't they?" We toast with our plastic cups, standing next the large *cazuela* where the cooked meat is placed. When I ask about the future of this tradition, somebody answers that traditions in Xochimilco will never die but rather improve in the future. The young will carry them forth, all agree, changing them as necessary.

Orphaned in his native state of Mexico at the age of eight, Don Miguelito left his Otomí village and made his way to Mexico City to join some cousins and work in construction. "Allá dejé mi yunque de bueyes y de mula" (I left my plow pulled by oxen and mules there), he says. When he was a skinny little boy, everything was too heavy for him at work, he remembers. After injuring his foot, he was sent back to his village. "But I no longer liked it." He had developed a taste for the city and for earning money and soon returned.

"It was a Thursday," he recalls. He had just finished eating the last *gorditas* (patties of corn dough and pork lard) that he brought with him from home. He was leaning into the river to drink, crying because he had no money and no work. Then a mysterious stranger appeared who led him to Xochimilco and whom he never saw again. The man asked him why he was crying. He had been without work or money for several days himself. But he shared his tortilla with Miguel, pulling it out of his *morralito* (traditional woven shoulder bag). When they finished eating, they took the yellow train to Xochimilco. The man promised they would find work there. At the market in Xochimilco they bought some nopales and tortillas with the small amount of money that Miguelito had left. The man asked him for his last twenty-cent coin to pay for using a restroom. He never returned. "Desapareció y nunca más volvió. Fue Dios" (He disappeared and never came back. It was God).

Miguelito soon found a man who offered to employ him working his *chinampas*. They agreed on three pesos per day and that Miguelito could stay until he married. He did, lasting twenty years with the man, and has fond memories of those years. "Lo del sueldo era lo de menos; me quedé porque compartía parejo su comida" (The salary was the least of it; I stayed because he shared his food equally).

January 21, 2001: The Blessing

Before *la comida* (the midday meal) the priest blesses "the people of the house and the barrio." I am surprised to hear him urge people to recognize their *mexicanidad.* Their Mexicanness, he says, includes Spanish and indigenous elements, both the dance of the *chinelos* and the Niñopa tradition, that are beautiful and deeply rooted. After the blessing, one of the many people packed into the Niñopa's new house asks if the dance of the *chinelos* is of the devil (*del diablo*). "No," the priest responds, saying that alcohol in excess is the problem, not the dance per se. It is fine to dance, the priest indicates, as long as the intent is clear: to celebrate the presence of God. The question provokes a brief sermon against alcoholism and domestic violence, both of which plague the local community. I am left pondering the ongoing struggle of the Catholic church to keep Xochimilcas and so many others in Mexico who celebrate traditions of old within its fold. Problems related to excessive drinking drive Catholics to join the "new sects," as people call the evangelical Protestant groups in Mexico.

January 28, 2001: Cleaning Tamarind Seeds

It is Sunday, and the sound of church bells ringing atop the chapel permeates the *callejón.* I am the first in the house-lot garden this morning, peeling tamarind (*tamarindo*). I have the place to myself, with no one to talk to. Roosters crow, pigs snort. Looking up, I see cauliflowers on the *chinampa* across the canal. Huge clay pots (*cazuelas de barro*) surround me, along with stacks of bulk food purchased yesterday at the Central de Abastos: sacks of potatoes, crates of tomatoes (*jitomates*) and green tomatoes (*tomates,* called tomatillos in the United States), boxes of garlic, sacks of *tamarindo,* fresh green chiles, dried mulato chiles.

Women, mostly *abuelitas,* start trickling in, soon forming a circle of seven. Señora Josefina and *la comadre* Meme, Doña Claudia's mother-in-law, are among them. Peeling the tamarind for the drinks is the first task today. Hands are busy; the day is long.

As we work in the yard preparing food, the men clean the *callejón*. They cut down a dead tree and spend the day carrying it out in pieces. My eleven-year-old son helps with this task. The men string wires back and forth and hang lights and colorful *papel picado* on them to announce the arrival of the Niñopa. Many neighbors are painting their outside walls.

In the circle the listening is rich. Talk turns to how lazy women are today. One woman stops working to point at me with her finger. I am an exception: a young woman willing to work. Another *abuelita* goes further: women today are just cigarette smokers, short skirts, and crossed legs. "They buy a few pesos of beans and a few chiles rellenos at the *cocina económica* [inexpensive restaurant or food stand with traditional style daily fare] and take that home to their families." Yes, the rest comment, shaking their heads with disapproval. And yet, another woman comments, it is cheaper to buy food at the *cocina económica* today than to pay for black beans and the gas it takes to cook them.

Another complaint: young women are not respectful anymore; they refuse to be subordinate to men. "Ya no aguantan las mujeres" (Women just can't take it anymore), says one woman, referring to the traditional female role and the treatment which younger women are not always willing to tol-

Serious talk among women of the circle

erate. One woman complains of her son's failed marriage, blaming his lazy wife: she advised him to look for "una mujer que sí acepte sufrir" (a woman who would accept suffering). Apparently, for many though not all of these older women, suffering is women's lot. They all agree that it is getting harder and harder for young men to find women who "accept suffering."

"¡Ya no aguantan los chingadazos!" jokes another, with a clever twist of phrase, implying that what women are expected to tolerate is abuse that they are perhaps right in rejecting. *Chingadazos* is from the verb *chingar*, which is a part of most Mexican explicatives and can be loosely defined as "to screw." In the context of this conversation and social context, *chingadazos* can be interpreted as physical blows or beatings. Despite the occasional joke, the topic is a serious one. The women of the circle—including younger women—are perturbed by the loss of respect for tradition, though they recognize that some traditions in the household are not in women's interest. These circles of women working together at the fiestas also serve to rally support for abused women at times. More than once during my years in the barrio I heard of women confronting another woman's husband for beating up his wife.

Stories turn to cases of wife-beating and to women who do not tolerate domestic violence: some hit back, others leave the men that abuse them, and some even manage to reform them and achieve some kind of domestic peace, if not bliss. They chuckle at hearing of women who beat their husbands: this is clearly an inversion of the gender paradigm. While I heard several stories of women hitting their husbands during my years in Xochimilco, I never heard of men wearing aprons. One young man even told me that a man who goes to the market or helps his wife or mother in the kitchen is called a *mandilón* (apron-wearer), definitely a pejorative term.

When the talk about women physically abused at the hands of men gets to me, I make the mistake of assuming a "shared sisterhood" and open my big mouth. "That is why I do not have a husband," I say, implying that I chose not to have a husband because it was too much trouble. A sudden silence in the circle weighs on me like an elephant. Eyebrows are raised, and everyone looks at me as if seeing me for the first time. Señora Josefina, Señora Rosa's sister and a single mother who endures more than her share of public scrutiny, intercedes on my behalf, saving my reputation. "Of course she has a husband," she assures the other women, as if clarifying a minor point, "but he lives in Cuernavaca right now and she lives here." *Aaah*, the collective sigh of relief is audible as the women go back to work. Thank you, Doña Josefina. I may be allowed to return tomorrow after all.

Clearly it is unacceptable to these women that I should be unmarried. Perhaps in part because they know my ex-husband and my children, *los güeritos* (the blondies), everyone in the barrio insists on treating me as Pancho's wife even though many know we are divorced. In another collective outdoor cooking experience, several women ask me outright if I still let Pancho sleep with me. I explain that he has remarried and that I have a boyfriend. On another occasion, Doña Teodora, eighty-one and a widow of about forty years, insists that she would have accepted her husband back in my circumstances.[12]

January 28, 2001: A Woman's Handshake

"A woman's handshake," I've often thought to myself as women with hands full of corn dough offer their forearm to another's outstretched hand. As part of the circle today, my fingers sticky with tamarind pulp, I offer my forearm several times. Every time a woman joins our circle she first goes around and shakes every other woman's forearm. Then she puts on her apron and joins the circle. Rituals: I've never felt such a part of this community as when someone shakes my forearm in the circle.

This is not just a women's thing by any means, but I think of it as the women's handshake, because it is so common in these cooking circles. Mechanics with greasy hands do the same thing. With hands dirty but a handshake socially obligatory in Xochimilco, people at work offer their forearms in greeting. Shaking hands is so important in this barrio that people will do so twice in less than a minute, stopping and putting their basket down in the *callejón* to greet an elder appropriately: "Buenas tardes, tía [auntie]." And immediately again: "Buenas tardes." (Hello. Good-bye.) To do otherwise can be taken as an insult or a sign of broken relations.

February 2, 2001: *El Mero Día*

"¡Ya es tarde, güerita!" (It is late, blondie!) several women point out to me at once. The three women who made the *atole* began at 3 a.m., including *la abuelita* Olivares. Everybody noticed that I was not there. With the Niñopa at the center of their universe, I cannot explain that I have been in

Tetecala, where the Día de la Candelaria is also one of the most important community celebrations. My lack of loyalty would be unacceptable, a violation of our relationship. But I am here now and dive into the final preparations. Today we prepare to serve the large crowds and special distinguished guests: multiple menus and massive quantities. *Hoy es el mero día* (Today is the very day).

The sense of excitement in the air is almost as thick as the smoke. Everything is just about ready. Banners with the Niñopa's image flutter in the breeze overhead as I walk down the *callejón* from my house. Anyone in the main plaza by the church today could easily find the way to the Niñopa's destination: banners strung row after row above the main avenue mark the path. Three different arches are decorated with corn and bean *semillas* (seeds) and mark each turn. The first, at the entrance into the *callejón*, is beautifully decorated with flowers made of painted seeds. Camilo, one of Señora Rosa's sons, tells me that the seeds are used to ask the Niñopa for a plentiful harvest.

Another arch of seeds bearing an idealized image of the Niñopa amidst canals and *trajineras* marks the fork down the narrow alley at the end of the first and wider part of the *callejón*. The final arch has been set up over the entrance that leads into the house-lot garden where the final food preparations are now taking place and where the Niñopa's new house awaits him.

Walking underneath the final arch, I am enveloped in the smell of wood smoke and a mingling of delicious food scents: *barbacoa, atole*, chiles. After walking past the tables that have been set up in the front of the yard, I reach the women's circles in the back. I think of these women as the rearguard, dignified and somber. Like the female soldiers in the black-and-white photographs of the Mexican Revolution, the women preparing food in the house-lot garden are *soldaderas* in the trenches.

The *atole* has been left in the hands of the three elders. Each of them has two long gray braids tied together on her back. It is no easy thing to stir huge pots of *atole* nonstop for hours with big wooden spatulas. Besides the certain backache, there is danger of the *atole* spoiling in the cooking process. "El chiste es la movida" (The trick is in the stirring), the women tell me. "Si no, se pega, se corta, se hace bola" (Otherwise it scorches, curdles, gets lumpy). As expected, the three women have fulfilled their duty. They are victorious: seven huge pots brimming with *atole champurrado* (*atole* with cocoa, cinnamon, and brown sugar) sit steaming in the cool morning air.

Made of blue corn toasted on the *comal* and ground at the *molino,* cinnamon, and *piloncillo* (dark sugar), today the *atole* also includes fresh milk from Don Miguelito's cows. Blue corn, one woman leans over and tells me, "es más sabroso, más oloroso" (has a better flavor, better aroma). "My daughter brought me blue and white corn from the same soil," she says, "but it does not taste the same. Blue corn tastes better, smells better. You will taste the difference if you compare them." I am handed a cup full of hot *atole* and a *cocol* (bread from Chalma with anise seeds) as soon as I arrive: a delicious and warm welcome.

By 9 a.m., when I join the group, television crews from national and foreign stations have arrived to interview the women—"las que prepararon el atole, el mole" (the ones who prepared the *atole* and the mole). Their presence has caused quite a commotion, and everyone is repeating excitedly: "¡Que a las cinco y cuarto vamos a estar en la TV, en el 13, TV Azteca!" (We'll be on at 5:15 on channel 13!). The women proudly show the media representatives around the house-lot garden, telling them to point their cameras this way and that. "Que pasen a la cocina, que vean el arroz, que vean los peroles de carne" (Tell them to come into the kitchen, to see the rice, to see the pots of meat). The women of the circle are the heroines of the day.

The kitchen they refer to in this case is adjacent to the main cooking area in the yard. It seems to be attached to the house-lot garden, rather than vice versa: a small, dark, room. Only about three women fit in there at a time. The meat has been piled high in pots there, beef that was soaked in chiles and steamed overnight in the back of the yard in huge drums. All over central Mexico, these oil drums have replaced the traditional *barbacoa* pits, though the *pencas de magüey* (century plant leaves) are still used in the steaming process for flavor. I remember seeing *barbacoa* steamed in the ground ten years ago in Teotihuacan. Mexican and foreign tourists flock in droves to that nearby archeological site (which includes the famous Pyramid of the Sun and Pyramid of the Moon) to get a taste of prehispanic history, which many food vendors are happy to oblige.

Yesterday the men sat drinking and sharing stories in the little indoor kitchen as the women sat nearby in the yard working on the final food preparations. It had looked more like a storage shed a few days earlier, piled high with crates and *costales* (large sacks) of food. *La abuelita* sits in the yard at the entrance to the kitchen, tearing the meat into serving-sized chunks with her hands. It is usually the older woman or someone assigned and supervised by her who determines the portions and controls the distribution of the food—a task of tremendous responsibility. This small smoke kitchen is one of three. The other two are the large cooking area in the yard where the huge *cazuela* always sits over firewood and the relatively modern kitchen with refrigerator and stove.

This morning I count twelve huge *cazuelas* of rice (*arroz*) in a neat line, each on its own pile of rocks or bricks over a small wood fire and covered with pieces of plastic as it cooks: over two hundred pounds of rice for today's meal. There are eight *peroles* (big metal buckets) of meat: Antonio's uncle came back yesterday to help slaughter three bulls and three of the young pigs. The beef is for the masses, but the pork is for special guests: for *la mayordomía*, including the *posaderos* who take on the commitment today together with the chief *mayordomos*, Doña Consuelo and Don Miguelito. The *posaderos* will be honored with a special basket of food to take home (*su itacate*) as well, with a whole chicken and some mole, nopales, salsa, and tortillas. Finally, the breakfast food consists of the seven big pots of *atole* in addition to many large baskets covered with cloth, holding the *cocoles.*

The yard is buzzing with activity and expectation. One woman goes for water to dampen a stick that has caught fire under a *cazuela* of rice. Keeping the temperature under the cooking pot just right with firewood is no easy feat; I often hear women complain about it in all three of my research communities. The youths of the *estudiantina* who have been practicing their songs in the alley every day are now smartly dressed in gray and white slacks or skirts and blazers. Though some of them had never played music before organizing for the Niñopa, they are sounding very good today. The young men in charge of security are wearing earplugs and carrying two-way radios. The reporters from TV Azteca try to record an interview with the women of the circle but are interrupted time and time again by the sound of fireworks exploding overhead and the brass band playing somewhere nearby. They seem uncomfortable, disoriented, and out of place here, so close yet so far from their lives in Mexico City. Amidst the chaos, everyone is offered *atole* and *cocoles.*

The *mayordomos* prepare for today's official ceremonies, beginning with Mass in the main church downtown. *La abuelita* leaves the rearguard in charge: "Ahí les encargamos, tías, por favor" (We leave it in your hands, aunties, please). Her daughter provides final directives: have everything

Twelve pots of rice for the Niñopa celebration

ready, pick up the 220 pounds of tortillas ordered at the neighborhood *tortillería*, finish setting the tables, and—the most difficult and controversial task of all—do not let anyone past the gate into the house-lot garden. The family has decided at the last minute that it will be too difficult to manage the crowds in the narrow *callejón* and in their house-lot garden. Instead we should set up to serve the majority of the people at the first archway, where the alley begins.

The women urge me to go to Mass, which they consider the principal ceremony today. I am more interested in the final food preparation that continues behind the scenes. In the end I participate in both. Mass is a dramatic event, with many Niños Dios besides the Niñopa as well as many human babies and small children, all taken to receive the priest's blessing. This is also the day when farmers take their seeds to be blessed. The courtyard of the main church (*la parroquia*) is a spectacle this morning, with Mass held outdoors, like the services held for Indians in colonial Mexico. A tarp has been put up to provide some shade, though entrepreneurs of all ages are making a killing by selling paper hats and hand-held fans as well. I am struck by the symbols of syncretism: baby Jesus figures sitting in baskets with the corn, dressed in everything from white gowns to *chinelo* outfits.

Niño Dios in a basket of corn for blessing

I find a seat next to Marta, one of Doña Claudia's daughters, and we chat for a while before Mass begins. She tells me some of her family's stories about the Niñopa from the time when her grandfather's brother was *mayordomo*. "¡Como es de travieso el Niñopa!" (What a mischievous boy he is!), she begins. "When my grandfather's brother had him, he would leave his toys strewn under his crib. And his shoes would be scuffed in the morning!" Marta tells me that all the Niños Dios that are here this morning must have new clothes or at the very least newly washed clothes. The water from washing those clothes is special and is sprinkled around the house-lot garden, much as the water from boiling the corn is used.

I leave Mass early to go help with the food, only to find the women facing an unexpected problem: how to get the dozen huge and very heavy *cazuelas* from the yard to the entrance of the *callejón* where the food is to be served. This is a new challenge due to the last-minute displacement of the dining area from the house-lot garden to the street. Several women are scrambling around, looking for burlap sacks to put under each *cazuela* so that they can carry them without the risk of the handles breaking off and the rice spilling.

Here begins the final escapade of the day and probably the most fun I will have all year—despite my knowing full well that I am seriously transgressing gender barriers. Earlier I had seen among the pots a bike with three wheels and a small platform that the father and grandfather use every day to work with their animals and plants. I am aware of the scandal that will ensue when I offer to use the bike to transport the rice. They are all happy with the suggestion until they see that I actually mean to ride the bike rather than walk beside it. Several older women offer to push it with me so that I will not have to straddle the seat. Time is really pressing upon us, however, and I decide to go ahead in the name of efficiency—very American of me. Though bicycles and even bicycle taxis are very common in this town, in all my years in Xochimilco I can only remember seeing one woman riding a bike alone rather than riding side-saddle on the back.

The idea of women opening their legs is relatively scandalous among the older women. Just yesterday in Tetecala, Doña Eustoquia shared her opinion of the young woman in her house, criticizing the way she carried her little girl on her hip, with her legs "wide open" and wrapped around the mother. So, knowing I am making local history, I cart the *cazuelas* one by one down the alley past the people who stand outside their doorways to observe the spectacle. Señora Rosa later tells me that she heard the gossip before I even reached her door with the first load—though it took me less than two minutes to get that far. Another young woman with a baseball cap joins me, and together we move the rice in time for the feast, much to the collective relief and surprise.[13] Doña Nati, Raquel's mother, chuckles and pats my arm as I ride past her little store at the bridge. Another woman offers to take a picture of me with my camera.

Later, after thousands of people have been fed in the street, those who want to visit the Niñopa in his new home line up and file into the *callejón*. Many are offended that they were not allowed in earlier: "People who come to visit the Niño should never be turned away; it is an offense."

Some fume at the further delay at the entrance to the hosts' property, where the young members of the security crew allow only a few in at a time and escort them out before letting another group enter. For the most part people are astonishingly patient. But some of the neighbors from the *callejón* who have been stuck on the wrong side of the makeshift barrier at the second archway for hours are upset that they were not informed of the change in plans. This will be the topic of heated discussion in the neighborhood for months, if not years.

For now, tensions are high at the third and final arch, where the young men are trying to keep people out, including some older people who have been visiting the Niñopa for longer than the temporary guards have been alive and who are clearly offended. Different social classes and ethnic groups mix but do not blend in the line. Some come from villages just outside of town or farther away. Some are indigenous people in traditional clothes, bringing their own Niño Dios and corn before the Niñopa for his blessing.[14] Some elegantly dressed Xochimilcas feel they have a particular right to the Niñopa and expect preferential treatment, wanting immediate access not only to the altar but to the dining tables set up in the house-lot garden. Names are checked against a master list, and in the end everyone who has come to see the Niñopa has a chance to come in, kneel before him in front of the hundreds of flower arrangements that have been placed at his feet, and then leave.

In the house-lot garden, meanwhile, the special guests participate in the ceremony that transfers the responsibility for the appropriate care and celebration of the Niñopa traditions from one *mayordomo* to the next and for-

mally introduces the new *posaderos*. My name is not on the list, but someone hisses at me, "Pssst, ¡güerita, pásale!" (Pssst, blondie, get in here!).

February 26, 2001: *Hoy Cocinan los Hombres*

Tomorrow the tour guides are in charge of the fiesta of Xaltocán. Like the
other groups, barrios, and pueblos of Xochimilco, they organize and finance the events for one day, beginning with a special Mass in the morning
and ending with a meal for all in the streets. Today they are gathered to
prepare the meal. The collection taken up to fund the event was 500 pesos
(about US$55) apiece from the eighty members of the organization of *guías*
(tourist guides) in Xochimilco. The *guías* wave you down, sometimes riding
alongside cars on their bicycles, and ask if you are looking for the embar-
cadero or a *trajinera*.[15] The collection amounts to a total of nearly US$4,500
for the party, not counting the *promesas* that people fulfill by bringing a
contribution like the 550 pounds of tortillas that will be donated by devout
followers of la Virgen de los Dolores. As several *guías* proudly tell me today,
no matter how much they prepare, it is never enough. People love this fiesta
and flock to this particular meal, which has historically been one of the best
parties in the month-long celebration honoring the Virgen de Xaltocán.

This is apparently an event where men break some gender barriers in
kitchenspace, though by no means all. I was so interested in observing the
guías cooking that I came to Xochimilco for the day, despite having just
returned from the all-night hike to Chalma on a pilgrimage with a group
from Ocotepec. My knees are so sore that I can hardly walk. I take the opportunity to bring Señora Rosa's family the *cocoles* that she has requested
and that everyone from Xochimilco who goes to Chalma is expected to
bring back to share.

Señora Josefina accompanies me to the preparations for the fiesta. Like
her mother, *la abuelita* Daniela, who never missed a fiesta (walking around
town and on pilgrimages to Chalma and other sites in bare feet for her
entire life), and unlike her sister Rosa, Señora Josefina is the stereotypical
Xochimilca. With her black hair hanging in braids behind her back and
her apron over her dress, she is always ready to contribute to a community
event. Despite her announcement at the beginning of my year of fieldwork
that she was not willing to participate in my research and that I should not

expect to interview her, she is an invaluable ambassador and cultural interpreter in events like this one.

Señora Rosa's *compadre* Don Benjamín, who has been a *guía* for forty years in addition to his job as a clerk for the local government, asked his colleagues for permission to invite me to this event in Xaltocán. When I arrive with Doña Josefina, he welcomes us at the door and proudly announces that I can take pictures of anything I want, something he has obviously cleared with his fellow *guías* in advance. Stepping through the archway into the inner courtyard, I know it is going to be a fruitful day.

Several neighbors in the barrio told me about this event, the tour guides' day in the month-long Fiesta de Xaltocán. They knew I was studying cooking, and some understood that I was looking at gender roles, so they thought I would be interested in an event that, though traditional, included men cooking. When I discussed this with Don Benjamín last week, I was thus surprised to learn that the men "do everything" but have six women to *guisar*, a word which I had previously understood to mean "cook." "Los hombres hacen todo" (The men do everything), he explained. They pay for things, carry things, chop things, prepare the meat, set the tables, serve the food—everything but make the rice or anything else that is *guisado*. In fact, the men do everything for the rice but cook it. They clean it, chop the carrots, peel the peas, and prepare the tomatoes for grinding in a blender. I was stunned, having never seen men cooking in this town except at commercial establishments.

"Hoy cocinan los hombres" (Today the men cook). Yet women fry the rice in oil before adding the tomato puree, stir it, and make sure it is seasoned correctly, because, I learn today, they are the ones with *sazón* (a special touch). *Sazón* is the secret ingredient in every successful dish, the seasoning that gives food flavor. All year I have been hearing people say that the recipe is somewhat irrelevant, that each dish is different "según el sazón de cada quien" (depending on the personal touch of each cook). Today I learn that the magic and essential ingredient that makes things taste right is in women's hands or touch, an opinion that people in my other two sites later support. Essentialized notions of gender roles are clearly part of the recipe.

Yet, as I find out today, men are expert at flavoring as well. I drink the first delicious pulque in my life—way too much of it, as I discover when I stand up to take my leave several hours later. It is *curado* (cured) with fresh

Men cleaning hibiscus for the Fiesta de Xaltocán

tangerine and sweetened condensed milk. I am told that the tomato-cured pulque also on hand is amazing as well: it is served with hot sauce and lemon, somewhat like tequila with *sangrita* (spicy tomato juice). Later my neighbor Beatriz tells me that those are the people who really know how to cure the pulque—so that even people like myself who are ill-disposed to its slobbery texture or bitter taste will ask for more.

Don Fermín, the man who serves me a glass of pulque from the pitcher, says he that he has been drinking pulque instead of water ever since he was four years old. "Xochimilco antes era un lugar de pescado y de pulque" (Xochimilco used to be a place of fish and pulque), he says, lamenting the changes. The fish are mostly gone because the city took the water, and the young no longer drink pulque because they have become professionals, he says, and pulque smells too strong afterward on people's breath and is not tolerated in offices. Others later told me that young people prefer "brandy" because of the status associated with it, which clearly requires leaving pulque behind. Most people consider pulque an indigenous drink that the older generation—*los antigüitos* (the ancient ones)—drank but that is not appropriate today. It is often served, however, at traditional fiestas in Xochimilco, though frequently in a back room or in the back of the same house-lot garden where women are preparing the food. Don Fermín tells me that the pulque I drank on other occasions was a type cultivated and prepared in Huitzilac in Morelos. I am surprised at his accuracy: indeed, not only was it from Huitzilac but I actually drank it in that very town. He says that it was not the same pulque; that was *clachique,* young pulque made from *aguamiel* (maguey juice: literally, "honey water"). The pulque preferred in Xochimilco was *pulque mexicano,* pulque made in barrels or in *pulquerías.* One man says that you can tell a good pulque right away by the thread it draws when served (in other words, it pours in a single strand rather than dripping), but Don Fermín says that you can also tell a good pulque by its name: Velásquez and Romero, for instance, are trusted brands.

May 3, 2001: Day of the Holy Cross

I visited Xochimilco briefly this morning before driving back to Ocotepec for *la comida de todos los barrios* (the meal of all the barrios) at María Teresa's. Today is Día de la Santa Cruz (Day of the Holy Cross). It is also el Día del Albañil, the day when people celebrate construction workers, cooking a special meal for them and giving them the afternoon off, usually to get drunk. It is one of those days when I need to be in three places at once, including Santa Cruz, one of the four barrios of Ocotepec.

New colored plastic flags in the style of the traditional *papel picado* have been hung in Xochimilco among the now tattered flags leftover from the Niñopa reception in February. They were put up a couple of days ago for the barrio celebration of the Día del Niño (Children's Day), April 30. Always a big day in the *callejón,* it has brought thousands this year to see Xochimilco's favorite child of all, the Niñopa. Neighbors always set up booths with miniature food portions along the side of the alley; this year Niñopa followers set up food booths as well. Señora Rosa was impressed with the amounts eaten. Beatriz made a killing by selling her Niñopa candles.

It is a time of renewal: fiesta upon fiesta, layers of color and sounds and smells. I am reminded of the slogans on local tourism propaganda: "¡Xochimilco, siempre de fiesta!" (Xochimilco, always a fiesta!).[16] This town is always celebrating something. At the end of the *callejón* several men—young and old—are building a *torito* from wire and fireworks to be burned later this evening in the plaza in front of the neighborhood chapel. People will finish the day's celebration with the excitement of running to avoid the *bus-*

capiés shooting along the ground and exploding at their feet. The man carrying the *torito* and running through the crowd may have the most fun of all. Some people will most likely be burned, but if they are from Xochimilco they may show their scar with pride and come back the next time, maybe even to carry the bull. Strangers to Xochimilco, like the ex-boyfriend of Señora Rosa's comadre's daughter, who burned his testicles in one such event, are not likely ever to return or to understand why anyone would want to run such "barbarian" risks.

Like the bullfights in Spain, Xochimilco's traditions are hard for outsiders to comprehend. Despite the accidents that occur every year, the government has not been able to stop the fireworks, just as the church has not been able to stop the drinking. Few politicians are stupid enough to risk their political career trying, despite the ban in Mexico City on sales of fireworks and indiscriminate burning. In Xochimilco, as in Ocotepec and most pueblos in Mexico, men's role in making, launching, and playing with fireworks is like women's traditional roles in kitchenspace: both are essential ingredients in local celebrations. As such, they are untouchable, a site of cultural resistance.

2 Ocotepec

"Not Letting the City Eat This Town Up"

In Ocotepec, known for its celebration of the Day of the Dead as well as the Posadas preceding Christmas, each of the four barrios celebrates its own patron saint in the annual *fiesta del barrio*. Each barrio formally participates in the fiestas of the other three barrios as well as over thirty additional fiestas, including the celebration of the town's patron saint, San Salvador, on August 6. Local residents are proud of their community's traditions (Díaz 1995; von Mentz de Boege 1995), which have become more familiar to outsiders thanks in part to a series of documentaries about Palm Sunday (Domingo de Ramos) and the Days of the Dead, produced in conjunction with the state school of anthropology and history (Escuela de Antropología e Historia).

Fiestas in the community are very complex and include a series of ritualized visits by representatives of other barrios and neighboring communities, both in preparation for the celebration and during the event itself. On each occasion the host barrio receives the visitors with a special meal. When requesting permission to participate in the festivities, the outside guests leave their *estandarte* (a banner with the name and symbol of their barrio) in the host barrio; they retrieve it on yet another visit, again celebrated with food. The new *compadres* and *comadres* from each town established through such visits meet and share food and drink, as do the old ones from previous years.

Ocotepec welcomes visitors and has developed a large roadside economy selling food to tourists. Many locals have sold their land at lucrative prices to refugees from the smog and stress of Mexico City. Nonetheless, the people strongly oppose outsiders—including governmental authorities from Cuernavaca—who "steal" their land. Local agrarian issues and organized opposition to changes in land use or ownership make the newspaper nearly every day. Several key government-sponsored projects have been effectively stopped. I was even told that when a recent and much despised governor arrived for a visit, the people did not allow him to speak and instead asked him to leave. During my stay, the Zapatista Army for National Liberation (EZLN), based in Chiapas, led a peace march from the south of the country to the capital city. When the caravan came through Ocotepec on the way to Cuernavaca, where a demonstration was planned, the people of Ocotepec barred its passage. They held an unscheduled meeting with the indigenous *comandantes,* who agreed to include Ocotepec's petition demanding respect for their communal land among the many grievances they were bringing to national attention in a formal and dramatic session with the national Congress.

This chapter is based on my participant-observation in two of Ocotepec's celebrations, Palm Sunday and the Day of the Holy Cross, in the barrios that bear their names: Los Ramos and Santa Cruz. I narrate events leading up to the principal celebrations and events on the following day, when I returned to help clean up. The two experiences differ in several important respects. I had no prior contact in Los Ramos and had to return several times before I was able to speak with the women I wanted to interview. I was linked to the barrio of Santa Cruz by a previous acquaintance, whose introductions set a familiar tone for the encounter. Additionally, the hostess of this second fiesta had a daughter who was studying anthropology at the university nearby and had the perspective of a semioutsider because she had lived outside Ocotepec for some years. For her, hosting the *comida de todos los barrios* (meal for all the barrios) was an important "coming out" of sorts, a ritual meant to demonstrate her belonging. Not surprisingly, in these circumstances, my questions and observations were better understood and welcomed. In contrast, the hostess in Los Ramos was a long-time resident; her own meal was not intended for a group as large or as public as the one in Santa Cruz but was an expected component of the celebration of Palm Sunday year after year.

March 25, 2001: The Barrio de los Ramos
Two Weeks before Palm Sunday

With Palm Sunday only two weeks away, I intend to find a group of women in Ocotepec's barrio of that name (Los Ramos) who will allow me to participate in their food preparation for this community celebration. Los Ramos is one of the four barrios in this town, the second on the north side of the road that cuts through Ocotepec, leading from Cuernavaca to Tepoztlán.

Knowing that the chapel representatives meet every Sunday at 8 a.m., I drag my youngest son out of bed and head out with him in tow, hoping they can point me in the right direction.

We drive up Francisco I. Madero Street to a brightly colored chapel that is the outstanding point in the immediate landscape. I ask a man and a woman standing outside of their house next to the chapel if they know where I can find the people in charge of cooking for the upcoming fiesta. The barrio representatives just left, they say. The man runs to the corner and whistles at four men walking two blocks ahead on the dirt road leading away from the chapel. They cannot hear him, but another man closer to them does and in turn calls out to them. In this first welcoming encounter with Los Ramos, the barrio appears to be a network, a whole made up of individual but synchronized parts.

We catch up to the men, who surprise me by assuming that I intend to work for the upcoming fiesta: "¿Va a usted a prestar servicio?" (Are you going to lend service?). This strikes me as unusual and positive, because in Xochimilco I was only allowed to lend service in preparation for the Niñopa's fiesta after years of prior residence and months of direct offers. Ocotepec has many newcomers, both middle-class environmental refugees from Mexico City who have bought up land in the community and poor indigenous migrants from the southern state of Guerrero, who are also interested in supporting local traditions. Perhaps that is why many neighbors that I interact with this morning assume that I am seeking to contribute money or work for the upcoming fiesta.

The whole barrio seems to be aware of our presence before I can locate the chapel representatives on top of the hill, el Cerro de la Cruz, cleaning a plot of land with a cross on top. I explain that I am a student studying *las tradiciones en la comida* (food traditions) and that I would like to help prepare food for the upcoming celebration on Palm Sunday. On the Cerro de la Cruz overlooking Ocotepec and Cuernavaca below, an older man comes forward to receive us. Right away he offers the information that four *mayordomos* are in charge, as well as several other key organizers for the upcoming celebration. He does not know who is in charge of food this year, because many people participate. There is a list, he says, with different families signed up for different meals or portions of meals, such as the rice, the breakfast, or the dinner for the musicians, for instance. It is too much for one family, he adds. When I say that I want to help with the food, he asks: "¿Usted tiene un predio por acá?" (Do you have a plot around here?). He seems to assume that I belong to the neighborhood somehow and want to take responsibility for an entire meal.

I explain that I want to help with a meal that somebody else is hosting and that I am a student studying food preparation. He gives me the name of Doña Rosalinda, a woman who hosted a *comida* last year and will know the many people who have that responsibility this time around. "She can direct you to the right women," he says, "and may even allow you to help her cook this year. Tell her the church representatives sent you." I am in luck: such an introduction will certainly ease my entry into the barrio.

I arrive at Doña Rosalinda's, but she is out for the day. Her house is adjacent to the barrio chapel: it is new, with two stories made out of adobe bricks and a *carnicería* (butcher shop) and *tortillería* on the edge of the lot. She appears to be a woman of means, though later she tells me that her income came from selling her land (cornfields) off parcel by parcel and that she has none left. At one point she asks me if I will help her obtain used clothes from the United States that she can sell at the market.

The women in the butcher shop try to answer my questions. "Who is in charge of cooking this year? Is it Doña Leti or Doña Laura?" They do not know and suggest I return in the morning.

I leave with a curiosity about how this growing town with shrinking cornfields maintains its traditions. In all three of my research sites, outsiders—be they rural immigrants or city refugees—apparently play a key role in supporting and transforming traditions. They come eager to belong and adopt a local identity to which they can contribute with different types of resources.

March 26, 2001: Meeting the Cousins and Doña Rosalinda

Back at Rosalinda's house this morning, I chat with her cousins. At first glance the two seem to embody the differences that I find between the older and younger generations in my sites. Susana—*la güera*—has long blonde hair and wears tight jeans. Doña Adelita has two black braids hanging down her back and wears an apron over her loose-fitting dress. She is sweeping the house-lot garden but edges closer, interested in joining the conversation.

Doña Rosalinda's lot adjoins Susana's at the back. About five kids between the ages of four and thirteen run around us in the yard, chasing each other. The introduction from the chapel representative is very important; but it is the people's pride in Ocotepec's reputation for celebration of Palm Sunday and especially Semana Santa (Holy Week) that really opens doors to discussions on town life and food traditions. It is no surprise to anyone that a student should come to inquire about these. They are anxious to spread the town's reputation and attract even more visitors to their fiestas.

This family has a long history of hosting meals for Palm Sunday and is proud of it. "Huy, eso viene desde muy antes" (That comes from way back), says Doña Adelita when I ask how long their family has been preparing food for Domingo de Ramos. "Nothing has changed," she asserts, a statement that I hear many times over, sometimes a little defensively. "Aquí es el mole, esa es la tradición" (Mole is the thing here, that is the tradition). When I mention that in Xochimilco mole is traditional but increasingly replaced by meat in many festivities because of the cost of chiles, she softens her stance with a statement that is often repeated here as in Xochimilco: "Lo que uno pueda dar" (Whatever you can give). She means that any offering is well received. But in their house, she says, even if they serve *pancita* (tripe) in the morning,[1] they serve mole for the main meal.

I realize then that people may be eager to talk to me about their traditions but are often apprehensive about my observing any deterioration: change is synonymous with loss or failure. For instance, when I met the woman who cooks year after year for an annual town fiesta in Tetecala, her first words were an embarrassed apology for not preparing the food according to tradition. It is a double-edged sword to inquire about traditions, opening doors but tightening the discourse. In any case, under no circumstances will complete strangers lead me into their kitchens and tell me what and how they cook for their family. Food preparation for community celebrations usually takes place in the more public sphere of the house-lot garden and is definitely the place to start with people I do not know. If I am lucky, the relationships that I establish there will bring me closer to accessing women's homes and learning more about their everyday cooking.

The cousins explain that different families are asked by the church committee to receive different *promesas*, as she calls the pilgrims who have ongoing commitments and relationships with the local celebration and who come from other neighborhoods inside and outside of Ocotepec. They mention the town of San Francisco (in the state of Mexico), Xochimilco, and the other three barrios of Ocotepec as examples of places that send regular emissaries. Of course, they are formally received with a meal.

Doña Adelita stresses that they do this out of faith. "Primero Dios, luego nosotros. Si Dios nos da licencia, aquí estamos para colaborar" (First God, then us. If God grants us life and the means, we are here to collaborate). With her hands on her heart, her eyes dreamy, her face blissful, she expresses that it is out of love ("es por amor") that people continue the tradition. No wonder any perceived loss of tradition is such an emotional thing.

I am finally about to leave when Rosalinda arrives. I see her walking up the dusty street, carrying her groceries in one of those colorful bags made of vinyl-weave that you see in markets all over Mexico. Obviously tired and busy, she is nonetheless kind and curious. She invites me to return that afternoon to join her and a group of women who are gathering to make decorations for the chapel. She also tells me that they start preparing food this coming Thursday and Friday. The group always meets at five in the afternoon, after all the women have gone to the market and finished cooking for their families. I am welcome to come help, she says.

March 29, 2001: My Visit to the Home of Doña Rosalinda and First Real Conversation

It has been a long day, but I drive straight to Rosalinda's house from Mexico City, where I am participating in a seminar at Mexico's National Autonomous University (UNAM). With Palm Sunday barely more than a week away, I cannot afford to go home and take a break. I am early: it is only 4 p.m. I find Doña Rosalinda eating with her family. Bad timing, but it is the first day I am free, and I am getting more persistent as the year goes on. Reminding Rosalinda that she said to come on Thursday and Friday afternoon, I mention that I have arranged childcare in order to come as we agreed. She says that if I give her ten minutes we can have a brief conversation. I am heading out to my car to read while I wait, but she invites me into the house and offers me a glass of water while they finish eating. At the table sit Doña Rosalinda, her younger son, her elderly mother, and her cousin, Doña Adelita. Doña Rosalinda offers me a taco. I am in the door, so to speak. What a relief!

After the women clear the table, I join the circle and help peel tamarind, the beginning of the preparation for the feast on Palm Sunday. Little do I know that I will be in charge of making the tamarind water myself when the day comes.

I try to explain my research, the purpose of my visit. Knowing Ocotepec's tradition of opposition to encroachment from nearby Cuernavaca, I explain my work from the perspective of food traditions as rural resistance to urban growth in towns on the outskirts of big cities, like Ocotepec outside Cuernavaca and Xochimilco outside Mexico City. Rosalinda understands the angle and chimes in: "Es más que nada que la ciudad no se coma a un pueblo, que no nos invada la ciudad" (It is more than anything about not letting the city eat this town up, that the city not invade us). She wants to be sure that I am aware of the town's struggle against the Soriana supermarket that some people (including the governor) want to build on "tierras de Ocotepec" (Ocotepec lands) and of their successful struggle against a gasoline station that the city tried to open there earlier. I have heard of both. The first is an ongoing issue still making headlines daily. The second is now reduced to a landmark, an abandoned PEMEX (Petróleos Mexicanos) gas station sitting at the edge of town.

Rosalinda gives me a detailed explanation of the preparation for the upcoming fiesta. She wants me to stop peeling tamarind and take notes. Several times she tells me that I do not need to help. I peel some and write some, my pen sticky with pulp, and try to explain that one way to understand something is actually to do it. I stress that I want to help prepare the food and not just be a guest. We clearly have different ideas of what my role should be but end up coming to a compromise. She finally gives up on me and continues, explaining why she wants me to write rather than peel tamarind: "Nos gusta que den a conocer nuestras tradiciones por otro lado" (We like people to make our traditions known in other places).

The patron saint of Ocotepec, she begins, is San Salvador, the name of the main church; therefore the festival for the town is August 6. Then there are the barrio fiestas: May 3 for the barrio of Santa Cruz; February 2 for La Candelaria; Palm Sunday for Los Ramos or Tlagoapan. Rosalinda knows the original Nahuatl name of her own barrio but cannot recall the original name of the other two older barrios of Ocotepec, which she considers important for me to write down. She calls her cousin—Doña Adelita—to tell me. "El barrio de la Candelaria se llama en mexicano Tlalnihuic" (The name of La Candelaria in Mexican is Tlalnihuic),[2] she says. Conversation turns to which barrios have the best fiesta. The women sound like sports enthusiasts arguing about their favorite teams. Rosalinda says that Culhuacán's is the prettiest of all these days, though about seven years ago it was La Candelaria's. The fiestas of Santa Cruz and Los Ramos are small, though things are improving thanks in part to the work of Rosalinda and her group of women in the church. "Hay mucha competencia" (There is lots of competition), Rosalinda says, as the barrios try to outdo each other in their celebrations.

Los Ramos is the smallest barrio of the four and used to have the smallest fireworks display. "Our fireworks display was so small that the rains would put it out. It was all smoke. But now there is a group in charge of the fireworks, and they made a five-year promise to keep them going. They have their own saint and everything," the women explain. As in Xochimilco, young people have organized to maintain and even create traditions that include most standard elements such as fireworks, pilgrimages, and rosaries. After the rosary, people share food and drink provided by the hosts. All of these traditions revolve around a religious figure.

Like my neighbor Antonio's group in Xochimilco that makes the pilgrimage to Chalma every year, this group is run by young men in their late teens and early twenties. They have to take care of their holy image with the expected rituals and worship, consisting mostly of regular rosaries at different people's homes. The involvement of the young men alongside the older people clearly helps to keep these traditions going. The *castillo* group that Rosalinda mentions began three years ago. The men that started it later put their sons in charge. "Ahora están sacando un castillo bueno, no de humo" (Now they have a good fireworks display, not a smoky one), she says proudly.

Rosalinda provides many details about the groups in each chapel that plan, organize, and finance the different components of the barrio fiestas. Each barrio has one committee for young people, but they participate in other groups as well. Rosalinda's sons are an example: one is very involved in a committee that requires much time and labor; the older one, who has a paying job, prefers to be involved in a group that requires more money and less time—the one that brings the *castillo* to the barrio celebration.

One group of relatively older people is ironically called the *grupo juvenil* (youth group). As young people twenty-some years ago, they added a new element from Mexican popular culture to the Domingo de Ramos tradition: a wrestling match. A few years ago they raised the funds to purchase a ring that they assemble each year on the empty lot across from the chapel and in front of Rosalinda's house. Rosalinda says proudly that they started with only a *torito* (fireworks bull) and now they have a wrestling match. Her son once had the excitement and honor of carrying the *torito:* like many before him, he too was burned when *buscapiés* went inside his pants leg.

One group is in charge of the arch made of fresh flowers that marks the entrance to the barrio. The men have been working together to build the arch for about forty years; now they are teaching their sons, Rosalinda says. Carrying these traditions forward is not just about labor and money, it also requires skill, as manifested by the beautiful arch welcoming visitors to the barrio on Palm Sunday.

A *chinelo* group is sponsored by a neighbor, Miguel Izquierdo. This group is about fifteen years old and is also in charge of paying for the musicians. A *grupo de la mojiganga* (parade including giant puppets/figures) used to bring *gigantonas* for street parades. (In Tetecala these are still part of the community celebrations.) Here it lasted three years but died out for lack of money. Another group brings the bulls, looks for *caporales* (managers), and makes *agua loca* (crazy water), which Rosalinda describes as similar to *agua de jamaica* but full of cane alcohol. She says that this group feeds lots of people, more men than women. It also must bring a band to play in the bullring. Each of the groups has to cover its own costs—which they can do by fundraising or, usually, by dividing the costs among themselves. No wonder the community is eager for newcomers to help share the costs of their celebration, I think to myself.

"We are from the women's group [*el grupo femenil*]," says Rosalinda, referring to herself, her cousin, and a neighbor who has also been helping us peel tamarind and shell peanuts for the mole. But Rosalinda is involved with several other groups as well, contributing to all of them with labor, time, and money as well as her obvious leadership and organizing ability. Her younger son has been with the group that builds the arch for one year, she tells me proudly. He gives his time and energy in addition to a contribution of 200–250 pesos (about US$25). Like the wrestling group (*el grupo de las luchas*), they have their own Christ figure that they honor with flowers and candles on a particular day.

The women's group was formed three years ago by fifteen women. They organized because they did not like the old-fashioned and depressing decorations that the men made for the chapel. "We wanted something more festive," Rosalinda says. This is an example of resistance through change—a group formed precisely to change things in order to carry on the tradition but in a new way. "It was not easy," Rosalinda adds. One problem was the money: they had counted on a person who left Ocotepec—as so many do—to work in the United States. The person had promised to send 10,000 pesos and then sent only 5,000 (approximately US$555). Rosalinda, her niece, and that person started the group. Rosalinda and another "compadre que se va a Estados Unidos" (*compadre* who goes to the United States), a regular temporary migrant, had to come up with extra money and covered the contract that they had already signed with a band from the neighboring state of Mexico. They needed to come up with the money somehow to fulfill the commitment. Rosalinda counts in her head and concludes that the cost was about 18,000 pesos (US$2,000): her niece put in 5,000 pesos; Rosalinda contributed 4,000, and they got 5,000 from the person in the United States. The group that builds the arch gave 2,000 pesos; the *compadre* temporarily in the states gave 1,000; and somehow they rounded up another 1,000. Rosalinda had signed the contract with the band and planned to honor it, no matter what.

The extensive organizing and fundraising to fulfill the commitment made to the musicians last year was only the beginning. The band members had to be housed and fed during their stay in Ocotepec: fifteen musicians and another ten people carrying their instruments and equipment, bringing the total to thirty-five. They arrived on the Saturday prior to the fiesta.

"Doña Laura housed them, my niece fed them the main meal on Saturday, Sunday Laura gave them breakfast and lunch. I gave the main meal that day, chicken in tomato, because they said they did not want mole because it did not sit well with them when they played. On top of that, I always butcher a pig that I make with red mole," Rosalinda says.[3]

This year Rosalinda will make mole again, using chiles that she purchased in September when she was going to open a store. The store never got off the ground, and now she is glad to have at least one component of the costly meal already paid for. She will make the principal midday meal (*la comida*) and also a dinner, as she does every year.

Rosalinda draws on multiple strategies for funding the festivities, including making her purchases where she can get better prices at a bulk rate. Another unexpected strategy this year was a debt that a political party owed her. She says that she was working as a volunteer with a political party that told her that it would give her something if it won ("quedamos que si ganaban me ofrecían algo"). She asked for aid in purchasing building materials for her house. When the party failed to come through on that, she asked for musicians for the fiesta. She will have the musicians for three hours that day and will be feeding them, of course.

All fifteen members of the *grupo femenil* are asked for 150 pesos apiece. "Not all contribute, however," Rosalinda says; "some give only 100." "We purchased 1,800 pesos [US$200] of artificial decorations; in addition we made flowers made of paper and plastic straws." The only thing that was missing was the fireworks. "We needed two dozen whistling rockets to announce our arrival," she says. Somehow they scraped together some more money for the indispensable fireworks.

March 30, 2001: Fifth Friday of Lent

Doña Rosalinda told me that the serious cooking would begin on the Thursday and Friday a week before Palm Sunday and that I should come help. I show up early Friday evening after a long day in Tetecala and easily find the yard where she said the women will be making tortillas for the dinner.

This evening is important because it is the first official meal offered as part of the barrio festivities for el Señor de los Ramos, the patron saint of the neighborhood chapel. The figure (*imagen*) is about eighteen inches high, representing Jesus entering Jerusalem on Palm Sunday. It sits on a little donkey carrying palms. People come from different towns and barrios to pay him homage, bringing flowers, candles, or fireworks. They are welcome to share a meal with host families in this barrio. *Gente creyente* (believers, meaning Catholics in this context)—visitors and residents alike—know that the Christ rewards their intense devotion and *promesas* with miracles and support in their lives, Rosalinda explains. As in Xochimilco, people in Los Ramos make a point to tell me that their Cristo is a representation of Jesus Christ: "Es el mismo" (It is the very same one). They know that the intense devotion surrounding a holy image differentiates them from the non-Catholic *sectas* (sects) that are increasingly taking hold in Mexico and that their folk traditions have drawn criticism from these groups as well as from the hierarchy of the Catholic church. In fact the priest who had been in Ocotepec for decades was recently transferred to Cuernavaca, people tell me, because the church hierarchy felt that he was too involved with the barrios. Nonetheless, he was still invited to say Mass at parties in people's homes, and his replacement did not come close to taking his place in the hearts of the people.

Rosalinda insisted that I join her and her crew tonight and take some pictures of them. She was excited because she said the tortillas would be made "the traditional way," by hand and over a wood fire. When I knock on the black gate she told me to look for, one street down from her house, I am quickly ushered past the long tables set up in the yard that stretches along one side of the adobe house. I can smell the wood fire and the sweet smell of tortillas made from fresh-ground corn toasting on the *comal*. Half a dozen women are working in the yard, some making tortillas, others preparing the *pancita* for the evening. Still others are running around hectically, setting the tables, making sure each has the necessary condiments: chopped onion, lemons, toasted *chiles de árbol* (a particularly spicy type of chile), and salt.

The children who open the gate take me to the very back of the yard, where Rosalinda and her crew are making tortillas. They use a metal tortilla press to flatten little balls of dough made with their hands. Then Rosalinda's sister, sitting on the ground next to the fire, pats and stretches them a bit between her hands before laying them on a clay griddle (*comal*). Ocotepec is the only one of my sites where I find griddles made of the traditional clay, apparently because vendors from the state of Guerrero to the south come here to sell them door to door. They are easily accessible and cost about thirty-five pesos (approximately US$4).

After I take photos as Rosalinda requested I am sent to talk to the oldest woman here, the hostess, who is making tortillas on another wood fire. She piles the hot tortillas in baskets and covers them with cloth napkins and plastic bags to keep them warm until the guests arrive. As in Xochimilco, I am struck by the indispensable role of plastic bags in "traditional" cooking today.

This evening I am aware of the diversity among the women preparing food for the dinner, ranging in age from about eighteen to sixty-five. Some look relatively well-off, with gold jewelry and two-piece polyester suits, while others wear flip-flops and ragged, mismatched clothes. Most have short hair, perhaps because it is a relatively young crew, but a few older women have the traditional long hair in braids. Many are not wearing aprons. Some are neighbors and some are family, but all are working together to receive the *promesas* appropriately and bring honor to the host family and the barrio and its patron, the Christ in the chapel.

Making tortillas on a clay *comal*

This particular evening the dinner is for the *padrino* (godfather) of el Señor de los Ramos. I am surprised that this role is not rotated but has been in the same family as long as anybody can remember. Doña Emilia, the hostess (who says that she was born in 1943 when I ask her age), tells me that the current *padrino* is the son of the previous *padrino*. That family is responsible for taking care of el Señor de los Ramos on his day: they bring flowers, music, and fireworks and pay for the Mass. Unlike some of the commitments in Xochimilco that last for a full year (such as the *mayordomías* for the Niñopa and the Niño de Belén) and have a long waiting list of future hosts, different families in Los Ramos take turns preparing the meal for these *padrinos*, the musicians, and anyone else who might be accompanying the procession. Tonight the women are preparing food for fifty people.

Doña Emilia tells me proudly that this barrio receives *promesas* from San Francisco in the state of Mexico; from Tlanepantla, Puebla; and from La Magdalena Contreras (one of the *delegaciones*) in Mexico City, as well as from the other three barrios in Ocotepec. I ask how long the reciprocal relationship with San Francisco has existed, since it is the first place everyone in this neighborhood mentions in slightly different but overlapping lists of who visits for Domingo de Ramos. Doña Emilia thinks back for a minute before responding that it has been about twenty-five years. People from Magdalena Contreras, another favorite, have been coming for about eighteen or twenty years, bringing flowers, candles, money, and flower holders. Representatives from Los Ramos make a reciprocal visit to Magdalena Contreras in Mexico City every May 15 to celebrate the Virgen de la Fátima. They take *chinelos*, which people have come to expect from the state of Morelos. Doña Emilia says that fewer people from Los Ramos went to Contreras this year, because the bus fare went up and many could no longer afford it.

Doña Emilia makes tortillas without interruption as she talks. Meanwhile the women around us rush to finish preparing the meat, cutting the *pancita* into small pieces. Someone comments with pride that it is a whole stomach, and Emilia responds that it is fresh from La Carolina, the market in Cuernavaca preferred by many women in this neighborhood. The city's central market freezes and sells old meat (*carne vieja*), the women tell me, while at the Carolina market "hay carne del día" (they have fresh meat killed that day).

The women are in a festive mood, even before they serve themselves a drink of Brandy Presidente. They quickly gather around the bottle when the guests begin to arrive, saying that the servers must be served first. They mention *las chimoleras* and laugh hysterically when they see me write the word down, saying that it is a word they made up. *Chimoleras* is a word used only in Ocotepec, meaning the women who make mole. They say that *las chimoleras* must have a drink for the mole to cook ("tienen que tomar un trago para que se coza [*sic*] el mole"). Mole is tricky: it must cook slowly and never boil or scorch. "If there is music, the cooks must also dance around the pot!" they say, giggling.

One story leads to another. They tell me that the tamales will not cook right if people fight or argue. "Tamales will come out crazy [*se hacen locos*] if there is fighting; some will be done and others will be raw." Having heard this many times over the years, I ask the women if it is a *creencia* (belief) or if it is actually true. "No doubt about it," they all chime in. "It is true, we have seen it!" With other things, women sometimes tell me in confidence that it is just a belief of the *abuelitos* or elders, but not with mole or tamales.

According to a book dedicated to tamales published by the Museum of Popular Cultures as part of its series on food, *tamal* or *tamalli* signifies *envuelto cuidadoso* (carefully wrapped) (Pérez San Vicente 2000: 21). The book mentions the 370 different types of tamales made in Mexico, including the various *mixiotes* (meats wrapped in parchment paper, foil, or maguey leaves and then steamed) so often cooked in Xochimilco.

I ask the women how important cooking is in Ocotepec. They clearly think this a strange question and respond categorically: "If no one cooks there is no fiesta." They seem to conclude that I am an alien and look at me strangely. One woman asks: "¿Usted es católica o es hermana?" (Are you Catholic or are you a sister?). After my response ("I am Catholic of course!"), they all burst out laughing, teasing the woman who so diplomatically used the term *hermana* in reference to evangelical Protestants. They let loose, criticizing *los evangélicos,* particularly because they do not take turns hosting the fiestas. The women are particularly upset that people who join the new *sectas* criticize their behavior and do not contribute to the community celebrations but nonetheless consume their food. "No hacen fiesta, no toman, no bailan, pero sí comen" (They don't have parties, they don't drink, they don't dance, but they do eat). Worst of all, they say, they do not fulfill barrio obligations ("No cumplen"). When I ask if there is a non-Catholic chapel in Ocotepec, the response is negative: "¡Ni lo mande Dios!" (God forbid!).

Our conversation takes place amid several curious kids who are hanging around, eating fresh, warm tortillas. They giggle shyly and ask about my camera. Suddenly we hear fireworks. These announce that the group of pilgrims has left the main church on the other side of the main road three blocks away and is heading our way. "Are the tables ready?" somebody asks. The women set the remaining tables in a final flurry of activity. Before we know it the tables are full of guests, and we are forced to give up the one we were using to cook. The brass band that accompanies the procession continues to play for a while, with the musicians standing around the edges of the house-lot garden.

When I leave shortly thereafter, though not before having eaten my bowl of *pancita* alongside the other kitchen helpers, I walk through the feasting guests to the other end of the yard by the gate. I am struck by the clear lines in this gendered space. At one end of the yard, in the back, are the women cooking, laughing, and drinking. At the table in the middle is a mixed crowd, with special guests, young and old, male and female, musicians and dancers. At the other end, by the gate, are only men, drinking and talking. They stop talking, surprised, when I come through. "¿Y esa güera?" (Who's that blondie?) they ask each other. "Ay, mamacita" (little mother, meaning hot momma) someone mutters. "Mother" is everything in Mexico, even a sex object.

March 30, 2001: Doña Emilia's Reflections on Change

"Women used to have ten or fifteen kids only to have most of them die of disease. Before, the diapers were made of rags, old aprons, and pants. Now they are disposable! Today even cats and dogs—not just children—are vaccinated!"

Doña Emilia describes how changes in Ocotepec have benefited women. She appreciates the vaccinations, *tortillerías,* and disposable diapers. Even the diet has changed: "Before we ate only beans, the tortillas were always handmade . . . Now we do not eat beans every day. The kids hardly like them anymore. They like their soup with a little chicken wing or gizzard in it at least."

In contrast to Xochimilco, where people in the old days pretty much lived off their vegetables and corn (and fish from the canals), Doña Emilia says that nobody in Ocotepec ate vegetables except during Lent. More recently, they have been eating more vegetables, as opposed to the trend in Xochimilco, where meat is increasingly replacing vegetables among the new and wealthier generations. I ask about squash. "Yes, squash we ate more of, but only once a year at the time of the corn harvest, in September. It was grown in the milpa between rows of corn."

Doña Emilia is glad not to have to make tortillas by hand (at least not most days), for reasons of both time and money. "I do not make tortillas; better to go to the *tortillería*. Today is an exception because it is evening and the *tortillerías* are closed.[4] But you have to spend money on the firewood, fifty sticks for sixty pesos (about US$7). It is much more expensive and takes longer: you have to buy your scoop of corn, put it to boil with lime, and pay the mill to grind it. They charge ten pesos to grind ten *cuartillos*" (a *cuartillo* is a scoop used to measure corn when purchasing in bulk). She has not ground corn by hand since 1959. "I used to grind corn on the metate. I was about sixteen when I stopped because I went to Cuernavaca to learn to sew. It was the way to get clothes, since women did not work back then and had to make their own clothes."

Doña Emilia has observed many positive changes, including women increasingly working for a salary. When she was young, the only women who worked outside of the house were those who made and sold tortillas. "No tenían derechos" (They had no rights), she recalls bitterly. "Before, women did not work and did not go to school. Now the majority around here work, though they still do not go to school. Men must learn: they have to cook for themselves and for their children too."

The clay *comal* on which she makes tortillas as we speak costs her about thirty-five pesos (about US$4) today. The last one cost twenty-five pesos. It should last her anywhere from six months to two years, Doña Emilia explains, "depending on when a child runs into it and breaks it." The women around us compare notes on how much their *comales* cost and how long they lasted. Instead of the aluminum *vaporera* that is now commonly used to steam tamales, they once used clay pots (*ollas de barro*). "Not the *cazuelas*," she clarifies. *Ollas* are used for making coffee or beans, while *cazuelas* are used for cooking rice or mole.

Doña Emilia says that about ten families from this barrio help with meals for Palm Sunday: "Musicians are fed dinner; the *promesas* are given break-fast, lunch, and the main meal at midday." She assures me that the fiestas have improved with time: fine bottled liquor is now served instead of the sugarcane grain alcohol for which Morelos is famous. "Las fiestas cada vez mejoran. Hasta en Santa Catarina [Tepoztlán] daban alcohol del 96 y ahora puro Presidente y Tecate" (The fiestas keep getting better. Even in Santa Catarina they used to serve grain alcohol and now they serve Presidente rum and Tecate beer). *Itacate,* she says, mispronouncing the beer, caus-ing the other women to erupt in laughter: "¡Quiero mi Itacate para llevar!" (I want my Itacate to go!) they chime in. Of course the beer is Tecate, but *itacate* is the Nahuatl term regularly used here and in Xochimilco for the food that is wrapped up to go: given to guests after fiestas to take home or taken to men working in the fields. Even the menus have improved with the steady income that comes from salaried employment, Doña Emilia contin-ues. "Before, people served meat in chile sauce, whether pork or beef. Now they serve chicken in mole. Sometimes they used to serve green mole, but now it is red mole." Red mole is much richer than green mole, with many ingredients, including several types of dried chiles, seeds, and spices; green mole has primarily pumpkin seed and chiles (usually fresh serranos) and sometimes tomatillos.

I ask Doña Emilia if the *tortillerías* use *nixtamal* (corn boiled in lime water). "Sí, pero quién sabe de dónde lo traigan. Es transportado. El bueno es el criollo de por acá. Ese es el bueno. Huele. El de allá huele, pero a olote; creo que lo muelen con todo y olote" (Yes, but who knows where it comes from. It is transported in. The good one is the local variety from around here. That is the good one. You can smell it. The corn that the *tortillería* here uses smells, but like corncobs. I think they grind it with corncobs and all). Most of the people I interviewed referred to the smell of corn at one time or another and evaluated its quality on that basis. The change in its smell and place of origin (it is now mostly imported from the United States) was the source of much heated conversation. In particular, many expressed anger that genetically modified corn from the United States was entering Mexico and flooding the market.

Sitting on the ground at Doña Emilia's feet and listening to her talk as she makes tortillas, I am struck by her lack of nostalgia for the old days, de-spite her criticism of some of the changes. In the process, it becomes clear that fiestas—while still considered traditional—have grown over the years in Ocotepec as in Xochimilco, thanks in part to decreased dependence on agriculture for a living. Fewer people used to offer meals years ago because they could not count on having anything to offer, Doña Emilia says. She stresses the uncertainty of the old days: "Los señores trabajaban en el campo y a veces se daba la cosecha y a veces no. Solo la gente que criaba pollos daba comida" (The men worked in the fields, and sometimes there was a harvest and sometimes there was not. Only the people who raised chickens hosted meals).

Saturday, April 7, 2001: The Day before Palm Sunday

The streets of Ocotepec are filled with vendors selling all sorts of traditional clay cookware. Traffic on the road from Cuernavaca to Tepoztlán is nearly at a standstill. I am struck in particular by the size of the *ollas* and *cazuelas de barro*—the biggest I have ever seen, almost large enough to sleep in. Like Doña Rosalinda and those preparing to receive the *promesas,* most of the families in the barrio of Los Ramos (or Tlagoapan) are preparing a special meal for family, *compadres,* and friends.

I arrive with my son Mario at noon and spend the first three hours cleaning ten pounds of rice while I observe women preparing other foods. Rosalinda's sister María is making mole at the same time. To my surprise, she does not hide the recipe. Mole in Ocotepec is different from the sweet *mole rojo* (red mole) from Xochimilco that I am used to. This recipe is simpler and has fewer ingredients. María is not as talkative as her sister, but she answers my questions. Only later do I learn that she is mourning the recent death of her niece's baby, born with her umbilical chord wrapped around her neck. "They did not pay attention to her at the Social Security clinic," she mumbles.

This upsets me. Every home that I visit in my research communities has had one or more deaths in the family that seem avoidable and unjust from my privileged perspective—deaths due to accidents, disease, violence, or just plain neglect. The family's passive acceptance of mortality always strikes me. I know that most women in Ocotepec—like my neighbors in Xochimilco, who have been telling me horror stories for years—have no choice but to have their babies in a government clinic if they want any medical attention at all. The quality of that attention and the conditions of the clinics and hospitals are often appalling, with women piled up in the hallways, lying two to a bed, and bullied or neglected by nurses and doctors during labor. I am angry. My son Mario was born with his umbilical chord looped around his neck too, but in a private clinic in Mexico City, where a doctor was paying attention and flipped the triple noose over his head before it was too late. One of the more painful differences of which I am excruciatingly conscious, which separates me from the women I interview like a dark canyon, is their lack of access to adequate medical attention. "Participant-observation is a farce," I think as I sit cleaning the rice beside María in Rosalinda's new outdoor kitchen. I can choose to participate in some aspects of these women's lives and not to participate in others, leaving me with a partial and skewed impression of their world.

When we arrive, we find Rosalinda and María on top of the roof cooking. Before I know it, Mario and I are up there with them. The *cocina de humo* (smoke kitchen), as Rosalinda calls it, used to be in her house-lot garden below us. Due to the shrinking space as a result of construction, she had it put on the flat roof, where it now provides the women with a bird's-eye view of the festivities below. This highly unusual and clever strategy seems to work out well.

Rosalinda explains that when the men finished building her adobe house they offered to put a fence between her and her brother's house next door and to put a *cocina de humo* on top of the other structure on the side of her house-lot garden where she rents space to the *tortillería* and butcher shop. Now she has all she needs to continue to provide meals for fiestas and can also offer her guests a spectacular view of the chapel and the lot just across the street, where many of the community festivities take place. Although Rosalinda had no more money at the time, she says, the men agreed to finish the job on credit with the remaining material.

The little kitchen is piled high with the usual cooking implements: huge *cazuelas* stacked upon each other. People from the barrio come in several times during the morning to borrow one. Rosalinda laughs when I point this out and says that she has yet another room full of cookware. A pile of wood contains both scrap lumber and dried tree branches. In the back I see a *manojo* (bunch of corn husks) that I will later be responsible for soaking and preparing to make tamales.

A large *olla* with a small mouth sits in the corner where we will later build one of two fires and set the *vaporera* with the tamales. I ask what it is for but get a vague response: "For whatever you want, for coffee or beans."

Of course it is not really "for whatever" ("pa'lo que quiera"): you would never make anything but beans or coffee in it—certainly never mole or rice. But it seems that the boundaries of culture are invisible until transgressed—for instance, if I tried to make coffee in the *cazuela* and mole in the *olla* or wanted to serve meat on the first day of a wake in Xochimilco with a body present or serve tamales *nejos* with red mole instead of green in Tetecala, all practically taboo.

Rosalinda is about to light the charcoal under the little grill (*anafre*) and put a huge kettle of pumpkin and *piloncillo* (cone of brown sugar) to make *calabaza en dulce* (sweet squash) on the fire. This and the *elotes* (corn on the cob) cooking downstairs are being prepared to sell tomorrow at her food both on the street corner outside the butcher shop. Sales of some kind—often food—make up part of the multiple economic strategies of every woman with whom I am working in my three communities.

María is stirring a pan full of sesame seeds, toasting them over the gas grill. I begin to clean the rice, to observe, and to ask questions. Every now and then I pull out my notebook and scribble a few things. The women always refer to the two different sets of ingredients in mole: the chiles and the *olores* (everything else). Here is María's recipe for this mole. First the *olores:*

- 7 fistfuls (about 4.4 pounds) of sesame seed
- 2.2 pounds of peanuts
- 1.2 pounds of almonds
- 1.6 pounds of shelled pumpkin seed
- 1.2 pounds of nuts (pecans in this case)
- ½ head of garlic, peeled
- 5 hard rolls
- 7 hard tortillas

Next come the 15 pounds of chiles, about equal parts mulatos, pasillas, and anchos. All this is fried separately in lard, beginning with the peanuts and ending with the tortillas, being careful not to burn anything. Avoiding bitter mole—and the danger of it separating like butter when it is beaten too long—is a challenge. As I hear in several fiestas in Ocotepec, mole is also supposed to be stirred from start to finish by the same cook—even though this can easily take four hours, depending on the size of the *cazuela*.

In Tepoztlán, where Rosalinda and María have a sister, they make sweet red mole, the sisters tell me, using chocolate, *galletas Marías* (cookies), and even ripe plantains. Though I have been eating mole for fifteen years, I thought red and black moles were practically defined by having chocolate regardless of regional variations. I was wrong.

Preparing the traditional pumpkin that Rosalinda is making to sell is also a detailed process. To begin with, the pumpkin itself must be hard and dry. Rosalinda has had hers since January. She was planning to prepare it in brown sugar to sell in the market. Now it is perfect. I am surprised to hear that when she sells food she has prepared at home it is usually at the Mercado Carolina, where the women went to buy the *pancita* for the dinner last Friday. She sometimes sells at the central market in downtown Cuernavaca but never at the local market in Ocotepec. Does anyone ever shop at the local market? Every time I go by, it is eerily empty.

María appears younger than her fifty years. She looks like Rosalinda except for her long hair and apron, which give her the appearance of a traditional indigenous *cocinera*. She has four boys and two girls, ranging in age from eight to thirty-four. María also has a husband, unlike Rosalinda and her neighbor Laura, who is also with us today. María's daughters are helping us out most of the day. The youngest is eight; the other one is in her twenties and expecting a baby. María is very proud that her older daughter is an accountant and that she still cooks, although she says that her daughter does not spend as much time as she does in the kitchen.

"I spend the whole day cooking!" says María. She shares some menus with me. As in all the recipes that women give me, quantities are never precise but are based on intuition or feel. "No más le tantea uno" (You just kind of get the feel of it) is the usual response when I ask how much or how many. But the details are key: you do not rub the chicken with chiles until it has started to brown and release juices, she warns me.

María's house is down the street; she has three fruit-bearing trees: tangerine, peach, and avocado. All her children live on the same plot of land, though some live separately (*aparte*). Separateness is usually defined by whether or not they eat from the same kitchen.

María tells me that she loves her sister's new house. In fact she spent the night here last night, after cooking and drinking late. This becomes clear as her adult children filter in and tease her about it. Her husband was apparently not amused.

"Ya están los olores" (The *olores* are ready), María announces to her sister at mid-morning, "but I still have to soak the chiles." I help her rinse out the chiles, flooding a tub with water several times. The stems and most of the seeds have been removed, but the remaining seeds now float away, with lots of dirt. The inconvenience of having a kitchen on the roof becomes clear to me as I spend the day climbing up and down the stairs to use the water from the house-lot garden below.

Throughout the day I am drinking water from one of the huge water bottles labeled "Agua de los Ángeles." I assume that it is the same water that I pay to have delivered to my house once a week for drinking and cooking. Not until the next day when I am asked to make the tamarind water with water from the faucet in the yard do I realize that the plastic jugs are only used to store regular tap water. In a short while my stomach hurts and I feel nauseous, a feeling that does not leave me for a couple of days. My intolerance for the water that most people consume is another difference between the women I work with and myself. From here on out I stick to beer.

I leave around 3:30 and return that evening to find Rosalinda and her group of women hard at work in the chapel. They are hanging the final decorations, some made of paper and straws, some of fresh flowers. The sweet smell of flowers fills the tiny chapel and overflows into the open space where the few pews are lined up and the musicians are playing. Purple and white are the dominant colors. The women are beaming, pleased with their work.

Everyone who is working to prepare for the fiesta is invited to dinner at another neighbor's yard, and I am welcome to join them. They serve *tacos al pastor* (tacos made of thinly sliced pork covered in chile and roasted on a skewer, gyros-style), the very same tacos sold on street corners everywhere in Mexico, with grilled onions, pineapple, cilantro, and salsa. Soft drinks and alcohol are offered.

As I walk back to my car later, I meet two little girls aged ten and eleven. They are playing in the empty lot where two greased poles have been set up next to the wrestling ring. Tomorrow there will be a contest and those who manage to climb to the top will win prizes, including plastic dishware and alcohol. The girls are very excited about the festivities. "The wrestlers get dressed at my house!" says one, thrilled. She lives just up the street and caught sight of my son earlier today. "Where is he?" The other girl asks, "Is he cute?" "Yes!" squeals the first in response. When it comes to boys, pre-teen girls seem to be the same everywhere.

The chapel in Los Ramos on Palm Sunday

April 8, 2001: Palm Sunday in the Barrio de los Ramos

I arrive just after 6 a.m. The people from Cuentepec (a Nahuatl-speaking community nearby) are already weaving their palm crosses and leaves in front of the chapel. A brass band plays on the chapel patio, and fireworks are already being launched into the sky. I help Rosalinda and her sister carry a table from the church that we will use to make the tamales. Rosalinda stops to barter with the palm weavers (*los tejedores de palma*). One woman wants ten pesos (about US$1.00) for her woven leaf. Rosalinda goes to the next one, who wants five pesos, and offers her ten pesos for three. She accepts. Rosalinda chooses her three and asks me to return for them later after we get the table set up in the smoke kitchen. A *compadre* will make a cross out of the three and attach a flower to the center, to decorate the outdoor seating area that has been arranged on the roof beside Rosalinda's fiesta kitchen.

Rosalinda's sons, ages fifteen and eighteen, are setting up food booths on the sidewalk outside of the butcher shop and the *tortillería*. They have been chilling cans and bottles of beer in buckets of ice all night. The boys will sell beer, corn on the cob, and the sweet pumpkin, which cooked slowly over the fire most of the day yesterday. Today it is still warm and smells delicious, its pulp a dark brown. Rosalinda gives me a sliver to taste. I manage to sneak quite a few delicious pumpkin seeds from the *cazuela* before she takes it away for the boys to sell.

"Madam, your dough is ready!" the woman from the *tortillería* yells up to Rosalinda. The beans and *habas* (fava beans) have been taken to the *molino* and are nicely ground. We are ready to make the tamales.

Laura joins us to help, as does María del Carmen and a *comadre* from Santa María de Aguacatepec, another traditional town on the periphery of Cuernavaca. Six women (including María and her older daughter but not counting myself) are working together most of the day in the little smoke kitchen on the roof. Doña Adelita, their cousin, is cooking in the house, and two young women (María's daughters-in-law) help make the drinks, watermelon water and tamarind water, on ground level below.

"¿Ya escojiste el frijol?" (Did you pick through the beans?), Rosalinda asks. "Ya" (Done), someone responds: the pebbles have been removed. María puts the beans on the gas grill to cook. Several times in the day we have to heat up more water to add to the beans so that they do not dry out; apparently it is not acceptable to add cold water directly.

The women work all morning long, taking many breaks to look out the window at the goings-on in the church and commenting on the splendor of particular *promesas* as they arrive, each announced by church bells and fireworks. Such and such a barrio has brought beautiful flowers, or so many fireworks, they exclaim. The church public address system has been squeaking and squawking since 6 a.m., announcing the festivities of the day, inviting one and all to take part in the events in Los Ramos on this Palm Sunday.

"¡Carnicero, la manteca!" (Butcher, the lard!), somebody yells. We are waiting for that in order to finish preparing the masa for the tamales. We have ten pounds of corn dough in all, at least five of lard, and two batches of ground beans and *habas*.

The work requires several pairs of hands. The masa is spread out, smoothed, and patted into a big rectangle on the borrowed church table. In places where it is too thick, a hand swoops in to pinch the excess and add it to the edge of the rectangle. A layer of beans or *habas* is spread out on top, about the same thickness as the dough. Both the masa and the beans and *habas* have been mixed with lard and salt. Then somebody draws a finger across the masa, subdividing it into smaller squares, which are rolled up and pinched into one-inch to two-inch swirls.

By now I have completed my first task, which necessitated running upstairs a few times to check on more detailed instructions. I was asked to soak and separate the dried corn husks, but even this relatively simple task requires expertise that I lack. I am afraid to break them; it is not easy to pull apart the dozens of husks that have been neatly tucked one inside the other and dried in a beautiful and compact bundle. They must first be soaked until soft and then gently pulled apart. Before the day is over, I am pretty good at it. Laura jokes: "Now you can get your diploma in soaking corn husks!"

Making bean tamales is a long process. The pattern continues for at least three hours: spread the masa as thinly and evenly as possible, spread beans or *habas* on top, cut the masa using a finger, roll it into a little log, cut it with your hands into small *tamal*-sized chunks. A final trick is the last step in making the two-tone *tamales de frijol:* the corn husk is twisted and pushed into the body of the *tamal*. Bean tamales are the only ones with an *ombligo* (belly button). According to Dr. Sergio Cordero Espinosa, an amateur historian in Xochimilco, this is because corn and beans are the key elements linking humans to life, like a mother to a baby in the womb.[5]

I am struck with the very careful patting and almost caressing of the *tamal* at each of its stages, nothing like I've ever seen in the preparation of meat or sweet tamales. Finally, as we are several hours into this process and only halfway through, I take courage and start rolling them too. The trick to the belly button is to put the little pat of masa halfway up the husk, at least an inch and a half from the bottom. The masa is pushed down when you tuck the husk inside the center of it, forming its belly button.

Talk among the women involved in this ritual today inevitably turns to stories of tamales that did not cook right due to some kind of discord: people arguing, fighting, in a bad mood. Cases supporting this are discussed in detail. "It's because they had a fight!" says one woman. They scorn such foolishness. "What was missing was for the cook to drink wine," says another. "No, she did drink wine, but she should have danced around the pot" is the response. The final solution for undercooked tamales in Ocotepec is for the women making them to drink alcohol and dance.

When I ask if men ever make tamales, the laughter that is a key ingredient in this collective cooking process reaches another level. *"Compadre,"*

Bean tamales with "belly buttons"

they joke hysterically, pretending to be men, "let's make tamales!" Apparently the answer to my question is "no." But this leads to stories of exceptions, men who cook "women's" food. One woman volunteers that she has an uncle who makes mole—"no más que es del dulce" (but it is the sweet kind)—which he sells on the street to tourists, most of them from Mexico City. The talk turns to how expensive his food is: last year he sold his mole at eighty pesos (about US$9) per plate at the *carretera* (highway).[6] The mole had lots of turkey of course and was delicious, everyone agrees, but eighty pesos! The women are scandalized. They cannot believe anyone would pay such a price, no matter how good the mole.

Before the first *tamal* is laid in the *vaporera*, María holds it in her hand and makes the sign of the cross over the mouth of the tamale pot. No need for coins in the bottom or nails in a cross, as in Xochimilco, or chiles in a cross with salt over them on the fire, as in Tetecala. When I ask, she assures me that the pot has been blessed: "Ya lo santigüé" (I already made the sign of the cross over it). María is the designated *tamal* layer; when she is gone, the tamales pile up. Yet the women refuse my offer to set them into the pot. The person who begins must continue, as with the mole. Tamales are *tan delicados* (so sensitive), everyone says. María's daughter eventually does take over, because her mother is taking too long and we can wait no longer, but she is the only one allowed to fill in for María.

Men come and go as we do this, helping out where they can in different but related tasks. One of Rosalinda's *compadres* is building the tables and setting up chairs for the new "dining hall." Another comes to check the gas tank and asks if we plan to use it all day. "This tank will not last," he says. Everything is closed today, but he brings a spare from somebody's house. One by one, young men arrive, sent by their wives to borrow *cazuelas de barro* or other fiesta cookware. The new smoke kitchen on the roof is a hub of community activity.

Nobody here except for María's pregnant daughter has ever eaten *tamales de haba,* much less made them. She tried them on her reciprocal *promesa* to the town of San Francisco. Because she is pregnant and *de antojo* (having cravings), her aunt Rosalinda decided to surprise her with the special tamales. It is considered essential for a pregnant woman to satisfy her food cravings—otherwise the baby will be born wanting. She watches her mother fry the pork meat that she and Laura cut into chunks. After it is fried, it is removed from the pan, and more lard is heated to fry the mole ingredients.

María's daughter recalls the last time she made mole herself for a fiesta, about ten years ago, under her grandmother's tutelage. She still remembers her sore back: "I told my grandmother: 'I am going to make mole!' And I started to make mole. But later your back hurts terribly! And my grandmother, she says: 'Didn't you say you wanted to make mole? Now you will finish what you started!' You see, there is a belief that the same person must finish; otherwise the mole curdles and spoils." Her grandmother insisted that she finish the job. She addresses her story to the other women cooking, though the clarification at the end is for my benefit, not knowing that I have heard this several times already. "You have to stir it about three or four hours," she groans. Not surprisingly, many young women refuse to devote the time and energy to cooking that their grandmothers did. Maybe the women of the circle in Xochimilco were right about young women "refusing to suffer" these days.

I can certainly sympathize, especially after my own experience today making the tamarind water. At first, when the smoke in the little rooftop kitchen became absolutely intolerable to my throat and eyes, I welcomed the chore, but I soon found it unbearably tedious. Unlike fiesta situations prior to this one, I was not surrounded by other women whose company and conversation helped pass the time and make it more enjoyable.

As the morning goes on, the delicious smell of the *carnitas* cooking on the street corner below wafts up to us. The cook is a man, as always in the case of *carnitas*. In our own small kitchen on the roof, the tamales are steaming, the mole and the rice are sautéing: all food from women's domain. Finally we are fed, but only after the male relatives, of course. A woman brings us some fresh blood sausage and beans with tortillas: "Un poco de morongita y frijolitos aunque sea" (A little bit of blood sausage and beans at least). As usual, the women are surprised that I eat blood sausage. I tell them the story about having a father-in-law from Michoacán and eating *carnitas* every Sunday at family gatherings. That and living in Xochimilco have prepared me for eating all sorts of things, including animal parts I have never seen before.

I take a break after the food is finally ready and I have finished the seemingly impossible task of separating the tamarind pulp from the seeds. I am exhausted and go home to take a nap. Rosalinda insists that I return later with my sons to eat.

I am the only one with the luxury of a nap. Yet when I return to enjoy the fiesta that evening I am still tired long before the wrestlers finish insulting the public and hurling each other around the ring. Now this is embodiment, I chuckle to myself, thinking of the contrast between theory and reality as the two sets of women wrestlers pull each other by the hair and smack each other on the behind. Nobody seems particularly excited about the contrast with traditional gender roles, though they are excited about the wrestlers' extraordinary costumes and masks and push closer to the ring. Very much a part of Mexican urban popular culture, wrestling is a favorite spectator sport made even more popular by Superbarrio, the hero of low-income housing rights in Mexico City. As recognizable in and around the capital as the Zapatista Subcommander Marcos is in the entire country, Superbarrio appears with his wrestling get-up at street protests and political rallies. When the mats finally clear, several dozen little boys, including my son, have a turn hurling each other around and bouncing off the elastic cords that surround the ring. The festivities culminate in a spectacular *castillo* display sometime before midnight.

April 9, 2001: Last Day of the Fiesta in Los Ramos

Today is the closing day of the fiesta. It is celebrated with a meal called *la marrana* (literally, "the sow"). I want to find the family hosting this meal, which accompanies the events in the bullring. The committee in charge of the bulls and everything associated with them is totally independent from the women's committee with which I have been working. Again, all aspects of the festivities are coordinated by the barrio's representatives to the church. Everything related to the bulls, as with the committee in charge of the fireworks, is in the hands of the men. Women have little to do with it, except the cooking.

I follow the directions that Rosalinda gave me yesterday to her *compadre*'s house. She said he would know for sure who is hosting *la marrana* this year. Nobody is home, but I track Don Mario down at the church, where the men have been drinking almost without interruption for several days and nights. The band continues to blast away, so I cannot hear myself speak. I barely make out his response but walk down the street in the direction he is pointing, toward a pink house.

I introduce myself to the women cooking in the house-lot garden first, explaining that I am studying food traditions and would like to speak with somebody about that. They immediately point out the host. As in Xochimilco and in Doña Rosalinda's house, women who are part of the cooking crew attend to guests by serving them food. If anybody has questions, only one speaker has the authority to represent the group. Only after chatting with the host for a few minutes—with the four or five women cooking nearby listening intently—do I ask him for permission to speak to the woman in charge. The male-dominated space contrasts with all the other meal preparations I have observed, perhaps because it is for the bull-riding festivities. I obtain a very tentative space; the conversation lasts no more than fifteen minutes. Buying time, I ask if I can photograph the clay pot full of nopales on the firewood. My argument is that I have plenty of pictures of rice but none yet of nopales, even though they are such a part of traditional food in this region. Indeed they are a regular part of the menu at home as well as in fiestas.

Before introducing me to his wife, the host explains that his group has about twenty-one active members who front the costs of the bull festival. There are additional members, he says, but not all contribute their share.

Things have changed, but the group continues its tradition as well as it can (*como se puede*). The host himself has only been a member for seven years, but this is his first time to host the meal. Later his wife tells me that she has been in charge of several other barrio meals during the Easter Holy Week in the past, though never for Ocotepec's main fiesta on August 6.

A few of the changes in the celebration that the host mentions catch my attention. They no longer use horses for the *jaripeo* (rodeo), because it was costing too much money to pay their owners when bulls injured them. They no longer serve *agua loca* (crazy water) before the bull spectacle. *Agua loca* is the grain alcohol drink that the researcher at the Morelos Institute of Culture mentioned when he recommended that I explore the uniquely macho food rituals in *la marrana*. He said the point was to get the guys who were going to ride the bulls ready for the day. Lots of chiles and alcohol to give them courage (*para dar valor*), he told me. They still drink "crazy water" in Tetecala; but the bulls are not always real (see Chapter Three), and the greatest danger seems to be the drinking itself. The man hosting *la marrana* tells me that they stopped making *agua loca* a few years ago because the men were getting too drunk to ride the bulls and "it was becoming dangerous." "Can you imagine?" he asks me. They used to make up to ten big barrels of *agua loca*, with fruit water like *aguas frescas* but consisting primarily of pure cane alcohol. "Not anymore, nowadays we stick to beer."

Before leaving Los Ramos, I stop by Doña Rosalinda's to say hello. Rosalinda and her sister María are busy sweeping and collecting the leftover Styrofoam dishes, plastic cups, chicken bones, and cold ash from yesterday's party and putting them in big plastic trashbags. I help finish the job, coughing at the fine ash in the air and remembering how thick the smoke was yesterday. It is very hard on the throat, lungs, and eyes, especially on long days like that one, when some women spend nearly ten hours in the smoke kitchen. I know I was surprised when I came back in the afternoon yesterday to find the same women cooking, only wearing new party outfits.

Though brief, this is an important stop. I have come to thank them and express my appreciation for their letting me participate. I am not here to ask questions. I thank them for their generous sharing and for offering me the best seat in town.

Best of all, I have a chance to chat with María, who seems only now to understand that I am involved in all the kitchen activity and discussions for school. This is very important to her. "¿Es su trabajo?" (It is your work?) she asks, amazed. I assure her that I enjoy it, that when I lived in Xochimilco I sometimes helped my neighbors before the fiestas, but that now I am focusing intently on food preparation for my *tesis*.

María, suddenly concerned that I do a good job in school, advises me that in the future I should tell people that this is for my studies (*para mi carrera*). She warns me to be wary of people who might lie to me. María reflects on the questions I asked her two days ago while she was making mole and I was cleaning the rice. Somewhat apologetically, she says it tired her (*es cansado*) to talk so much. Before I leave, Rosalinda insists on my taking more food home: *frijoles en mole,* which they are reheating for the main meal today. They are a perfect accompaniment to the *tamales de frijol* that she sent me home with yesterday, which I have not yet had a chance to eat.

May 1, 2001: Barrio de Santa Cruz

I took my dog to see our old vet today, not only because she was sick but because he is from Ocotepec. León has been a friend of the family's for over six years; he knows our current lab, Tequila, and knew our previous dog, Zenda. He knows my kids well also and offered them one of his dog's pups as a gift a few years ago when Zenda died.

León is very friendly and helpful. I explain my research and ask him if he would introduce me to his mother or sisters. Better yet, he offers to take me down the street right away to meet his cousin, María Teresa. She will be hosting an important meal for the annual *fiesta del barrio,* the Feast of the Holy Cross, this Thursday. "Va a dar la asistencia" (She is going to give service), he says; she will offer the meal for all the barrios on that day. Later she tells me that this was initially her father's commitment, not hers. The old man had signed up to give the *asistencia* at last year's planning meeting. María Teresa recently moved back into the community to care for her mother before she passed away. She was now supporting her father's commitment. "El apellido hay que lavarlo muy bien" (The family name must be scrubbed very well), María Teresa joked with me later. Younger family members not only listen to and obey their elders; they do everything possible to protect their honor, which is theirs as well.

After taking care of my dog and eliminating the possibility that she was stung by a scorpion, León and I walk down the street and visit his cousin.

He introduces me as an old friend (*una vieja amiga*), which makes all the difference in the world. María Teresa's family immediately addresses me in informal register, rather than the formal treatment I was given by the women at Doña Rosalinda's. I feel like part of the family. Being part of the family will also mean that I do not have to deal with men making passes at me and the ensuing tension that causes among the women, thank God.

The next day when I arrive to work, María Teresa is busy receiving guests in the chairs set up in her house-lot garden just outside of her house. She is offering them drinks and formally inviting them to the meal the next day. I am sent directly to the kitchen to chop carrots. Before the collective work party is over in a few days and after the meal for eight hundred people, I would end up scrubbing gigantic kitchen pots in the yard. Today María Teresa and I briefly discuss my research and interest in participating with the women tomorrow and Thursday. Given the more intimate terms (*de confianza*) of the introduction, I tell her that I am interested in following up the fiesta with interviews of women about their everyday cooking. That, as she warns me, would be much more difficult.

María Teresa is glad for my help, especially since she will not have the support of León's mother and sisters. They will be preparing a meal in their own house, because they have construction going on and the Día de la Santa Cruz is also the Día del Albañil (Day of the Construction Worker). León jokes that I am his representative, since with his regular government job he will not be able to help his family that day either. Even today, the Día del Trabajador (Worker's Day), which is an official holiday, he takes the opportunity provided by his day off to do house calls to ailing animals. Like most in Mexico's precarious economy, male and female, León employs multiple economic strategies to support his family. Although he may not be able to help with the meal for the barrios with his time and labor, I tell him that I am sure he has already contributed. His cousin says that of course he has—both by paying into the neighborhood collection and in other ways.

María Teresa's house is typical in a sense: it is under construction like her cousin's and like about one of every five homes in Ocotepec. We arrive at the small house by walking through a plot of land that includes a milpa full of corn drying on the stalk. I mention to León that growing corn here seems to be important symbolically rather than economically. He agrees and says that the old man who planted this—María Teresa's father—does it for pleasure. "If you do the math," he assures me, "and figure the costs of production, it makes no sense whatsoever to grow your own corn today. People do anyway because it is meaningful and important to them." I ask if any young people grow corn now. "No," he says, "they prefer to buy it at the market, where it is much cheaper and less work." I wonder if corn and fiesta traditions (which seem one and the same) will die out in this community with the older generation, thanks to free trade and the loss of agricultural land to speculation and construction.

May 2, 2001: Last Day before the Fiesta

María Teresa's family has been preparing to host tomorrow's meal for the past year. Over the last six months in particular, the family has been stocking up on nonperishable items and making decorations by hand. These include the *banderitas de papel picado* (traditional paper banners) that are the domain of the *abuelo*, the grandfather and family patriarch. He is the expert and cuts out all the designs with scissors. María Teresa's 22-year-old daughter Lucía, who is helping with everything, tells me that he has taught others in the family how to do it, but none have obtained his level of skill. Rosalinda says later that this family is well known around town for its skill with handmade decorations. At one point I overhear María Teresa telling one of the women who is helping with the food and decorations that she will gladly advise and help her with an upcoming wedding. She assures the woman that she has a lot of experience making floral arrangements and decorations. As in Xochimilco, the small-scale, informal economic activities linked to both community and life-cycle fiestas provide women with opportunities to earn a little cash to help support their household.

I assist María Teresa this morning and again in the afternoon. When I return in the afternoon, my job is to help two neighbor women glue paper banners onto dozens of long strings which have been strung like a clothesline, zigzagging across the house-lot garden. Early tomorrow morning the banners will be strung up above the street and along the pathway to the house. The colorful *banderitas* will mark the entrance to the yard and lead everyone down the field directly to the altar with the Santa Cruz, the Holy Cross that is at the center of this celebration. It too will be adorned with brightly colored paper. As I work with the other women gluing banners onto the strings, I comment on how lucky we are that it is not raining, given that the last two weeks have brought unusual rainstorms every afternoon. One woman interrupts her task with the glue to look up at the sky with her arms outstretched and exclaim: "Thank you, God is great!"

Besides the paper banners, María Teresa has been preparing the baskets for the tortillas and the napkins that will be used to envelop them. She also decorates saltshakers and napkin holders. They look exactly like those you might find in a fiesta in Xochimilco, except that the family name is not printed or embroidered on anything. María Teresa is constantly interrupted by people coming to the door to inquire about the upcoming meal for all the barrios and thus is only able to join us at the kitchen table for moments at a time. She tries to finish the decorations, using an electric glue gun to stick the dried white flowers and blue ribbon onto the remaining napkin holders; but her obligations as hostess require her to get up time and time again to greet guests at the back door and welcome them to tomorrow's meal. During the hour or so when I am working in her kitchen this morning, she only spends about ten minutes on her task. This is typical of women's work—full of interruptions. Pulling off a reception like this one requires women to organize among themselves to cover all the tasks despite each one having other things to do and other people to care and cook for.

As in every other collective food preparation for a community festivity that I have attended, the host coordinates the preparation of the main meal and also makes sure that her helpers are fed and take food home with them when they leave. María Teresa says that today she will serve *chicharrón en chile verde* (pork rind in green salsa) and beans, an everyday, low-budget meal. Later she tells me with horror that in nearby Ahuatepec you have to pay people to help you cook. Here, she says, it is still the custom for people to help out and for the host to send them home with a taco—"le manda uno su taquito." In Xochimilco you would call that your *itacate,* but the practice and expectation are the same. Indeed one of the changes in tradition that I heard people grumble about in Xochimilco is that the *itacate* has gotten smaller and smaller, coinciding with the increased number of guests.

As I sit at the kitchen table chopping carrots for the *arroz a la mexicana* (Mexican rice), I take the opportunity to interview Antonia, the young woman next to me, who is peeling and cutting the ends off the carrots. I am interested in her perspective on the loss of food traditions, which the older women generally blame on young people. She is quiet until I strike up a conversation but is friendly and willing to talk when I do. First we talk about carrots, of course: the best way to get through the forty-pound bag on the floor next to the table. She peels, I chop. Antonia is helping out today because María Teresa went across the street to her house and asked her to support her family's efforts for this big commitment (*este gran compromiso*). When I tell Antonia that I am studying food customs in Ocotepec, she interrupts me to say that she is not from Ocotepec. She has lived here for twenty of her twenty-five years, however, so I tell her that her perspective is valid for my purposes: she has been observing how things work in this town practically her entire life.

Only true locals (*los que sí son de aquí*) have the power to speak for the community in Ocotepec and to influence controversial decisions over land use, such as the gas station that was halted or the attempts to launch the governor's supermarket project on community lands. One woman who married into Ocotepec told me that people like herself who are not *de aquí* are not even allowed to participate as observers, much less vote, in the town's *asamblea* (assembly), where members heatedly discuss issues such as sale of land to outsiders—*tierras comunales* or *ejidatarias* (communal and *ejido* lands). This is key to understanding the attachment to place that these food traditions and celebrations are all about. It is in part the need to belong that pressures María Teresa to meet social expectations and carry off this collective meal after years of living outside the community.

Antonia says that many young women do not cook anymore. When I ask why, she replies that they are busy outside the home and even if they are married often have mothers or aunts or mother-in-laws to cook for them and take charge of family responsibilities. "No les gusta cocinar, es muy laborioso" (Some just do not like to, it is too much work), she says; they prefer to buy prepared food at the *fonda* (family-style restaurant). "What is it they buy?" I ask. "Comida típica" (typical food), Antonia says: the usual *sopas y guisados* (soups and stews) that other women make every day in their homes.

I continue this discussion over brunch (*el almuerzo*) with María Teresa's family two days later. Her father, son, daughter, brother, and sister-in-law had been working all morning to clean up the previous day's fiesta and prepare for the *recalentado* (literally, "reheated," meaning leftovers) the next day. The *recalentado* seems to be the dessert for every fiesta (though served the following morning) in the same way that the meal served to those who help prepare food for the fiesta is the appetizer. It became clear in the conversation that passing on traditions to younger generations is a top priority in this family. Cooking is an indispensable component of these traditions, inseparable from others.

I take my leave after chopping only about twenty pounds of carrots, but already my hands are sore and I have a huge blister on my thumb. Before I depart, I jot down tomorrow's menu: chicken with mole, rice, beans, and *tepache* as well as soft drinks, brandy, and beer. The *tepache*, a traditional drink made with pineapple peel and other ingredients, has been fermenting for three days. For the meal, María Teresa has gathered the following quantities: 265 pounds of chicken; 220 pounds of tortillas; 44 pounds of carrots; 44 pounds of rice; two crates of *jitomates* (red tomatoes, not the green tomatillos); 66 pounds of mole; and green peas, onions, and garlic for the rice.

When I leave the indoor kitchen and step out into the house-lot garden, I find the *abuelo* sitting at the edge of the cornfield drinking liquor with several men, including a son and a grandson. They are admiring the beautiful milpa—all reds and golds with several trees in bloom. The few ears of corn left on the stalks to dry for *nixtamal* are outlined harshly but elegantly against the sky. The small milpa surrounded by the construction on this lot and just beyond seems a fragile but definite symbol of resistance. The *abuelo* invites me over to the group, proud and pleased with his milpa; he enjoys contemplating it and seizes the opportunity to talk about it. There was about twice as much planted earlier, he says, but he cleared the rest in February to make space to receive the guests at the fiesta tomorrow. I take several pictures before I leave, but I am sure they will not capture the beauty and emotion of the experience. I cannot even imagine how I would feel if I had planted and tended this milpa year after year and had once helped my father and grandfather do the same.

May 3: Día de la Santa Cruz

Tired of eating mole and hanging out with his mother in kitchenspaces, my youngest son talked me into leaving him alone at home after I picked him up from school. His brother Juan is on a field trip visiting museums in Mexico City. I go to María Teresa's alone to celebrate the meal, very conscious of how inappropriate this will appear, though I am anything but alone once I get there. While my research focuses on food preparation and not on the feast itself, none of it makes any sense without the final consummation, so to speak. The hostess would be extremely upset if I did not show up for the meal. It would be a violation of the tacit agreement underlying the reciprocity network in which I too am participating. A person contributes however he or she can (with work or money or both) and is not only welcome but expected to participate with family and friends in an event that recognizes and celebrates the community, generating and confirming a common bond.

I arrive at the cornfield to find row upon row of tables covered with white tablecloths. Young girls carry trays full of plates loaded with chicken and mole and rice and beans to the several hundred guests seated at the tables. María Teresa's family rented the tables, tablecloths, and chairs, paying for them months in advance. With her family's honor at stake, she did not want to risk coming up short on a day when many people in the barrio would be competing for the same items. A big welcome sign hangs by the gate, with the words formed out of the stenciled letters that María Teresa's son and daughter were still cutting out last night when I left. The hostess and several of the women with whom I have been working on the previous days welcome me and usher me in.

Rosalinda and her crew from Los Ramos are here. She quickly points out that this meal is not like the one that I helped her prepare, though both occasions involve an annual neighborhood fiesta. This is the *comida para todos los barrios* (meal for all the barrios), hosted by the barrio of Santa Cruz for all of Ocotepec, while Rosalinda's meal was mostly for family and friends this year. In both fiestas plenty of people in other households hosted meals for specific groups, like the musicians or the *promesas* from other neighborhoods. Almost everyone in the barrio celebrates in both cases, but some have greater community responsibilities than others. On this day, while the barrio has its annual fiesta, people throughout the country are cooking for the construction workers in their homes.

As soon as she sees me walk onto the lot, Rosalinda sends her young niece running to bring me to their table. She calls the serving girls to make sure that I have a plate of food and hot tortillas right away. Although somebody brings me a glass of *tepache*, Rosalinda guesses correctly that I would prefer beer. She orders three cold bottles via her niece, so we can share a toast. She and her friend chuckle at the resistance that the little girl gets from the beer man; Rosalinda makes him hand signals to indicate that the three bottles are indeed for us. They cackle at the idea of the man assuming an eight-year-old girl might be running off to the corn rows to drink three bottles of beer by herself.

Rosalinda is enthusiastic and grateful for the pictures that I dropped off with her cousin several weeks ago, a little album of the shots I had taken during the week I spent with her before the Palm Sunday meal. I was happy that she asked me to take pictures, because it gave me a formal role in the preparations—not one I particularly wanted, but clearly one that she liked for me and that gave me a chance to contribute. Rosalinda says that she was sad to see me leave and hoped I would come back to visit. She suggests that I come for Muertos (Day of the Dead) next year, because a good friend of hers lost her mother this year and she will be helping prepare the *ofrenda de cuerpo entero* (full-bodied offering) that is traditional in this town on the one-year anniversary of the death. In Ocotepec an altar during the Days of the Dead for a person who died during the previous twelve months includes a representation of the person with a life-sized body shaped out of hay or pillows and dressed in the clothes of the deceased. When I leave today, Rosalinda almost insists on going back to the servers to ask for a few plates for me to take to my boys. She is practically scandalized that I would leave without asking for my *taquito:* not only do I have a right to expect it because I helped prepare the meal, but I owe it to my children at home.

As I leave, Lucía is at the gate, saying good-bye to each of the guests, asking them if they were well attended ("¿Los atendieron bien?"). I assure her that the feast was excellent, and she says that she hopes everyone else thinks so as well. Her mother is crying when I leave—from the emotion and excitement, her daughter explains later. I ask Lucía to thank and congratulate her on my behalf. It is clear that hosting *la comida de todos los barrios* is a huge physical, emotional, and financial effort for the hostess and her support network.

May 4: Día del Recalentado

María Teresa invited me to the *recalentado* and meeting of the barrio representatives on the day following the fiesta. Lucía told me that the meeting would begin at 10 a.m. I spend the morning washing dishes and helping set up tables, but it still has not started when I leave at 2 p.m. Nobody seems in the least concerned. Everyone assumes that people are still discussing things after the Mass at the neighborhood chapel and trying to get the numbers straight before coming to the formal meeting.

When I arrive, the men are sweeping up trash and all the women are in the *cocina de humo.* Someone is filling two huge barrels with water from a hose so that we can wash dishes. A young female in-law arrives and sits down to chat with the *abuelo* for a minute. When she gets up to join the women, Lucía teases her, joking: "Niña, ¿qué andas haciendo ahí? ¡Las mujeres en la cocina!" (Girl, what are you doing there? A woman's place is in the kitchen!). The young woman explains apologetically that she could not ignore the *abuelo* when he invited her to sit with him. Spaces may be gendered, but the authority of elders supersedes all.

Gloria, the woman who cooked and served the rice the day before, tells me she went home at 9:30 p.m. and headed straight for bed, complaining to her husband about her aching feet. She got home comparatively early because she made sure to serve her pot of rice first. She is the first one outside of the immediate family here to help this morning. Tía Lupe, who arrives soon after I do, says that her arm hurts from stirring and serving the mole all day. All the women have sore feet from standing and sore backs from stirring with heavy wooden spoons. Among the casualties, María Teresa hurt her foot by stepping onto a large splinter from the firewood; she picks at it now, trying to remove it. She went to bed after midnight.

The moment Tía Lupe arrives, she drains some of the water that the younger women have put in the rice to reheat it and scolds: "¡Cuidado que así va a salir como arroz con leche!" (Be careful, that way you are going to have rice pudding!). Nothing is considered worse than mushy rice, except perhaps burnt mole or half-cooked tamales. Rituals and beliefs that make a cook personally responsible for her dish help prevent these disasters in collective situations. Just as the *abuelo* is clearly the authority to whom everyone defers in the fiesta preparations and family matters, Tía Lupe is the ultimate authority in the kitchen. Nobody here comes close to matching her reservoir of knowledge.

I wash several plastic pitchers that were used to serve the *tepache.* Then I gather up over eight boxes of empty beer bottles and more than a dozen empty bottles of Presidente. When I ask why pulque was not served, I am assured that, although it was not served, it would all have been consumed. Until recently they used to serve *tepache* made with pulque or pulque *cu-*

rado. If the *tepache* had pulque, they explain, the children would not have been able to drink it. Today the women do not serve alcohol until the meeting is over and the representatives are satisfied with the clear accounts (*las cuentas claras*) and the commitments lined up for next year. María Teresa's brother, who made the *tepache*, gives me the recipe and tells Lucía to invite me in advance next time they are going to make it so I can see how it is done: "You use pineapple, peeled and chopped; also the peel, but you remove the tail. Orange, chopped with the skin. Tamarind, without the peel but raw. Limes, the ones with the 'titties' so you know what I mean. A bit of clove. You cover that with water and leave it to ferment for three days. Strain it, and you get the concentrate like the stuff you buy. It is very sour, but you add water and sugar to taste. We got about three hundred quarts. The fermented concentrate lasts for a week."

I ask about proportions and quantities, since the recipe has none as usual. The answer: six pineapples; thirty-six oranges; twelve large limes (not what are called limes in the United States, but large fruits like grapefruits that are bitter but not sour); about two to three ounces of cloves; and about six and a half pounds of tamarind. Covered with water, this makes concentrate for about three hundred quarts or more, when diluted with water and sugar.

Everybody wants to join this conversation about how things should be made and how they should taste. Tía Lupe comments on the changes in *mole verde* and how disgusting it is that some people now make it with cilantro. "In this town, green mole was made with pumpkin seed and pasilla chile that was toasted and ground, nothing else. Cooked in chicken broth." All variations are inappropriate and inferior from her perspective. María Teresa's brother, who is forty years younger than Lupe, disagrees, arguing for newer and richer versions with more ingredients.

Independently of the recipe, it takes skill to make mole. "Not everyone knows how to make it," she says. "Se corta, da asco, hace daño" (It curdles, makes you nauseous, doesn't sit well on your stomach). They all agree with her and have a story to tell about somebody's mole that made them sick. "Besides the recipe, what is the secret?" I ask Tía Lupe. One detail, she says, is that you do not add the salt until it is well cooked; otherwise it curdles.

The conversation turns to home-raised pigs, which María Teresa's brother says are still very common in Ocotepec. Tía Nacha insists they taste best because they are raised on corn, including the water from boiling the corn for tortillas: "No hay como criar su marrano en casa. ¡Qué rico! En casa es maíz, tortilla, agua de masa" (There is nothing like raising your pig at home. How delicious! At home they get corn, tortilla, and water from the corn dough).[7]

Before I leave, I ask María Teresa how barrio events are financed. "The neighborhood representatives go from door to door raising funds. They ask for 280 pesos [about US$30] per house, regardless of how many families are in each house. Some give more, some less. I paid my father's contribution in addition to mine, so he would not be removed from the list. At the committee meeting, they say such and such a family gave this amount, and such and such family gave nothing."

This very important list will be read aloud at today's meeting, announcing to the public who gave and who did not. That is why María Teresa, despite everything she put into the meal herself, paid double for her household, so both her husband's and her father's names would be heard.

"Why contribute?" I ask. "Si no cooperas no puedes exigir" (If you do not contribute, you cannot make demands), María Teresa says. And if you do, you can count on the community to give you a hand when you need one ("Si necesitas ayuda, te echan la mano"). This is key to understanding how gendered spaces of food preparation are at the center of the community. She gives the recent example of her mother's death. People immediately stepped in to support them, as members of the community in good standing. They began by ringing the church bells. At that point, the women ran to find out who had died and what they could do to help prepare the nine-day burial ceremony (*el novenario*). "They help you with the wake; they bring coffee, sugar, candles. For the nine-day ceremony in this town we offer bread, coffee, chocolate, and *atole*. When you take up the cross after the wake, you go to Mass, leave the cross at the cemetery, and then go share a meal together."

With the stress of preparing the big meal behind us, today is the best day for conversation with the family and the helpers. Everyone is in the mood to reflect and comment on the previous day's events. The meal had been planned for five hundred, but they conclude that eight hundred came, given the extra boxes of disposable dishes that had to be opened. I began the morning scrubbing cooking pots with pumice stones and concluded with a delicious meal of leftovers. I listen to everyone talk, leaving the table to write in my notebook now and then. Something the *abuelo* says as he sweeps up trash with his grandson catches my ear: "Una cosa es ponerse la corbata, otra es ponerse a trabajar" (One thing is to put on a tie and another is to put yourself to work). That seems to capture the aftermath of yesterday's celebration.

3 Tetecala

"Here Mangos Used to Be Like Gold"

Each year Tetecala de la Reforma celebrates two principal fiestas: Día de la Candelaria on February 2 and the day of St. Francis of Assisi, patron saint of the town, on October 4. February 2 is one of the most important dates in both Xochimilco and Ocotepec and, not coincidentally, marks the onset of the planting season. A series of events occurs in Tetecala on that day and the preceding day, including a parade and a spectacle in the bullring. Unbeknownst to most residents, a special meal takes place prior to the parade, in conjunction with the neighboring town of Coatetelco.

While this fiesta and most nationally significant fiestas—such as the day of the Virgen de Guadalupe on December 12—are part of the calendar in Tetecala, they are celebrated primarily within the confines of the church and in the civic space of the central plaza. As is often the case in Mexico, the plaza (*zócalo*) is bordered by the somewhat daunting physical structures of the lay and ecclesiastic authorities. Like the bullring, it is a very public and highly supervised space.

Most people in Tetecala consider themselves mestizo and want little to do with the "exaggerated" indigenous traditions that the people I interviewed claimed never existed or were quickly disappearing. Magdalena, the woman who owned one of the two long-standing *misceláneas* (mini-marts), told me she had observed the waning significance of the Day of the Dead through people's purchases. She no longer sold the vast quantity of candles, bread, and *piloncillo* used for the offerings that she once did. Instead, she said, children make *ofrendas* at school and put them out on tables in the plaza for others to admire.

Despite the rejection of indigenous identity in Tetecala, part of the Candelaria celebration is based on what I call a case of borrowed ethnicity. The woman who has hosted the meal for nearly twenty years is originally from an indigenous community in the state of Puebla, and the majority of the people who partake of it are pilgrims originating in the neighboring indigenous community of Coatetelco. According to legend, a man from Tetecala found a small statue representing the Virgen de la Candelaria in the nearby Coatetelco lagoon. He took it to Tetecala and built a chapel in her honor. Soon the rains stopped, and the lagoon—which locals depended on for fish and agriculture—dried up. The people of Coatetelco blamed the catastrophe on the absence of the Virgin. An agreement was reached: every year they take her home to Coatetelco for a week-long celebration resembling the type seen in Xochimilco and Ocotepec, after which they hope to regain her favor and guarantee enough rain to fill the lagoon. A group of pilgrims returns the *virgencita* to Tetecala on February 1, again in a solemn and formal procession. She is back in her chapel on her day, Día de la Candelaria. The procession that delivers her is received with food by a group on the outskirts of Tetecala, in the neighborhood closest to Coatetelco. This legend describing the theft of Coatetelco's water by the more powerful Tetecala and the animosity reflected in the anti-Coatetelco discourse firmly identifies Tetecala as center (powerful, dominant) and Coatetelco as periphery (weak, dominated).

This chapter provides glimpses of three different fiestas—or four, if we consider the parallel Candelaria fiestas separately. We begin with a typical life-cycle celebration marking a girl's transition to womanhood on her fifteenth birthday, the *quinceañera* or *quinceaños* (as the fifteenth birthday celebration is commonly called in Mexico, to differentiate it from the *quinceañera*, meaning the girl). Next I share my surprise and difficulty in investigating the Candelaria celebration. We conclude with an *elotada*, a family's celebration of the corn harvest with delicious tamales made of sweet corn. The women who guide me through these fiestas, Doña Eustoquia and Esmeralda, appear again in the following chapter.

December 30, 2000: Fiesta de Quinceaños

Doña Eustoquia was thrilled to be invited to the party, happy to be treated as family by her friends from the market. She was also pleased to be able to invite me to a fiesta and to contribute to my research in this way. She had requested and obtained a special printed invitation for me from her "niece's" family. Smiling, she handed me the envelope with my name neatly stenciled on top. At her suggestion, I purchased and wrapped an appropriate present: a bottle of shampoo and conditioner for the long black hair of the *quinceañera*.

We go to Silvia's house early, but too late to help with the food preparation. The food is already cooking in the yard: several of the usual big drums used for *barbacoa,* and of course the *cazuelas* of rice placed over bricks and firewood. As I have come to expect, the men supervise the meat. The women are in charge of the rice and beans. Looking like a young bride, Silvia is gorgeous in her white gown; she poses for my camera with her plastic flower bouquet. Her *quinceaños* is an important celebration that cost her family a lot of money, even though they had different people help with the costs. It is one which the humblest families consider essential, though of course some spend a lot more money than others.

At the Mass, family and friends join the Catholic priest in thanking God for life and youth; he exhorts Silvia to stay in school and "improve herself." After Holy Communion the crowd moves to the party site next to the chapel, with a huge plastic tarp overhead. A disk jockey is already at work; loud pop music blares from the speakers on top of the stage. Coolers filled with beer and soft drinks await. Soon the guests file in and sit down. We are served *barbacoa,* rice, refried beans, canned jalapeños, and of course tortillas.

The party takes place in the shadow of the *ex-ingenio* of Atocpan (just outside the town of Tetecala proper), one of several sugar mills that once

Steaming *barbacoa* in oil drums

employed many men in this town. I see several cars with plates from the state of Tabasco, where most of Tetecala's sugar workers moved to work in the sugar industry when they closed the mills here. Doña Eustoquia is glad to have somebody to share a beer with her. I do not leave until after her sister, her brother-in-law, and their extended family join her at the table.

February 1, 2001: The Day before Día de la Candelaria

Today I took a break from the Niñopa preparations in Xochimilco to spend the day in Tetecala. I did not want to miss the chance to see how Tetecala celebrates. What an event! Both of this town's celebrations, Día de la Candelaria and the day of St. Francis of Assisi in October, are celebrated in a carnivalesque fashion, with a *mojiganga* street parade complete with giant doll-like figures called *gigantonas,* masks, and plenty of alcohol. There are no *chinelos,* though the giant figures dance and spin to jittery tunes very much like *chinelo* music. I am surprised to find that the most important figures in today's parade are imported cartoon characters: Woody, the cowboy from the U.S. hit film *Toy Story,* and Picachú, the character from Japan's popular Pokemon craze that swept the world.

Woody and Picachú in a Tetecala parade

As I was driving into town this morning, however, I caught the tail end of a very different sort of parade, which piqued my interest. It was clearly a pilgrimage, which none of the people I had been interviewing for months had mentioned. It looked more familiar to me from my experience with Xochimilco than the street festival that they invited me to share with them. As I approach the town, I see a large group of people near the health clinic on the side of the road. I will have to investigate later, because people are expecting me. I have come today because several of the people I have become close to invited me to see their parade. I was surprised that none of them were busy preparing food for the event. They planned to celebrate eating at the many food booths in the market.

The parade includes fireworks, though nothing like the extravagance of Xochimilco and Ocotepec. No *castillos,* just the basic whistling rockets shooting up in the sky, announcing the parade. We walk down the street, following the *gigantonas* to the bullring. I don't see any collective food preparation areas, though plenty of booths are set up in the plaza with delicious food for sale. It appears that the celebration here is in the street rather than in anybody's home.

Alcohol is a key ingredient today, in the form of *agua brava* (wild water). It is pretty much the same as Ocotepec's *agua loca* (crazy water), liquor made of grain alcohol from sugarcane. The parade winds through the streets and heads for the bullring on the edge of town, where many people wearing masks and disguises will participate in a contest. By the time we reach the ring, many of the men can hardly walk, including a "bull" consisting of two young men sharing a bull outfit: one stands in the front legs and holds the head on his shoulders; the other stand in the back legs, literally bringing up the rear. Both fall over so many times during the parade—sometimes dramatically—that more than once I become alarmed, sure that they are injured or passed out. Each time they fall, somebody resuscitates them by pouring more *agua brava* into their mouths. Somehow they make it back onto their feet and teeter forward, only to trip and fall again shortly thereafter.

Today is also the day when the *diablos* (devils) chase people—especially pretty women—all over the street, grabbing them with tar-covered hands. All those who want to play, and some who do not, end up covered in tar.[1] Devils notwithstanding, it does not feel like a religious celebration and seems very different from the solemn parades accompanied by brass bands in Xochimilco and Ocotepec.

March 22, 2001: Investigating La Candelaria with Doña Eustoquia

Nearly two months later I am still trying to understand the food preparation behind the Candelaria celebration in this town. I get an opportunity after a long day in the nearby town of Zacatepec—sugarcane central. I have been helping Doña Eustoquia, the sassy 78-year-old woman with whom I have been working most closely. She needed to claim her deceased husband's social security check in a nearby town, and I offered to drive her. I asked her if she would like to accompany me in my search for the woman at the heart of Tetecala's reception of the Virgen de la Candelaria. It is a good thing that she does, because I doubt I could have gotten past the front gate without her. Doña Andrea, a dark woman around sixty years old with long black hair, was easy enough to find. All the neighbors in her barrio know who she is. Several directed me to her house. Getting her to let us in was much more difficult.

As soon as we walk up to her black gate and I spot the huge *cazo* (a large metal tub used to cook *carnitas*) in her yard, I know we are in the right place. A younger woman, Nayeli, answers the door. She is extremely suspicious and does not seem to believe me when I say that I am interested in food preparation. She asks me for identification right away. I head back to my car for the letter of introduction from UNAM that I keep in the glove compartment for such cases. Before I can find it, Doña Eustoquia has talked her way past the gate. She swears to the woman that I am legitimate and introduces me as a student who is staying at her place. She says that I have been here all year. Again and again I am struck by Doña Eustoquia's cleverness. Today I am especially grateful to her for having adopted me and for being so committed to my research.

Still seeking to establish some connection with the women I hope to interview, and to reassure them that I am not from the Central Intelligence Agency, I offer another reference: Doña Magdalena, the owner of the *miscelánea*, who has been introducing me to people in this town. Until a new store recently opened right next to hers, the *miscelánea* was one of only two places where people could go to buy anything from milk and ham to soap and rope. I tell them that Doña Magdalena's daughter Alicia is my landlady in Cuernavaca. Once we are in the courtyard, where we sit down for a brief conversation, it becomes clear that both Nayeli and Andrea know Doña Eustoquia from having seen her around for decades. Doña Eustoquia very shrewdly asks about Andrea's daughter, from whom she used to buy beans at the market.

In this very tentative and unfriendly space—the first I have encountered in Tetecala—I inquire about food preparation for the Candelaria celebration. Doña Andrea is immediately on the defensive: "No lo hacemos como se debe" (We do not do it as it should be), she responds. Andrea is concerned that she is not an appropriate spokesperson because she is not from Tetecala. "No soy de aquí" (I am not from here), she declares right off the bat. As if to reassure her, Doña Eustoquia happily chimes in that she is not from Tetecala either. Doña Eustoquia is from the state of Guerrero, as are most of the people in this town. Andrea is from a little village (*un pueblito*) in Puebla. It is a place called San Miguel Tecomate, near Hueyapan and the crater of the Popocatepetl volcano. When I ask her to repeat the name of her town, panic and suspicion flash in Andrea's eyes. I drop the subject immediately. Given the region where it is located, however, I know that it must be a place where mole is the only appropriate way to celebrate. It is definitely an indigenous region. Her ethnicity explains in part why Andrea is at the center of her adopted community's collective food preparation for the annual fiesta.

Andrea has been organizing the barrio to support the arrival of the Virgen de la Candelaria for more than seventeen years. It becomes clear in our conversation that she feels guilty that in the last two years—under the pressure of the increasing costs and the reluctance of neighbors to help feed an ever-larger crowd accompanying the Virgencita—they do not even serve *carnitas* properly. And of course that dish is not mole to begin with and is not considered appropriate for such an occasion. As an economic strategy, Andrea had the idea of making *carne de puerco en salsa verde* (pork in green salsa) last year so that the meat would go farther ("para que rinda más"). And so for two years they have prepared *carnitas* in green salsa, with rice and tortillas, as well as the usual fresh fruit waters: *agua de jamaica, de tamarindo,* and *de sandía* (hibiscus, tamarind, and watermelon water). The first two drinks are the same ones served at most fiestas in Xochimilco. The watermelon water may reflect the produce readily available in this hot region. Andrea is not sure how long the tradition will continue in the face of rising costs and increasing numbers of mouths to feed. She is tired of dealing with the neighborhood resistance to contributing to the meal with money or work or both.

Andrea collects 150 pesos (about US$17) from each household in this neighborhood, which is a short distance away from downtown Tetecala. Everyone pays the amount, she says, but many complain. For fifteen years she made mole and *carne en adobo* (meat in a special red chile sauce), sometimes pork, sometimes beef. "Not any more; chile is too expensive and too many people come to the feast." Pork is the most common meat served for fiestas, she and Doña Eustoquia agree, because it is the cheapest and people can raise pigs at home.

Doña Eustoquia volunteers that she thinks that chicken or turkey, which is traditional with mole, is no longer served because "modern people" waste too much. They do not like getting the gizzard or foot or many of the other parts that are served along with the breast, leg, or thigh. Pork or beef can be served in a chunk of meat: everyone is happy and there is no wasting, she says. I ask Andrea if she raises the pigs that are used in the meal. No, she says, they purchase them with the neighbors' financial contribution. This year they used four pigs, two crates of green *tomates* (tomatillos), and lots of serrano chiles. Food seems to be a safe topic of conversation as long as I do not ask too many questions, so I keep them to a minimum and listen intently to what she offers. Andrea is happy to share the recipe and quickly tells me the ingredients, including cumin, garlic, and herbs. The vegetables are purchased at the central market in Cuernavaca. Some neighbors contribute more than the 150 pesos, and some bring rice or sugar. It is easier to get women to help cook, she says. One woman cooks an entire pig herself and brings it already prepared in the *cazuela*. Women and girls of all ages come to work together in Andrea's house-lot garden.

I ask Andrea why she does this, though I suspect that one reason why she is the one behind this meal and not somebody else is because she is from an indigenous community. This becomes clearer when I hear the women discuss mole in Tetecala and find that many of them do not make it from scratch, which would be unacceptable in most of the homes I have visited in Xochimilco and Ocotepec. While Andrea does not make mole for the huge community feast due to the cost of its ingredients, she says that she does make it for family celebrations of course. So the big *cazo* and other large *cazuelas* find use throughout the year in smaller and more private fiestas in her household. Meanwhile they are stored in the house of a neighbor, a woman with more space, who has offered to care for the big *cazuela*. Andrea is proud of her *cazuela:* she says that it has lasted over seven years now and has four handles. She bought it from a traveling craftsman. I recently saw one in the local museum in Tlayacapan, a town famous for its pottery, where it was probably made.

Our conversation takes place in the house-lot garden, inside a square space filled with ornamental potted plants that make the place feel cool and shady despite the heat. Doña Andrea eventually answers my question about why she organizes the annual feast. Because she made a promise, she explains. When she first arrived in Tetecala, she was asked by a "señora anciana de aquí" (an elderly lady from here) to keep the tradition and never stop receiving the Virgin ("Me pidió que no dejara de recibir a la Virgen"). While Andrea is still fulfilling that promise, she says that its nature has changed over time. Receiving the Virgen de la Candelaria nearly twenty years ago meant cooking for the dancers and the musicians; now it implies feeding the women and children who accompany them as well, at the very least. The neighbors have changed too, and now Andrea is beginning to feel alone with her commitment and especially the task of rallying everybody: "They no longer want to cooperate, they do not want to continue the tradition." "Cooperate" in this context means giving their share of the money (*la cooperación*) that each household in the barrio is expected to contribute.

Doña Andrea suggests that I speak to the family that prepares the other meal for the Virgen, making *atole* and tamales to serve around 3 a.m. That is when the people of Coatetelco come to borrow La Virgen for the week. Doña Andrea organizes the *comida* or main meal of the day when she returns to celebrate her fiesta. On each leg of the journey, the Virgin is accompanied by a large group of pilgrims. They carry her in the same way believers in Xochimilco carry the Niñopa, on two wooden poles supported by four people. No wonder I saw two different parades on February 1. They were two separate rituals with very different ethnic characters and uses of space: one mestizo, centered in the public space of the street, with food in the plaza for sale; the other hosted in the semipublic space of a house-lot garden with a neighborhood working collectively, if somewhat reluctantly, to maintain a tradition considered Catholic but with roots in prehispanic nature worship. The bigger fiesta is certainly the traditional reception in nearby Coatetelco, when the people there borrow the tiny Virgin from Tetecala and give her a week-long fiesta. Without their efforts, there might not be enough water for the smallholder agriculture and no more fresh *mojarras* (fish) or *tamales de pescado* (fish tamales) that so resemble Xochimilco's *tlapiques*.

July 19, 2001: Follow-up Visit with Esmeralda

Four months later, near the end of my year-long stay in Mexico, I return to Andrea's home one last time. I bring Esmeralda with me. While Esmeralda's style is vastly different from Doña Eustoquia's, not to mention that she is about fifty years younger, once again it proves crucial to have a neighbor along who can get me in the door. By now several people have told me that Doña Andrea is particularly suspicious of strangers for unique reasons. Her property is adjacent to the old hacienda marking the entrance to Tetecala, the Hacienda de la Luz. It is the place that reportedly belonged, and maybe still does, to the powerful drug lord known as el Señor de los Cielos (Lord of the Heavens). According to Mexican authorities and the media, he reportedly died in a recent plastic surgery operation on his face, but many do not believe it and fear his reappearance. The drug trade (*el narcotráfico*) has brought violence and distrust to this town and too many others in the region; it is a very sore point.[2]

Out of caution, I make it clear to anyone who brings up the topic of *las drogas* that I am studying food, not drugs. It is notable nonetheless that this "unimportant town with no history," as many refer to Tetecala, is smack in the middle of the drug traffic and kidnapping that characterize the region, due in part to its relative wealth. With all this in mind, I have come with my UNAM letter in hand this time. I wait patiently while Nayeli reads it carefully several times before calling Andrea. The opportunity almost evaporates when a colleague from the state university drives by with a car full of students from Tetecala. She recognizes my Texas plates and pulls up abruptly to ask what I am doing here. Nayeli jumps in surprise and only slowly regains composure.

Esmeralda later tells me how amazed she was at their suspicion. She also notices—as I do—that they much prefer to address her than me. I am lucky that Esmeralda, who is both my friend and my research assistant, is knowledgeable enough about my work that she is able to keep the conversation on track.

Andrea again complains of the heavy burden she carries because she accepted the responsibility for the fiesta long ago. The neighbors in her immediate barrio are the only ones helping with the funding and food preparation, but many other people come to eat, she says. Esmeralda asks how many people come to eat and is shocked to hear that over 1,600 accompany the Virgin. Not all of them eat here, Andrea clarifies. Some bring their food, and others buy it at the plaza. But plenty of them expect to be served in this neighborhood.

When I ask how they manage, Andrea repeats what she told me on my last visit: besides the cash contribution that goes to buy most of the ingredients, many women bring food from home to prepare at her place. Some clean the beans; others fry the meat. The pigs are slaughtered in the yard as well. Sometimes it is a pig that a neighbor raised for the occasion; at other times they purchase the pig.

Eventually talk turns to the fiestas in Doña Andrea's hometown and how different they are from those in Tetecala. Esmeralda cheerfully interjects: "People here are always looking for an excuse to party!" Indeed fiestas in this town tend to happen in private settings, where a family closes off a street or has music in the yard and invites friends and family.

March 31, 2001: Celebrating the Harvest

Yesterday, after a long day spent with Doña Eustoquia and another friend, Doña Magdalena, I stopped by to say hello to Esmeralda before heading back to Cuernavaca. The last thing I planned was returning at the crack of dawn the next morning to make tamales. But here I am, sleeves rolled up, ready to help.

"¡Ya están los elotes!" (The corn is ready!) Esmeralda exclaimed when she saw me yesterday. *Elotes* means sweet corn on the cob eaten fresh, as opposed to the corn left on the stalks to dry for making tortillas and other foods with corn dough. Her tone and excitement reminded me of the joy with which fresh wine is announced in France after the grape harvest: "Le Beaujolais nouveau est arrivé!" (The new Beaujolais is here!). Esmeralda said her family had been wanting to invite me to join them in making *tamales de elote*, which they do at the beginning of each harvest. They have two corn harvests in this region: this one in March is the harvest of irrigated corn; the rain-fed corn harvest is in September. This was the second batch of tamales they were going to make in a week. While it is a family affair, it is also a chance to celebrate with others, as campesinos always seem to do around the corn harvest in this region. Arnoldo, Esmeralda's brother, also invited a group of people from Cuernavaca to join the family. That night I will return home with a plastic bag full of a dozen or more sweet tamales and another with a dozen freshly cooked *elotes.*

When I arrive, I find Esmeralda's mother, Doña Fernanda, clearing dishes off the outdoor table and washing them in the basin facing the lemon trees (key lime in the United States, *limón* in Mexico). Clearing the table of dishes and scrubbing it down with lots of water and bare hands turns out to be a fairly regular ritual today. It is carried out by different women—Esmeralda, her mother, and her sister Sonia—at different times. Esmeralda is already peeling the outer leaves from the *elotes.* I join in helping her with this task right away. The food preparation takes place in the outdoor patio, from dawn until we leave for the river after 5 p.m. The space is dominated by a huge hearth, raised for comfort. Three separate but adjoining hearths heat the three huge metal, barrel-like tins of *nixtamal* which the family uses to supply the mill and sell masa. A chicken sits on her eggs undisturbed, in the middle spot, which of course has no fire today. Other chickens and roosters run around the patio all day, two asleep in the *chiquihuite* (a tall, cylindrical basket). At one point a rooster almost catches his tail on fire on the coals that we light for the tamales. This, along with almost everything else today, is a source of commentary, laughter, and enjoyment.

We begin husking the corn at 7 a.m. and will not finish until late morning; the tamales will not be ready to eat until 4 p.m. It is truly an all-day affair. At 11 Doña Fernanda is ready to mix the ingredients with her hands: "I am going to give it a little stir [*una movidita*]," she announces. The day's work is interrupted by the regular food preparation for the multiple family meals: breakfast, *almuerzo,* and *comida.* Finally, around 2 p.m., we put the tamales in the pot to cook. "You have to stand them up so they will not spill their contents as they cook," Doña Fernanda explains.

Three pairs of hands work together, seamlessly interweaving at different times of the day. The process includes husking the corn, cutting it off the cob, grinding the kernels in the *molino* with pieces of cinnamon, breaking fifteen eggs and separating out the yolks, and opening cans of sweetened condensed milk. We beat all the ingredients together in the masa for a long time, tasting and adjusting the dough several times. Next we fill the husks with the masa, using a large spoon for measuring, and sprinkle raisins on top. Finally, we fold the husks to enclose the dough. We stand the tamales neatly on end in the pan—three layers' worth—and cover them tightly to be sure the vapor stays in. Of course we tie ears of corn husk strips on the pot handles so that the tamales will not absorb any strife that would prevent them from cooking fully or well, a tradition that persists throughout central Mexico.

Doña Fernanda takes the freshly cut corn down the steps, made of old worn-out grindstones from the family mill. She carefully grinds a few slivers of cinnamon stick with each batch.

Because we need the best husks to make the tamales, we take care to cut the bottoms off the ears of corn before peeling them. The outer leaves are thrown into a huge *costal* to feed to the cows later, but we put the nicer large, inside husks into a big tub so we can use them for the tamales. Unlike other tamales, *tamales de elote* always use fresh, green husks. After tasting the masa, the women decide to adjust it by adding another pound of butter and a bit more sugar. "¿Va a querer otro poquito de azúcar? ¿O ya estará bueno?" (Is it going to want more sugar, or is it good already?) asks Doña Fernanda. "Ahorita la pruebo" (I'll try it right now) both daughters volunteer.

Celebrating the corn harvest with *tamales de elote*

Pure pleasure: hands in batter, batter on the tongue. Time seems to have stopped, and worries have evaporated. The world begins and ends here. The tamales cook on high heat, coal in this case, for one and a half hours. "Listen," the sisters tell me at one point when the fire is whistling, "that means visitors are coming" ("¡Va a venir visita!").

Conversation at the table turns to immigration, which is a tragic story and often the only hope in Tetecala. Esmeralda has many women friends from Tetecala who are working in the United States—not all in one place, but always in a place where family networks already exist: Los Angeles, Phoenix, Chicago, Houston, Dallas, San Francisco, New York City. Some swim across the border; some walk across the desert. Esmeralda laughs, recalling one friend's story of how she fell on a prickly pear and stuck her rear end. Another had trouble getting over the wire fence at Sonorita. Esmeralda concludes the conversation by announcing that she would like to go to Chicago, where she has an uncle who has a restaurant. But, she muses, it would be difficult to leave and stay away. "Como México no hay dos. La tierra llama. Siempre regresan. Ganan dinero y regresan, aunque sea en ataúd" (There is no place like Mexico. The land calls. People always return. They earn money and then come back, if only in a coffin).

Our talk turns to the subject of death. Many of Tetecala's immigrants do return in coffins, killed by AIDS, accidents, or violent crimes in the United States. Some returned alive and introduced AIDS to the local population. "Everyone who has died of AIDS in this town brought it back from the United States," Esmeralda claims. The *mujeres públicas* (public women)—as the government calls prostitutes here—were also infected by returning migrants.

Finally, after eating lunch, everyone at the table disappears, only to reappear thirty minutes or so later, ready to pile into the old pickup truck and drive to the river to eat again. Soon after we arrive, Esmeralda's father lies down by the side of the river to take a nap. Eventually the women (including myself) wade into the river with our dresses on. The kids jump in; the young men play ball and test their strength by swimming against the current.

Some very nicely dressed local girls and older women walk by, crossing the river at the spot where we sit. Esmeralda's mother explains that they are Jehovah's Witnesses. Several people come by to swim and to set traps for fish. Though this mango orchard is private property, it is play space used by all—or recreation and rest space anyway. Reflecting on changes in the region, Doña Fernanda tells me: "Aquí antes los mangos eran como oro" (Here mangos used to be like gold).

Before I leave town I stop to say hello to Doña Eustoquia. She, the would-be sister-in-law who ate with us, and my landlady Alicia are all quick to tell me that *tamales de elote* are not usually as sweet or rich as the ones we made today. They should be served with cream and green salsa, everyone stresses. Yet these are the best I have ever tasted—and I have had more than my share over the years.

Tamales Nejos, Traditionally Eaten with *Mole Verde*

As we prepare the *tamales de elote,* Doña Fernanda shares the recipe for a traditional *tamal* that is typical in Tetecala: *tamales nejos.* I recently sampled some at the Tuesday market (*el tianguis*). These white tamales are made with ashes and wrapped in banana leaves instead of corn husks. Unlike most tamales I have seen and tasted, they are not light and spongy, because they are not made with baking powder. Perhaps they are more like what tamales were like before baking powder existed. The women at the market told me that formerly they used the water from boiling the tomatillos (in their husks) as a rising agent.

"Son muy trabajosos" (They are very difficult), Doña Carmen says. You have to stir ash into the *nixtamal* very carefully to avoid getting burned. For five *cuartillos* of corn you use five *cuartillos* of ash. "Tiene que ser ceniza buena de palo, porque hay ceniza que no sirve" (It has to be good ash from clean wood, because some ash is no good). Ash from charcoal will not do. After boiling the corn for one hour, "se descabeza" (literally, the head is taken off or separated from the kernel) with the ash. Usually you do this by boiling lime with the corn. You have to put the ash in by the fistful very carefully. "Once the boiling kettle is full of ash, it splatters and burns. Next you take the corn out and scrub it until it is white. Then you grind it. Finally, you add salt and lard and wrap the dough in banana tree leaves. After the tamales are cooked you eat them with green mole. Bean tamales go with red mole, *tamales nejos* with green mole."

Like other tamales, these spoil if people are angry or fighting around them or "si les tienes muchas ganas" (if you desire them too much). It is like the *mal de ojo* (evil eye) that afflicts cute babies in Mexico who attract too much attention and envy. "No se cocen, o se cocen locos. O si las personas que los están cuidando se van, dicen que los tamales se van también, no se cocen" (They will not cook or will come out crazy or half-cooked. They say if the person who is taking care of them leaves, the tamales leave too; they do not cook). You cannot leave them alone. Like children, tamales require constant attention and care.

Many tricks are used to avoid such problems, such as tying corn husk ears onto the pot handles. Today I learn another trick: make a cross of guajillo chiles, cover it with salt, and put it directly on the fire underneath the pan. I have seen Doña Josefina in Xochimilco make a cross out of nails and put it in the bottom of the pan when we made chicken *mixiotes,* another type of tamal. I have also observed several women in Ocotepec and Xochimilco make a cross out of salt, but never one made of chiles. In any case, the ritual is essentially the same: it is about blessing the pot to ensure that the food is both good and plentiful.

Finally, Doña Fernanda says, you should put the *molcajete* (stone grinder used for chiles and seeds) on top of the tamales "para que no se cozan locos" (so that they do not cook crazy). Interestingly, in Xochimilco people use the *mano* (hand) of the *molcajete*—also called the *meclapil*—for the same purpose. The tamales are usually covered with an embroidered tortilla napkin, then with plastic bags, and then with the lid of the pot. Today we have too many *tamales de elote* for the lid to fit, so we use some tough plastic bags to seal in the vapor. "¡Tantos secretos de la cocina!" (So many kitchen secrets!) marvels Esmeralda, only partly in jest.

PART TWO

Kitchenspace Narratives

This section presents individual women's perspectives from kitchenspace, making evident my hosts' hospitality, knowledges, and creativity as well as some of their food-related beliefs, recipes, and economic strategies. It includes descriptions of several home kitchens and several maps that women drew at my request. The selections here (as in Part One) are drawn from a much larger group. As women reflect on their lives and the losses and gains they have experienced from the kitchen, we hear voices communicating a vivid sense of place and change. Not surprisingly, food practices linking the living with the dead are a recurring theme.

Gendered perspectives from kitchenspace

Whereas Part One provides glimpses of collective experiences, Part Two focuses on individuals. Chapter Four
features women in Tetecala; Chapter Five women in Xochimilco; and Chapter Six women in Ocotepec. Nowhere do I
attempt to portray an imaginary "typical" woman. Instead I
present people with different perspectives that bring to light
some of the issues that I encountered over and over again in
my work. Older women comment on what they consider the
pereza (laziness) of the young, while younger women express
their frustration and exhaustion with traditional gender
roles. To stress the social nature of kitchenspace in these
communities and that the women here are part of a web of
relations to which they are firmly attached from the kitchen,
I include other voices as well.

This section overlaps with Part One to some degree. Just
as that section allowed us glimpses of women's everyday
lives through conversations that took place during collective food preparation, some women here talk about fiesta
food preparation, though in private conversations with me.
One interview in Chapter Five takes place during a fiesta:
I take the opportunity to learn more about food in Xochimilco from one of the *abuelitas* considered a guardian of
tradition. Some characters overlap as well. Once again we
encounter Esmeralda and Doña Eustoquia from Tetecala,
Señora Rosa and Doña Teodora from Xochimilco, and Isidra,
Dolores, and María Teresa from Ocotepec. New people are
introduced: Señora Linda in Xochimilco and María Soledad
in Ocotepec. In order to present women's narratives with
minimal interruption, this section includes some short
monologues in the first person. These are usually taken from
several different conversations. In the case of Esmeralda
(Tetecala), Doña Teodora (Xochimilco), and María Soledad
(Ocotepec) portions of their narratives (including parts in
Spanish, with translation) are taken verbatim from their
written or tape-recorded responses to my questionnaire.
This provides space for women's voices and for forms of
expression embedded in the language itself.

Kitchens—whether the community kitchens in the house-lot garden that are the focus of the first three chapters or the less visible home kitchens presented here—remain at the center of cultural reproduction and at the heart of family and community relations. Some of the women who speak here are fully aware of this fact, despite the lack of social recognition that they experience.

4 Women of Tetecala

"You Have to Be Ingenious in the Kitchen!"

This chapter on Tetecala begins with entries from Esmeralda's own ethnographic notebook. I include her mother and her father, because Esmeralda's kitchen is in her parents' house and her story makes no sense without them. I conclude with Doña Eustoquia, a woman and neighbor much her senior who was introduced to me by a professor from Mexico City who rents a part of her house for weekend visits. If Esmeralda's cooking is at the center of her family and even the marketplace, Doña Eustoquia is a relatively lonely widow, though she too shares her table with others on a regular basis. Both women are very expressive and full of energy, opinions, and insights; both were particularly supportive and involved with my research. I rarely visited Tetecala without eating with each of them, whether I was hungry or not. Esmeralda always sent me home with something—a bit of home-cooked stew, perhaps, or a chile relleno full of spicy pork and drowned in fresh cream and always, always, those delicious, handmade tortillas which I can still smell today as I type these words. Doña Eustoquia made sure to save something for me that she had gathered in the fields, or she would knock down a papaya or soursop from a tree in her house-lot garden. Neither ever let me leave empty-handed.

Esmeralda and Her Family

Esmeralda is a remarkably candid and intelligent young woman whose talents in the kitchen are recognized by her family and others. People from surrounding towns who visit Tetecala on market day eat at the booth where she and her sister serve food that they and their mother prepared at home the day before or early that morning. Esmeralda is caught between the heavy demands of a traditional household and her desire to live beyond the parameters of the kitchen. To her frustration, she spends most of her time preparing food for her parents and brothers, the two men who periodically help her brothers and father with the land, and any guests who drop by at mealtime. On Mondays she cooks all day in preparation for the Tuesday market. In addition, sometimes she helps prepare food that her family members sell in the evenings on the sidewalk just outside their house.

Toward the end of my research year, Esmeralda offered to help me interview women in Tetecala. I gratefully accepted but insisted that she answer the questionnaire herself as well and write her responses in the notebook that I provided for her work. Her 22-page response, including family recipes in addition to several maps and charts of her kitchen, informs much of what I present here. Other parts come from our endless discussions over her kitchen table or by her stove. Esmeralda is not typical of Tetecala: there is no other woman quite like her there or elsewhere; but of course every one of the women with whom I worked is unique. At the age of twenty-four, however, Esmeralda is representative to some extent of her generation's attitude toward the kitchen.

Esmeralda's Narrative

I remember when I was little, we spent our time jumping from mango tree to mango tree, my brothers and I. We had a little orchard in our yard with lots of mangos and a grapefruit tree. The grapefruit tree has dried up since then. We also had an avocado tree. My parents raised pigs and lots of chickens, and I recall we used to have lots of goats as well, about a hundred. My father taught my older brother how to milk the goats. The milk had a real authentic taste. The taste was so strong it seemed like you were eating the whole goat!

My father always farmed the land. He grew tomatoes, squash, rice, onions, tomatoes, beans, and corn. I remember my mother used to take him his midday meal out in the fields. She would cook a tasty chicken in chile sauce and garlic, rice, a pot of beans, and some hot tortillas. And off she'd go, together with the five of us kids. It looked like a parade, each of us carrying a box so we could eat together in the fields. I especially remember that I always carried a bucket of lemonade, and how we used to walk one behind the other until we reached the fields. On those walks I loved to close my eyes and listen to the special sound the water made as it ran downstream. I always asked myself if that water ever passed by the same place again or if the sound it made was a farewell.

I remember Tetecala when there were no paved roads. When you walked, it was so dusty, it seemed like you had put talcum powder on your feet! In the springtime, I recall lots of pigeons of many colors—and the children running after them, including myself of course. So many friends visited us every day! *Hace mucho se los llevaron al norte* (They were all taken north a long time ago). They never came back. Their parents were very poor, so they all left. I remember how, when it rained, the dirt turned to mud and we would play in it. We ended up with such fat feet (*¡unas patotas!*) that it looked like we had boots on! We could hardly run, but it was lovely (*¡era bonito!*). What I remember most was the smell of wet earth. I think Tetecala was a magic place.

Things have changed, people have changed. The ones who keep the traditions, like making tortillas by hand, are the old folks.[1] My father says: the population goes up, but our *molino* business goes down. *Dice mi papá: "Ya las mujeres son modernas, ahí van con su pan Bimbo y su mayonesa. Antes molían"* (He says: "Women are modern now: there they go with their white bread and mayonnaise. They used to grind corn").

Mamá was always a good cook, and Papá was very responsible with our daily expenses (*el gasto*). He still is to this day. What I most remember was the smell of *elotes* boiling with *tequesquite* (a mineral). And a pot full of *tamales de elote*. Those were my favorites. Mamá also made a delicious pork in plum sauce. *¡Uy, qué rico!* (Yum! That was so good!).

I was always standing next to my mother by the stove, observing how she cooked. She would say: *"Fíjate bien* [pay close attention] so that when I am sick you can take me a plate of soup to my bed *aunque sea* [at least]." She would touch my head and say: "I am proud of my children but especially of you."[2] My mother taught me to cook. I think I cook pretty well, but I do not prepare things the same way she does. I have combined things a bit.

Nowadays my family plants corn, beans, and sugarcane. We used to have chiles and epazote in pots in the yard. Now we only have *ruda* (rue, *Ruta graveolens*) left because the chickens got to everything. *Se dice: "¿Prefieres patas o plantas?" No se puede todo* (They say: "Do you prefer paws [animals] or plants?" You cannot have everything).

These days I help my mother prepare the meals. I go to the plaza to buy food and chat a while with the woman butcher and other acquaintances. I have been preparing the everyday meals for over five years. Of course, sometimes I punish Mamá and make her cook, but then she gets angry.

I hate it when the beans boil over. And what bothers me most of all in the kitchen is beating egg whites: that is the most tiring thing. Everyone says you should not get angry when you are beating the eggs if you want them to get stiff. And that when you cook tamales you must make sure to tie ears on the pot so they will cook well. Otherwise they get crazy (*se hacen locos*) and end up half cooked, half raw. [Beating egg whites until stiff, for use in one of many typical dishes, including chiles rellenos, seemed to be on everyone's list of least favorite kitchen tasks.]

Cocinar es como un reto de no fallarle (Cooking is like a challenge that you must not fail). You have to obtain the right flavor and fragrance, and the dish must also look so appetizing that when you see it you feel you just have to have it (*que al verla se te antoje*).

I like to cook. What I really hate is sweeping: I feel like a pile of dirt is going to swallow me up. *Lo que más me gusta es poder compartir la comida con personas que aprecian a uno* (What I like best about cooking is sharing a meal with people who appreciate you). What I do not like is when they abuse you and act as if you are their maid. In my house there is always plenty of activity, so you can spend the entire day cooking. *Tanto trabajo que da preparar la comida para que te la comas en un ratito. ¿Qué chiste es ese?* (It takes so much work to prepare food, and then you eat it right up in no time at all. What kind of joke is that?).

When I am angry, I think my food comes out very spicy. When I am happy, I try to please my brothers and cook what they like. I think I only cooked with lots of love (*con mucho amor*) one time. Lots of good it did me. I think cooking is an art capable of conquering any heart from the stomach. The problem is that sometimes you get the wrong heart and you want to run! But without food perhaps life would be boring.

My brothers say I am a good cook. They are so demanding! *El sabor de mi comida lo tienen bien identificado y les gusta mucho lo que les hago; es raro que lleguen a renegar* (They recognize the particular flavor of my cooking, and they like what I prepare; rarely do they complain). They are pretty obnoxious if somebody else cooks besides me or my mother.[3] But with me they rarely complain. When they especially like my *comida* (midday meal), they ask for more at dinner or simply eat a lot.[4]

Imagine a day without *cocineras* (cooks), with nobody to wait on those demanding men. It would be such a mess! I think no matter how hard men would try, things would not come out right. So we are a necessary evil for everyone. I think we are more active and creative than they are.

The trick to cooking delicious food is to season things slowly, have just the right amount of salt, and take things off the heat at just the right moment, when the food is just right (*en su punto*). For mole, you give it the master's touch by cooking it in a clay pot and adding all the ingredients like sesame seeds, almonds, bread, tortillas, chocolate, tomatoes, onions, tomatillos, and raisins.[5] To cook beans you have to be sure not to uncover them very much and to mix two types of beans, one for flavor and one for appearance. For great rice, you cook it with a couple of chicken feet, a few livers, and make sure you use chicken broth instead of water. *Atole* is best with fresh [raw] cow's milk and cinnamon and cooked over low heat. For great pineapple tamales, you have to grind the cornmeal to just the right consistency, *pallenada* we call it, and beat it with plenty of butter and Royal (baking powder). Cook lots of pineapple with sugar separately to make preserves. In the green corn husk (*totomoxtle*) you put a bit of the masa that you prepared with a piece of pineapple and then you steam it for more or less an hour and a half. And then you are set (*¡lista!*).

Some beans that grow here in Tetecala turn out hard as rocks—like the *pinto* or *coconito*, which is nice and tender when it comes from Canada. When I was a little girl, I liked a sweet, tasty bean that we used to grow here. It was called raindrop, but it has not existed for about five or six years now. Another one we used to have is *bola;* now we have one called *recortado* that is similar. There was also one called goat's eye that was lost about twelve years ago; that one was similar to the *coconito*.[6] The bean called *canario* Sinaloa does not exist anymore either. You can buy a bean called *huevito* (little egg) that you cook with pork in *adobo*. All beans are different in terms of how they are cooked and how they taste. For instance, *el peruano* (the Peruvian) cooks until tender like a fava bean, but its flavor is bland—it does not taste like anything at all. People buy it because it is white and looks pretty.[7] Peanut beans get darker when they cook, but they are tastier. People here like to see their pot full of white beans.[8] But the secret in the kitchen is this: you use half Peruvian and half of another type to get pretty and tasty beans. The flavor and the appearance even out. And there you go. You have beans that are tasty as well as pretty, white. *¡La cocina es para ingeniárselas!* (You have to be ingenious in the kitchen!).[9]

I usually cook in clay pots, though I cook beans in an enamel one because it is faster. Normally I make tortillas on the gas stove on a *comal* made of tin. Sometimes I make them on firewood, but rarely on coal. I use a hand-press, a *tortillera.* We make them fresh daily at my house, and they are delicious. I use the metate only to *amasar la masa* (knead the masa), and the *molcajete* of course for a good salsa.

As for the blender, you know, sometimes I cheat and use it, especially when I make a peanut sauce. It is a lot of work to grind peanuts with chiles so I grind them a little bit in the blender, just until they are coarsely ground, and then I pour them into the *molcajete,* mash them a few times with the pestle, and pretend it is from the *molcajete.*[10]

Mi jefa me enseñó a cocinar, o sea mi mamá. Mi papá me enseñó a recojer productos del campo desde los cinco años, y mi mamá todo lo demás (My boss taught me how to cook, that is, my mother. My father taught me to harvest products from the fields from the time I was five years old, and my mother taught me everything else).

The Narrative of Esmeralda's Mother, Doña Fernanda

Tuve una vida pobre, triste de niña (I had a poor, sad life as a girl). My mother was ill. I had two sisters. *Mi mamá cocinaba muy sabroso, hasta un tlacoache nos hizo y nos chupábamos los huesitos* (My mother cooked very well, she even cooked a possum,[11] and it was so good we sucked its little bones). We were so poor. My father tanned cowhides. My mother raised chickens and turkeys.

I recall the time we ate a possum that fell into our water tank in the middle of the night. We all woke up. I held the oil lamp while my father and brothers butchered it. My mother cooked it with guava and mango leaves, avocado pits, bay leaf, garlic, onion, and salt. She brought it to a boil and threw out the water. Then she added fresh ingredients and brought it to a boil again. Three times she threw out the water. *Para que no estuviera cho-quiaque* (So it would not have that wild taste). After my mother died, my aunt took care of us. She cooked a *tlacoache,* but we could not eat it. *Daba asco* (It was disgusting).

Las mujeres modernas son flojas: sus maridos venden maíz y ellas com-pran tortillas (Modern women are lazy: their husbands sell corn and they buy tortillas). *Las mujeres ahora ya no quieren ni saben cocinar* (Women these days do not want to or know how to cook). And the men, well, now their wives buy them *barbacoa* that is already cooked and just put avocado on top. One of my in-laws is such a disgrace, her husband even has to wash his own clothes. She does not iron them either. He puts them on while they are still wet. He comes to buy prepared food from us at the market. *No me*

*gusta meterme, pero me dan ganas de decirla a la esposa: ¡báñate temprano
y pídele a Dios que te quite esa pereza!* (I do not like to get involved, but I
feel like telling his wife: get up early to bathe and pray to God that he take
away that laziness!).

The Narrative of Esmeralda's Father, Don José

My mother was a very good cook. She made some special beans, with lard,
so good that you could ask for nothing else. She would make my grilled
steak of beef or pork, my *cecina* (salted meat) from Iguala, or chorizo.[12]

People have changed. Now they buy canned beans! And they eat tortillas
made of powder from the *tortillerías*.[13] *Le ponen polvo y la gente no repela*
(They put powder in them and people do not complain). People will eat
anything these days!

Here, in my house, they make me beautiful tortillas and pig's feet with
eggs. Everyday they serve me a fresh dish. My wife knows how to cook
well—not like my mother of course. What wonderful bean *gorditas* she [his
mother] used to make me with epazote. They would bring them to my work
[the fields]; I would drink my pulque.

It has been fifteen to twenty years since they sold pulque in the market
here. In other towns it is still available. They used to bring me my little barrel, and I would drink it with chopped onions and chiles.

I do not eat artificial cream.[14] I am used to dairy cream. People are pigs
nowadays; they mix in artificial cream that costs three or four pesos per li-
ter and sell it to you at twenty (US$2.20). *Y los jóvenes ya se hizo harto mari-
juano* (And the young are all marijuana druggies). Not before. *Pura gente
fea a venido, sinvergüenzas* (Only bad people have moved here, shameless
folks). It has grown so much here that my house used to be at the edge of
town and now it is in the center.[15]

Tetecala *se está modernizando* (is becoming modern) with its surrounding neighborhoods. *Tetecala era la gente más honrada de ningún lado*
(Tetecala used to be the most honest people around). Folks that live on the
outskirts are bad; people who are from here live in the center. Over fifteen
years ago *llegaron gente porque aquí hay mucho que agarrar* (folks came
because there is lots to grab here): mango, avocado, maguey, banana. Many
supported themselves that way, by stealing. Once they robbed me of one
thousand mangos. I had two thousand. Only half were left. I used to sow
seven hectares, no more. *Mi hijo siembra tres ahora. Puro frijol y maíz* (My

son sows three now. Just beans and corn). He sells it at the market in Puente de Ixtla on Sundays and here on Tuesdays.

Kitchenspaces

Most of my conversations with Esmeralda took place in her kitchen. I showed up at her doorstep one day and told her father that I was a university student interested in food traditions. I asked him about the family mill that I could see from the street. I had seen people line up there every morning, many with buckets of corn in their hands. He ushered me into the courtyard at the center of the house and took me up the single step made of an old grindstone from the mill. There he introduced me to his daughter. Esmeralda was standing in front of a stove cooking. They offered me a seat, one of half a dozen plastic chairs at the table behind the stove.

The kitchen was in the shade, neither indoors nor out. Esmeralda had sewn several grain sacks together to make a curtain of sorts and keep the breeze from blowing out her gas stove. "Es bueno y no estás afuera. Entra aire rico, pero si está muy fuerte el aire, o llueve, se apaga el gas" (It is nice and you are not outdoors. A nice breeze comes in, but if it is too strong or it rains, the gas goes out). Although her kitchenspace had only three walls, Esmeralda would later express her frustration that older people expected young women like herself to live within the confines of "estas cuatro paredes" (these four walls).

Don José soon joined us for conversation, leaving his seat at the door, where he usually sat tending to the family's sale of grains, including the corn and beans grown by his two sons. Like most elderly people, he was more than happy to share his opinions about changes in food preparation in recent years. Disgusted with the stuff they sold in the *tortillerías* in town, he claimed that "modern" tortillas were not made from corn at all. He did not know what they made them from, he said, but it was certainly not corn. On several occasions trucks carrying what he calls "animal feed" from the United States tried to sell him grain for his mill. On many subsequent visits I would find Don José selecting the best seed from his own dried corn, scraping the kernels off carefully with his hands or rubbing two *olotes* (cobs) together to loosen them. Some he saved to plant in his fields. Some he sold as seed to neighbors for planting their next crop.

Esmeralda took over in the kitchen several years ago. She had to quit her studies at the state university in Cuernavaca after one year because her father was ill. She began cooking full time then, helping support the family from the kitchen. On Monday afternoons and early Tuesday mornings her sister joins her, and they prepare the food for sale at the weekly outdoor market (*el tianguis*) that sets up in the town every Tuesday.

When her mother, Doña Fernanda, is out, another family member minds the store. Esmeralda, her father, and Sonia (the sister that lives across the street) take turns attending to customers who come to buy beans or corn, dried corn husks, soft drinks, or masa. Another sister, a biologist, lives in Cuernavaca. The pay was so bad for professionals that she was trying to go to the United States to make more money performing unskilled labor. Esmeralda's two brothers, on the rare occasions when they are home and not eating or resting, step in now and then to measure out corn or beans for a customer. Diego spends most of his time in the fields and selling corn and beans at different weekly markets nearby; Arnoldo, an agronomical engineer, is in charge of a large mango orchard just outside the next town. The owner fled from his property after being kidnapped and now manages it from afar.

I joined Esmeralda's family at the kitchen table on several occasions throughout the year, sometimes bringing my children and on one occasion even my advisor from the University of Texas. I visited regularly once or twice a week and sometimes on weekends. Arnoldo showed me around the mango orchard, and I walked to the family fields with Diego once to observe how he prepared them for planting. Most often I came in the morning, when the young men were at work in the fields, Don José was minding the store, and Doña Fernanda was grinding *nixtamal* into masa for customers. I would talk with Esmeralda in the kitchen while she cooked, sometimes helping her grind spices in the *molcajete* or stirring the pots. As soon as I appeared, Esmeralda would call out cheerfully: "¡Güera! ¡Ya viniste!" (Blondie! You've come!) and make me a fresh, sweet tortilla. She would give it to me with the cream that she knew I loved—"de la buena" (the good kind), she would always say—and a bowl of delicious hot beans.

On several occasions I joined Esmeralda, her sister, and her mother to make tamales (see Chapter Three). Sometimes I made a few tortillas, though that was always a personal exploration rather than a contribution to the household. More often than not, I scribbled away in my notebook at the kitchen table while Esmeralda told me stories about the people, places, and food in her life. Doña Fernanda shared recipe after recipe with me, telling

me how to make them for my family and wanting to help me with my research. I always left with a plastic bag full of thick tortillas and a container
or two of the day's meal, or the mole, chiles rellenos, or *picadillo* (a delicious
dish made of ground beef with raisins, carrots, peas, and other ingredients)
that they sold at the market if I had come on a Tuesday. Sometimes I picked
lemons from the trees in the courtyard to take home with me as well.

Esmeralda's kitchen was a place where I felt at home. There I was always
cognizant of and grateful for the pleasure of having a year to eat my way
through my research. The generous spirit of everybody in her family—as
well as their astute observations—provided insights into the complex nature and role of the kitchen in an agriculturalist family in Tetecala. It was
also a place where I knew my family and guests were always welcome and
would be treated to whatever delicious food Esmeralda was preparing.

Esmeralda's house is two blocks away from the central square, on the
main street. Two wide doorways lead into the house, one to the *molino*
that is Doña Fernanda's space and one just to the right of that, where Don
José and his sons sell grains. Between the two is a Coca-Cola refrigerator
filled with sodas. Customers often help themselves and leave the coins on
the table, per the instructions that Esmeralda yells down from her place by
the stove. When walking into the covered area where the various economic
transactions take place or simply walking by on the street when the doors
are open (which they are throughout the day), you are likely to see Esmeralda cooking on the raised part of the kitchen to the right. From here she
can keep an eye on the street, the family business, and the chickens in the
yard as well as the food cooking in her pots and the tortillas on the *comal.*

Food preparation plays a key role in Esmeralda's household relations and
in the family's economic strategies. Not surprisingly, the house-lot garden
and adjacent food-related areas are extremely complex. Unlike many other
homes, which have an indoor and an outdoor kitchen, this kitchenspace is
somewhere in between and blends into the house-lot garden.

Esmeralda's kitchenspace includes the key elements that I found in most
kitchens in my research sites, though to an exaggerated degree in some
cases. These include an outdoor water source and a multitude of containers
for storing water; various hearths for cooking (seven in this case); several
spaces and items devoted exclusively to storing or transforming corn, such

Facing page: **Esmeralda's map of her kitchenspace**

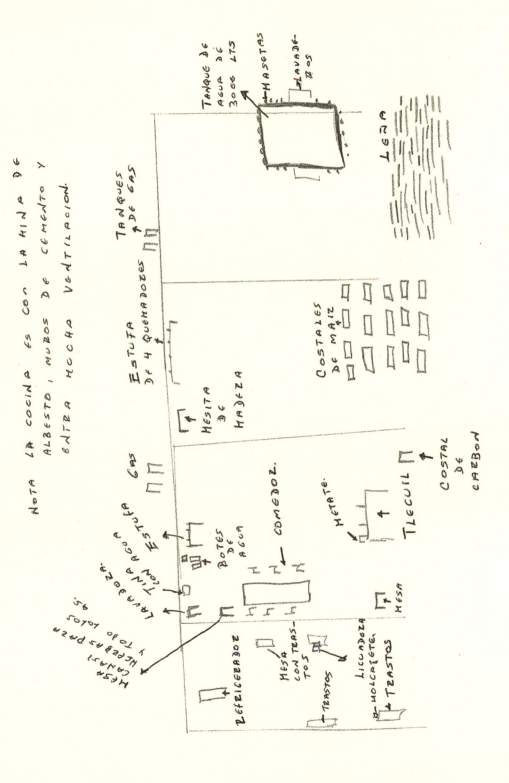

as grinding tools that are used on an everyday basis (like a metate, *molca-jete,* and blender); an assortment of fuel for use in cooking: firewood, dried corn husks, charcoal, and various gas tanks; a variety of cooking pots and dishes made of clay, plastic, and enamel-covered aluminum; live food (in this case in the form of more than sixty chickens and several fruit trees); dried foods and medicinal herbs for teas; potted ornamental plants; a caged bird; and, of course, a place to receive guests and serve meals.

This house and mill that once belonged to Esmeralda's grandmother has become the primary family residence. They have another house a few blocks away, where they lived before gravitating to the mill in the very center of town. Arnoldo, the older brother, stays there now and takes care of various pigs, goats, and cattle that he raises in the yard. The roof covering part of the kitchenspace is made of rock, brick, and cement. Iron rods (*varillas*) protrude from the top. Coke bottles cover the ends of the rods, *para que no llame los rayos* (so as not to call the lightning). Smoke is usually billowing out from under the boiling pots of *nixtamal* and fills the covered kitchenspace, filtering out the top at both ends.

The space is densely filled with an assortment of containers, tools, foods, and more. The following partial inventory of Esmeralda's kitchenspace focuses on the sections of greatest interest. For instance, behind the water tank—under the roof—are many piles of tools and containers. These include three *braceros* (small portable outdoor stoves); one *coladera* (colander) for washing vegetables and also for scooping out the corn or *nixtamal;* a basket for carrying strawberries; a large bar of soap; an old container for petrol (*una anáfora para cargar petróleo*) that is no longer used; an old door; several brooms; a wooden rung-ladder; and a large *guacal* (box made of wood) that belongs to a man who sells bread at the market on Tuesdays. Esmeralda's family keeps it for him because the *colectivo* (collective taxi) charges him extra to transport it. There are many plastic-weave and burlap sacks (*costales*) for storing corn, beans, and oranges as well as several shopping bags (*bolsas de mandado,* the usual colorful plastic-weave containers for buying food at the market). One *costal* is used for the trash, along with a trash can, which is dumped into the garbage truck that drives by every three days. Edible food scraps and compost are fed to the dogs, pigs, and chickens. One sack labeled "Frijol de Canadá" (Beans from Canada) is used to store the corn grown by Esmeralda's brother. The family also purchased several other sacks of corn to prepare the *nixtamal* for the *molino,* because the demand for masa is more than they can supply with their own production. Propped up on two crates lying on their sides is a sieve of sorts used to separate the chaff from the dried corn prior to boiling it with lime ("un arnero para ceñir el maíz o quitarle el tamo").

Closest to the main gas stove is another section, dominated by the large table which serves as a gathering and eating place for the family and guests. Behind it is the huge *clecuil* (firewood hearth) where the *nixtamal* is always boiled. Another large table is pushed up against the wall at the very back of this space. On top of it are a bunch of dried flowers, a toolbox that serves to hold money when they sell food or beans at the market, a plastic bowl with dried herbs (the usual *hierbas de olor:* thyme, bay leaf, and marjoram), cinnamon sticks and home-made breadcrumbs, a container full of pumpkin seeds, a bag full of beans (*frijol chino*), boiled mangos from Arnoldo's most recent experiment, a pot full of corn husks, a roll of aluminum foil, and vinegar. Hanging beside that table are two baskets and a bag. The bag has dried leaves from various trees for teas and home remedies: chamomile, arnica, black tea, and medicinal teas. The two baskets contain medicines from the local pharmacy. Under the table are a *vaporera* (large aluminum pot for steaming tamales), an enamel-covered cooking pot (*olla de peltre*), a bucket of lard purchased from the local butcher, and a cardboard box full of glasses (made of glass, not the more typical plastic) for special celebrations. Next to the table are a *costal* full of charcoal, several buckets, and half a dozen plastic chairs.

The *clecuil* (which Esmeralda says can also be called an *hornilla*) is raised and holds three large metal tubs full of *nixtamal* cooking over a woodfire. Chickens scramble next to them, and kittens and puppies play. Beside the *clecuil* is a metate, used mostly for kneading the cornmeal dough now (*para amasar la masa*), though sometimes used to grind ingredients for the mole. Near the table—which serves both as the main work space and to serve meals—is an old "Easy" brand washing machine with a manual wringer. There are also two small tables with three shelves and many baskets, containing odds and ends: perfumes and deodorants, matches, salt, chocolate, sesame seeds, cumin, black pepper, a tape recorder and music tapes, an electric mixer, and popping corn (to fry in a covered pan on the stove). Attached to the pillar next to the main stove is the forty-year-old parrot. The "Acroz" stove was purchased when Esmeralda's parents were married thirty-one years ago. It has a *comal* and four burners as well as an oven that is never used. When the family members bake bread or chicken, they use the baker's oven in town. Next to the stove, near the washing machine, are two large barrels of water with a lid and a large plastic tub (*una tina de agua*).

Esmeralda sometimes refers to a boxlike indoor room as the kitchen (*la cocina*), although it has not been used for cooking in years. It has four walls, no windows, and two doors: one leading to the semioutdoor space where the cooking and eating occur and the other to the front where the family business is located, also open to the courtyard. The room itself is largely empty, with the exception of a refrigerator and a few cupboards where the dishes are kept. Esmeralda says that her family pulled the table and gas stove out into the covered patio years ago because the kitchen was so hot. They never moved them back. Doña Fernanda's dream is to have a formal dining room in that space, with new furniture, where she can receive guests.

The center of the house-lot garden is under the open sky. It contains a barrel of water, a *chiquihuite* (large basket) of dirty clothes, two tall tanks of gas, two crates of empty soda bottles, a broom, and a dustpan. The potted plants include roses and other flowers. Food-bearing trees include lime, mango, lemon, coconut, papaya, guava, and *guaje* (a tree bearing small *guaje* or *hauxya* seeds in pods, which are very popular in this region and used in many local recipes). Plants in the ground include rue and aloe vera. Rue is the single plant—with the possible exception of aloe vera, always with little red bows tied to its leaves to bring good luck—that seemed to be in the yards of everybody that I visited. Used traditionally and around the world for earaches and for other medicinal purposes, rue is also employed for problems caused by "bad air" or spirits and planted to protect the household space from evil. To one side of Esmeralda's house-lot garden is a chicken coop with hens, roosters, and one goose. Many of the sixty or so *animalitos* (little animals, as Doña Fernanda lovingly refers to them) are loose. Esmeralda says that they used to have epazote and chiles, but the chickens ate them.

Las Cuatro Paredes

Esmeralda is truly an excellent cook; her food is favored by her family and regular customers at the market. Despite the compliments that she receives and the explicit recognition of her skills, she questions existing gender roles and the worthiness of her own activity. She is not happy to spend most of her day in front of a stove, making tortillas and preparing first breakfast, then the *almuerzo* (brunch), then the *comida* (main meal), and finally re-heating things for the *cena* (dinner): "The cook is not valued until they need you. At times it is necessary to punish them so they understand that they need you. The kitchen is sad because it is not recognized. It is lost work. I tell my mom: 'Here you gain nothing.' What bothers me most is when they ask me to serve them by snapping their fingers. People here think that women were bred for the kitchen!"

Esmeralda agrees with her sister Sonia that women are more responsible and concludes that women are doomed to their role in the kitchen. "La mujer ya traemos el don de la cocina, y somos más organizadas" (Women are born with a gift for the kitchen; we are more organized), she says. "Ya es como un mal que traemos" (It is like a sickness that we bear). Based on the sisters' observations, they conclude that women make feeding the family the top priority, which men do not. Men, they say, consider their own entertainment and even alcohol to be a right that comes before any responsibility to their family.

Esmeralda had an opportunity to experiment briefly with professional as well as student life, enough to know there is more to life than the kitchen. After a year of social service working for a lawyer in town, she spent another year working with the local government accountant. Despite her low position and pay, her math and people skills soon led to her practically running that office. After a change in government brought her a lecherous new boss and she refused to accept the rampant sexual harassment, Esmeralda quit her job.

Like many young people, Esmeralda is frustrated by the lack of employment opportunities in Tetecala. Her mother has willed her the house with the *molino* that once belonged to her father's mother, causing a certain amount of tension with her brothers that Esmeralda would just as soon avoid. Doña Fernanda insists that it is essential for her daughter's economic future, whereas the young men "tienen más oportunidades" (have more opportunities) and can make a living off the family land.

Despite having had a few suitors, Esmeralda is in no hurry to get married or to embrace the commitment to a life of hard work in the kitchen that marriage would most likely bring. Nor is she willing to accept domestic violence, which all too often accompanies marriage in Tetecala. She tells me the story of a younger cousin who married at the age of sixteen, disregarding Esmeralda's warning. "I told her that she was throwing her youth into the trash." "Le fue rebién" (She had it real good), Esmeralda jokes wryly about her friend's life before she finally left her husband and crossed the border illegally to seek work in the United States. Esmeralda is indignant as she tells her cousin's story of poverty and abuse:

> *La llevó a una casa de chinamal, de zacate y carrizo. Ni agua tenía. Tenía que lavar en el apantle y dormir en el piso, sin cama ni luz. Cocinaba en tres piedras, el clecuil, pero el original. Se iba por leña para cocinar. ¡Y además se la sonaban! Y se embarazó luego luego. ¡Le ha dado una paliza con su pancita! Me dijo que yo era una amargada, que por eso no quería que se casara, que yo era una quedada. Cuando vino toda golpeada, pues le dije "ya te dije. ¡Apenas estás en el mero apogeo y ya te van a tumbar las alitas!" ¡Yo soy enemiga de que si a palos te tienen, tú te tienes que aguantar los golpes! Quizás por eso no me casé. Yo le decía: no te dejes, no le muestres miedo. ¡Al fin se defendió con el machete, y entonces la suegra se metió a defender a su hijo!* (He took her to a house made of sticks with a dirt floor. It had no running water or electricity. She had to wash clothes in the irrigation ditch and sleep on the floor. She cooked on the three rocks—the original *clecuil*.[16] Every day she had to collect firewood. And on top of it all he beat her! She got pregnant right away. Even with her belly her husband hit her. She told me I was bitter, that was why I did not want her to get married, because I had been left behind. When she came all covered with bruises, I said to her: "I told you so. You are just reaching your prime and they are going to clip your wings!" I am an enemy of the idea that if they are beating you, you have to shut up and take it. Maybe that is why I never got married. I told her: stand up for yourself, do not show him your fear. She finally defended herself with a machete, and that is when the mother-in-law [who lived with them] stepped in to defend her son!)

Esmeralda was furious that the mother-in-law had stood by when her son beat his wife and only got involved when he was threatened. "Women have to outsmart men," she concludes, "since they have strength on their side." After giving birth to a baby girl, her cousin left the child with her mother and went to work in the United States. Esmeralda says that the young woman's brothers report that she has changed a lot.

Despite the pleasure and recognition that sometimes accompany her many hours of hard work in the kitchen, Esmeralda resents her lack of options and the demands—primarily from her family—that she satisfy the needs of her household from this space. She lumps kitchen work together with domestic violence as part of the gender roles assigned to women. Esmeralda is conflicted about her future, not wanting to betray her family's expectations of her but not willing to sacrifice her own dreams of a life outside the kitchen.

Doña Eustoquia

Doña Eustoquia does not eat much: coffee and bread for breakfast and dinner; vegetables, a bowl of beans, and her *memelas* (oval-shaped corn dough like tortillas) for lunch. She eats eggs, fresh salsa, and plenty of fruit, from mango to black sapote, depending on the season, and always drinks fresh lemonade. Anything edible growing in or near Tetecala finds its way into her kitchen: *guaje* seed, flowers from the *zompantle* tree, *cazahuatl* mushrooms that grow on fallen tree trunks. She gathers fruit hanging heavy on the trees—especially mango, black sapote, plum, and guava—and vegetables left in the fields after the harvest: tomatoes, squash, green beans, and corn. "Va uno a titichar, a recoger lo que dejan después de la cosecha" (One goes to glean, to gather what people leave after the harvest), she says. "When my husband was alive, he never let me go alone; with someone else, yes. Now I go with my dog, Duchesa. We join two or three other women and enjoy the walk."

Eustoquia loves to walk in the countryside. "Me alegra el corazón cuando veo un árbol" (It makes my heart happy when I see a tree), she says. "I never want to return. When I go out in the countryside I do not remember anything; here, at home, I remember everything. Like how much my husband suffered at his death." She exclaims with joy at nearly every plant she sees. On one of our walks together she finds a rock she particularly likes: "¡Como me gustan esas piedras boludas, y lo que pesan!" (How I like these big, round rocks; and they weigh so much!). She carries the rock home to put alongside the ear of corn on her porch.

Doña Eustoquia was always happy to have company when I visited. She generously shared her meals, taught me to prepare local dishes, told me endless stories, and patiently answered way too many questions. Once she bought me a cassette tape of *música ranchera* at the local market with a ballad on it about Tetecala that she had been telling me about for months. She introduced me to people and places she knew; she loved taking me to the market and having company on her walks. She told everyone she met that

I was staying at her house, that I was a student doing a "tés," her version of *tesis.* She hated missing an opportunity to help me gather the information and knowledge that I needed and was very proud to be a part of my research. After introducing me to somebody she knew—not only in Tetecala but in nearby towns—she would turn to me and offer to help me interview her contact: "¿Algún dato?" (Any data in particular?), she would ask, with head cocked to the side awaiting my response.

In the fields and marketplaces we visited she would eagerly gather samples of plants for me to put between the pages of my notebook. Her knowledge of the edible and nonedible plants around us was astounding: everything had a name, a use, and a season, which she eagerly shared. She would wait for me to write the information down, which I always did to oblige her. As I developed other relationships in Tetecala, sometimes I would visit her at the end of the day. Each time she had heard that I was in town and cooked something for me to eat. She often insisted on treating me to something to eat at the market—often one of the huge *gordas de chicharrón,* which truly live up to their name in this town (*gorda* means fat): huge corn patties filled with pork rind and served smothered in salsa and cream. When my advisor from Texas visited Tetecala with me, she was horrified that—due to a miscommunication—she had not prepared a special meal to receive him. While her recipes were simple, they were delicious and typical of the region. They represented the meals common to people of her age and income level and reflected what was available during a given season.

Doña Eustoquia's Narrative

Ya no tengo tierra. La vendió él. Lo único que me dejó es esta casa y el seguro de vida de la caña. Con eso me la voy pasando. Lo de Juan Carlos va para arreglar la casa . . . hasta que acabe el juicio. A ver qué pasa con la casa (I no longer have any land. He sold it. The only thing he left me was this house and the life insurance policy from the sugarcane. That is how I get by. The money from Juan Carlos [rent] goes to deal with the house . . . until the court case is resolved. We'll see what happens with the house). If I win the case, I am going to leave the house to his two daughters. Both daughters were from extramarital affairs—can you believe it? I always worked hard, as he earned very little selling his sugarcane. I sold the beans that we grew in the weekly market. *Dejaba la comida hecha y a vender* (I would leave our meal prepared and then go sell).

Cuando tenía cosecha en el campo, llevaba la bolsa con la olla de frijoles y jarros y cucharas y un plato. En el campo ponía la leña y a meter fuego—a calentar los frijoles y la tortilla y a cenar, y acuéstate, y a dormir. Hacíamos un cucurucho de zacate—amarraba las cañas con lazo y nos dormíamos en costales en el suelo. Ha cambiado mucho la cosecha, pues antes se usaba vara y ahora usan animales (When we had a harvest in the fields, I would take a bag with the pot of beans and pitchers and spoons and a plate. In the field I would gather the firewood and start the fire—heat up the beans and the tortillas and have dinner, and lie down and go to sleep. We'd make a little shelter out of the grass—tie some cane together and sleep on sacks on the ground. The harvest has changed so much: before we used sticks and now they use animals).[17]

Doña Eustoquia Did Not Always Eat Alone

It is impossible to visit Doña Eustoquia and not hear about one of her three husbands, all of whom she has outlived. Doña Eustoquia's third late husband was one of many sugarcane growers in the region who sold his crop by contract to the mill in Zacatepec. Now she is lonely. Her two beloved dogs—who are fed bean broth with tortillas and salsa—are her primary company. She also has several cats to keep the mouse population under control. Her dog Duquesa (a gift from the UNAM geography professor who rents a portion of her house) accompanies her everywhere, on walks through the countryside and to the market. Doña Eustoquia even takes Duquesa to visit her sister in nearby Cocoyotla, hiding the dog in a bag so she can ride the *colectivo*.

Doña Eustoquia, now seventy-eight, cooks mostly for herself, though she occasionally cooks for her nephew (a single father) and his daughter and for her sister and brother-in-law. Her only son was killed in a disagreement over a billiard game forty years ago. He was twenty-one. She has two stepdaughters, whom she visits frequently. Her first husband kidnapped her ("*me robó*") when she was fifteen, a traditional approach to marriage in the region until not very long ago. He was thirty-two at the time and was shot to death a few years later. Her second husband died, Doña Eustoquia explains, because a lover bewitched him. The woman sent him a cake that was full of worms. Soon afterward he died with a cut on his toe that would not heal. Doña Eustoquia saw the big black worm under his toe—proof of the evil spell that his lover had cast on him. The fear of being hurt through food is common in my region of work; it is one reason why sharing somebody's food implies a relationship of trust. While many claim not to believe in such superstition, most women I asked recalled at least one example of its occurrence. Worms commonly figure in such stories as symbols of evil.

Doña Eustoquia's third marriage lasted thirty-four years, until her husband's death. He was a drunk and a womanizer: her eyes sparkle as she tells stories about how she caught and slapped four of his lovers ("¡Era muy enamorado, le cacheteé cuatro mujeres!"). Doña Eustoquia was proud of having stood up to him. When he came home drunk or smelling like women's perfume, she would be waiting, hidden behind the curtain in the outhouse, with a bucket of water and throw it at him. She stayed angry for a month at a time, she says proudly. She was partly glad when he became a Jehovah's Witness: "Por un lado era bonito; les dicen que ayuden a la mujer, que no tomen, y que no cometan adulterio. Mucha disciplina, vaya" (On one hand it was nice, because they do not allow drinking or adultery and they tell the men to help their wives. Lots of discipline, you see). Her husband's change in religious affiliation also meant that Doña Eustoquia's social world was drastically altered. Almost all the people she introduces me to during the year (outside of some market vendors and family members) are Jehovah's Witnesses.

Living Spaces

Though her house consists of several constructions surrounding a courtyard, Doña Eustoquia's enclosed living space has been reduced to a tiny two-bedroom space on the ground floor. She moved into it after her third husband's death. The bedroom has just enough room for two twin beds pushed together, a small dresser, and a closet, which dominates the space. Her clothes and personal belongings are piled on top of one of the beds. When I spend the night, Doña Eustoquia has to move all her things onto the dresser to make room for me. When I ask her why she does not use the closet, she responds that she has not found the courage to go through her husband's things: sadness overwhelms her and makes her dizzy. Looking at his things gives her the feeling that he is still alive and spooks her. The only other room contains her kitchen table, cupboards with dishes and a few jars of basics like sugar and salt, always a couple of tomatoes, eggs, and chiles, her water jug, and a small television. At night Doña Eustoquia likes to watch the news and other programs on TV. At other times she keeps her radio on, tuned to *música ranchera* (ranchero music).

Beside Doña Eustoquia's stove on her small covered porch are a few plastic chairs for company. Whenever I eat with her, we pull the small table out there as well. On the edge of the porch she has a little flowerbed in which she grows chiles, a few flowers, and *pápalo* (a favorite edible local grass). *Pápalo* is also found standing in glasses of water at the food booths in nearby markets, for people to help themselves and put on their tacos. Her porch has some decorative elements, including a few rocks and a dried ear of corn. When I ask her why the corn is there, she contemplates it for a minute before responding simply: "Está bonito" (It's pretty).

The bathroom and water tank used for washing are outdoors. Doña Eustoquia shares them with a family that lives above her and the couple from Mexico City that sometimes comes on weekends. The people living above her rooms do not pay rent; she says she has them to keep her company and for protection. Doña Eustoquia is afraid of the next-door neighbors who took over a part of her house. They are relatives of her deceased husband who dispute her claim to inheritance of the property. Her "tenants" upstairs are a middle-aged woman named Evangelina, her son, his common-law wife, and their little girl. They too are Jehovah's Witnesses. The young man is a chief in the local police force (*el comandante*). Doña Eustoquia always refers to him and his wife in hushed tones. The little girl is primarily in the care of her two grandmothers and spends many days playing in the courtyard, often around Doña Eustoquia.

The principal drama in Doña Eustoquia's life today revolves around the legal battle to keep her house. A less worrisome distraction for her is the saga of the young couple on the verge of separating. She is certain it is because the woman is not assuming her wifely responsibilities. Each time I visit Tetecala she provides me with an update. The situation reflects the painful tensions in this household and many others in communities where young women are increasingly rejecting traditional gender roles. This young woman is the object of constant criticism by her mother-in-law, Evangelina, and Doña Eustoquia. Eustoquia is scandalized that the young woman does not cook for her husband and eats boxed cereal or drinks instant chocolate milk for breakfast. Worst of all, "¡Deja los trastes en la mesa como un hombre!" (She leaves the dishes on the table like a man!). Every morning the young woman rushes out to catch a bus to the university in Cuernava-ca, returning in the afternoon to work in a local pharmacy, which Doña Eustoquia cannot understand. She is particularly suspicious because the young woman's husband has what appears to be a powerful position and is able to maintain her. The young woman's reasoning that she wants financial independence for herself and her little girl makes no sense to Doña Eustoquia: her imagination runs wild at the thought of a woman supporting a man to keep him around for pleasure and decoration.

Doña Eustoquia gave up a large indoor kitchen that her husband had built in exchange for the company of Evangelina and her family. This did not seem to present a problem, because she clearly prefers to spend her time outdoors. She enjoys using her small covered porch and large house-lot garden for everyday food preparation. The indoor kitchen contains a table and a refrigerator in which she still keeps a few things. Eustoquia uses several different stoves located outdoors, including a gas stove that sits on her porch, a large smoke kitchen where she makes her tortillas over firewood, and a *bracero* that she uses with charcoal to cook beans to save on gas. In the summer months, when the sun is so hot that Doña Eustoquia claims the ground is like fire and she has to water it to cool it down, she loves to sleep directly on the ground.

Doña Eustoquia's house is located in the center of town, less than a block from the plaza (*zócalo*) that is the site of the city government, the jail, the church, the permanent market, and the weekly *tianguis.* On Tuesdays, when the *tianguis* is set up and Tetecala fills with buyers and sellers from around the region, trucks and vendors crowd the street and sidewalk in front of her house. Standing outside the gate, it is easy to see if Doña Eustoquia is home. If she is not, the little blue wooden door that leads into her rooms is locked and the gate to the street closed with a chain and padlock. On a market day she is always around; but if her door is locked on any other day, she is likely to be out of town visiting her sister or in Zacatepec picking up her monthly social security check. If she is home and somebody comes to the gate, the dogs immediately begin barking to warn her. From the gate you usually see clothes hanging on the line and a few ripe fruits lying on the ground.

The patio is strikingly neat and always well swept. Doña Eustoquia cooks *nixtamal* about once a week, boiling it again to keep it fresh as needed. She grinds it in a handmill attached to a tree and uses the masa to make fresh tortillas or *memelas.* Her yard is full of brooms that she makes from

Making *memelas*

Doña Eustoquia grinding *nixtamal* with a hand mill attached to her tree

brush she collects in the fields. Every morning when she sweeps, she uses her hands to sprinkle the lime water in which she cooked the corn, to pack the soil and keep the dust down in the yard, she says. I am struck by this ritual-like use of everything associated with corn. Like most courtyards, orchards, and indeed any piece of land in Tetecala, Eustoquia's yard has fruit trees: soursop and papaya. She dries papaya peel in strips in the yard and uses them to soak clothes before washing them in her outdoor sink, "para que afloje la mugre" (to loosen the grime). She rarely uses her hot water heater, but when she does—usually for guests—she heats it with a piece of firewood, although it is meant for gas, which is too expensive. Every time I accompany Doña Eustoquia on a walk through the countryside, she periodically exclaims about all the good firewood lying around going to waste, promising to come back to collect it later.

Women of Xochimilco

"It Is Better for the Pots to Awaken Upside Down"

In this chapter we hear from three women. Rosa, Linda, and Teodora have very different perspectives on cooking and food traditions in Xochimilco. Señora Rosa is the only one of the three to have spent much time outside of Xochimilco. At an early age she was sent by her family to Mexico City to earn her keep and learn a skill working for a hairdresser from Xochimilco. Her boss also taught her how to prepare traditional recipes and fed her Xochimilca beliefs and sayings. Working outside of Xochimilco for much of her life has given Señora Rosa perspective, some impatience, and plenty of nostalgia. Tired of the gossip and in-fighting that characterize the barrio, she says she hates the fiestas but loves Xochimilco's food traditions.

Linda, in contrast, scorns many of the local food customs and especially the closed-mindedness that she observes in the barrio. She is from the next barrio over and prides herself and her family on being open to new recipes and ways of doing things. Teodora, the oldest of the three, is from a *familia chinampera* (a family that still makes its living from working the *chinampas*). During a celebration in a neighbor's home for which she was invited to help cook, she shares her thoughts on the changing foodscapes that she has experienced and some very old Xochimilca recipes.

Señora Rosa

Señora Rosa's kitchen is always full of people, including extended family, *comadres,* and *compadres.* When her brother died, she raised her six orphaned nieces and nephews alongside her own five children and her sister Josefina's daughter. The house used to consist mainly of two bedrooms. One is now Josefina's sewing shop and bedroom; not long ago she shared it with her mother, Cleotilde, as well as her daughter Pilar. The second held Señora Rosa, her husband, and five children, two or three to a bed. Two of her children have since married and left the home, as has Josefina's daughter. Another son, Camilo, has built a little room out of scrap wood—his penthouse, he jokes—on top of the roof, while Jesús has built a separate bedroom room for his family, in part out of the space his mother's kitchen occupied. He also built a small kitchen for his wife alongside his mother's, separated by a thin wooden wall. The wall is very important for family peace and allows Jesús's wife some autonomy, even living within Señora Rosa's household. Señora Rosa shares her bedroom with her youngest daughter, Beatriz, Beatriz's common-law husband, and their two small children. Rosa's husband lives in a separate house with a married daughter and her husband and children, though he comes by regularly to bring tortillas and cash and to be fed. He also plays with his grandchildren and helps his daughter wash diapers. In this chapter we hear from Señora Rosa's daughter and her *compadre* Don Benjamín, who invited me to the fiesta where men did the cooking (Chapter One).

Señora Rosa's Narrative

My name is Rosa Sandoval López. I am sixty-eight years old. I am from the *callejón*, even though I do not like fiestas. I was born here. My father was born here. My grandfather had his cows here. You could say that I am a hairdresser by profession, because that is what I dedicated myself to full-time for seventeen years. Later I became a custodian at an elementary school for another twenty-five. Now I am dedicated to the home (*me dedico al hogar*).

For me, Xochimilco is in the countryside, not the city. It is full of flowers and vegetables. Its canals are not in very good shape anymore; people do not take care of them as they used to. We have ruined them. Even the *chinampas* have changed. A short while ago some folks took us to see our *chinampas* and we hardly recognized them. They did not even have trees on them anymore! Somebody stole everything on it, even the topsoil.

My mother died in the hospital because she did not want to eat what they tried to feed her there. She wanted her pork rinds in green salsa and tortilla and her ice cream. *La abuelita* Cleotilde was very traditional; she kept the customs. She did not wear shoes her entire life. I remember she used to make us *chicharroncitos* (little pork rinds) after grinding the *nixtamal* on the *metate*. We were too poor for real *chicharrón*, so she made ours from corn. She would make one big tortilla and put it on the *comal*. Before turning it over she would scratch it with a stick and put salt on it. When it cooled she would cut it into pieces and give them to us for breakfast with *atole* made of white corn dough with brown sugar in a little clay pot. She would just add a little bit of cinnamon stick.

Here in my patio I have only ornamental plants, all in their own pots. Right now the only animals we have are cats, but Josefina sometimes has a pig or chickens. Jesús raised a pig here too, for his daughter's *quinceaños.* When we do not have any animals, we give the waste from the kitchen to people who are raising pigs. Look, here I am saving things in this pot. The hard tortillas I save for Antonio's grandfather, for his cows. He soaks them to make them soft first before feeding them.

In Xochimilco food is the same as always, according to our traditions. The only thing that has changed is the way to prepare certain dishes. Before, we always cooked with firewood and charcoal and clay. Now we use gas and enamel and aluminum. We eat lots of vegetables, tortillas, and tamales. It is the custom to offer a meal when someone dies. My mother used to tell us that eating meat in front of a dead person is disrespectful; it is like eating the corpse. The custom is that the day a person dies you offer a meal. If there is not a lot of money, you make beans in red chile sauce (*frijoles adobados*) and rice. If there is more money, you make *romeritos* (patties of dried shrimp, sprigs of *romerito,* which resembles rosemary, and potatoes served in mole sauce) and the meatless white *tamal* (*tamalate*). On the ninth day you offer another meal, only this time something like mole with chicken or green mole with chicken. Some folks make *carnitas.* Everyone who comes to eat is given food to take home afterward, the *itacate. Si dan bien de comer en los nueve días, dicen "pasó a trabajar el difuntito"* (If they give a good meal for the "nine days," people say, "The dead person went on to work").[1]

I am always overjoyed when I am about to eat. I eat with great pleasure. Maybe it is because we suffered such hunger when I was a child. My father used to say we were worms—like those in dirty water—we were so skinny. What I most like is everything made from corn: tortillas, tamales, *sopes.* And cake. I love cake too, especially chocolate cake. Before, everyone here ate according to their means. Those with more money ate more meat. We ate more vegetables and drank very little milk. Instead we had *atole* made from corn dough. Now many of us work; and although we do not have much money, we do buy milk and bread. We eat better today than we used to.

I've always loved to cook. I love to cook everything—except for roasting the chiles for the chiles rellenos. What I really dislike is when I have to cook

Señora Rosa making *sopa de pasta*

with firewood or charcoal. I am not a good cook, but I like it. I went to work out of necessity; what I really wanted was to get married and stay home. I learned to cook from the woman I went to live with, the one who taught me to style hair when I was twelve. My mother did not teach me to cook because I was never here. That woman taught me to be useful to people who needed me.

I never learned how to make tortillas because I spent all my time working. That is the one thing I never liked about the kitchen—making tortillas. I do not even like to wait in line at the *tortillería*. Sometimes I come home and lie; I tell Josefina that they ran out so that she will go to buy them later. Before, we used to boil our own *nixtamal* (*antes poníamos el nixtamal*) and then take it to the mill to grind if there was any money. If not, well, we ground it on the metate. I have both of my mother's metates here—though I have not used them in at least ten years. They have not moved. Before, we used the metate, even if only to grind the beans for tamales. Now we take the beans to the mill. The blender does not work for that.[2]

My sister Josefina also has worked since she was little. She was sewing at the age of seven. One day as a little girl she stuck the needle right through her finger with the sewing machine. My father told her to put her finger in the *nixtamal* water so it would heal quickly. Josefina was raised by an aunt in a *pulquería* (pulque bar). She still makes *pulquería*-style salsas—really spicy. Josefina is the one who cooked for the household all the years I worked in the school. Now I am the one who cooks everyday. I spend about five hours a day cooking.

I taught all my children how to cook. They know how to cook, wash clothes, and iron.[3] They know how to make their nopales, their *quintoniles* (greens) with chile veins, their chicken gizzards, their sausage. They make their *botanas* (snacks).

We mostly eat vegetables at home: potatoes, carrots, poblano chiles, spinach, cauliflower, radishes, lettuce. And for tea we use cinnamon, chamomile, spearmint, guava with raisins and cinnamon. We also drink lemonade or *jamaica*. For meat we eat some beef and pork but mostly chicken and fish. We eat plenty of fish during abstinence periods, like Holy Week and Christmas. On Fridays my father always had his cold *tlapiques* (fish tamales) with hot tortillas and fava bean soup with nopales—so tasty! My mother ate fish and beans and eggs every day. She always had a few chickens, about four or five, and the egg basket filled up each day![4] Now the fish you get out of the canals taste bad because the water is dirty. They taste like damp earth (*tierra húmeda*). When someone gives us fish nowadays we

Making *tlapiques* (fish tamales)

prepare it in *tlapiques*. Pork also tastes terrible now: pure garbage—they feed pigs chicken guts full of poop these days!

What I cook depends on how much money I have to spend. If there is enough, I buy a cut of meat or a piece of chicken. If not, at the very least I make a soup (pasta or rice), beans, eggs with salsa, and tortillas. When my children were small and I had to use the money for medicine or cloth for school uniforms, I made lots of potato patties (*tortitas de papa*). For a special occasion I make green mole with beans and rice or *adobo*. We make a little mole when there is a fiesta in another barrio so that we are not left craving (*con deseo*) as my mother used to say, that is, wishing that you had been invited to a fiesta, since sometimes we do not know the people in another barrio.[5]

We also make *pipián* with the chile seeds that I save up. To make *pipián* for a week, for instance, I use chile seeds, two or three ancho chilies, anise seeds, raisins, peanuts, sesame seeds, a clove of garlic, a piece of onion, and four black peppercorns. You can eat it with pork or with nopales and potatoes.

When I was little I liked to eat fried fish with tomato sauce and tortillas from the metate (with home-ground corn). And plain corn dough *atole* with brown sugar, and *gorditas* made with lard. Today my family's favorite foods are mole, green mole, and *adobo*. For special occasions people make meat dishes like *carnitas* and *barbacoa* more and more often. They are leaving mole behind. There are many people today who do not like mole. My *comadre*'s children say: "¡Ay, guácala!" (Eww, gross!). That is so rude.[6] They like smoked pork chops and roast for a fiesta. People are eating more and more meat! But even though young people eat many things that I did not when I was a child—*carnitas*, chorizo, *barbacoa*, hot dogs, head cheese—the majority still do eat mole and many types of *antojitos* (traditional snacks). *Sopes* are something everybody likes, especially served with very hot salsa when people have a hangover.

I derive a lot of satisfaction from serving food that people like. My father used to say, "It is better for the pots to awaken upside down the next day"—that is, it is better to share food and not to have it left over. I like to send people home with their *itacate*—their taco to go. That is the custom here in Xochimilco, though it is not always the way it is in every home. My mother used to say that when you wanted to give something away, you had to give it before serving the meal; otherwise it was as if you were giving away leftovers—and that is bad manners. You give it all away: basket, napkin, and food. The exchange of food is like a sharing or coexisting of sorts (*es como una convivencia*).

Señora Rosa's Kitchenspace

The approach to Señora Rosa's kitchen is lined with plants. Visitors have to walk through a small blue wooden front door, along the long covered hallway with the bedrooms to the left and a row of plants in cans and plastic containers on the wall to the right. The plants lead to the back (and only) yard, where a large number of plants announce the kitchen door. Here assorted seating places invite you to stay: benches, a tree stump, chairs. It is where Señora Rosa's *comadre* Marcela sits when she visits every weekend and where family and neighbors and special guests often sit before or after they eat at the kitchen table.

Beyond the kitchen is a small room that was Señora Rosa's beauty salon. Though it still receives plenty of use—including the occasional haircut or permanent—it has become more of a storage area than a workplace. Beyond that are a row of latrines and showers with cloth curtains for privacy to the right and the multiple sinks alongside the adjacent canal to the left. At any given hour somebody tends to be at the sink: Señora Rosa washing her bucket full of dishes, Josefina washing vegetables or chicken, or another member of the household washing clothes.

Between the bathroom and the sinks are the animal pens or chicken coops, which have been in use off and on for years on end. They have alternately housed chickens, pigs, rabbits, or whatever other animal is being fattened for slaughter. The animals also serve as a source of amusement and education for the children who are always growing up in this house, running around the little yard and up and down the hallway.

In the center of the house-lot garden, there is sometimes a pot of tamales or *mixiotes*. On one occasion the pot of *mixiotes*—complete with its ears of corn husk on the handles—was fueled not by firewood but by the legs of some old furniture. This symbolizes adaptation and resistance in the house-lot garden or at least evokes the ghost of *la abuelita* Cleotilde sitting by the fire, toasting corn on the *comal* for *pinol* (cornmeal) to use in *atole champurrado*.

Señora Rosa's kitchen was always a place for tea and conversation for me, ever since I moved in next door to her after the 1985 earthquake. When

Steaming *mixiotes* in a pot with corn husk "ears"

most of the people in the barrio treated me with outright suspicion, she was always kind and generous. If I arrived on the unusual occasion when she did not have tea on the stove, she would put water on to boil right away, throwing in whatever leaves she had at the moment or a few plums from her tree or a *tejocote* (*Crataegus* spp., from the Nahuatl *texocotl*) and an apple and a cinnamon stick—maybe a few raisins. Knowing that I only drank boiled water, she usually kept a pot of tea going for my children and myself. She always offered *un tesito* (cup of tea) and something to eat. And if I did not visit on a given day, she might come knocking at my door, bringing me a plate of something she knew I liked: "Le traje unas enchiladas" (I brought you some enchiladas), she would say as she let herself in. My son Carlos, as a toddler, once climbed out of his bedroom window early in the morning and made his way to Señora Rosa's kitchen, where he got his warm tortilla and cup of tea. He was no dummy.

Señora Rosa's kitchen is unusually cozy, even though it is cramped and dark and has an uneven cement and dirt floor. When it rains, several pots are set up on the table to catch the rain that leaks in through the corrugated tile roof. There is only room to sit down at the table or stand in front of the stove when cooking. If anybody wants to get up from the side of the table close to the wall, everybody else who is sitting on the bench on that side must file out first. But when you sit down you are expected to stay a while. The kitchen used to be a bit larger, until Señora Rosa's son expanded his room next door to create a kitchen for his wife, Raquel. It is a bit more modern than this one, with a refrigerator as well as a stove, though Raquel also must take her dishes to the sink in the back yard to wash.

"Donde Come Uno, Comen Dos"

Señora Rosa says, "Donde come uno, comen dos; y donde comen dos comen cuatro. Aunque una tortilla, pero comen. Es un antiguo dicho que nos decía mi papá" (Where there is enough for one to eat, there is enough for two; and if there is enough for two, there is enough for four. Even if only a tortilla, but they eat. That is an old saying my father used to tell us).

It is impossible to come to Señora Rosa's house without being invited to share a *taquito* or a *tamalito*—whatever was cooked for the day or brought over by a neighbor or by Doña Josefina returning from a fiesta. Some mole, *frijolitos adobados*, a *mixiote*, and always, always some nopales. Señora Rosa goes out of her way to make everybody happy in her kitchen. When she makes nopales in salad, she keeps some without cilantro for me; when my kids are coming to eat, she makes them the *tortitas de papas* or *milanesas* (breaded cutlets) that they love and sends me home with some.

Señora Rosa always has a huge pile of tortillas in the middle of the table—nine or ten pounds—and a bowl of salt. She usually has a bowl or two of salsa or at the very least a jar of canned jalapeños. She likes to tell tales from her previous life as a hairdresser and in the public schools. Sitting at her kitchen table, you hear her views on life, men, power and corruption, and the dignity of the poor. "Somos pobres pero honrados" (We are poor but honorable) is one of her favorite sayings. Señora Rosa enjoys telling her stories. None of the people present ever dare interrupt. The kitchen is her space. When you sit at her table, you listen to her.

Señora Rosa shared her recipe for potato patties (*tortitas de papa*):

> You take about two pounds of potatoes, four eggs, two soup-spoons of flour, four ounces of grated white cheese, salt, and oil. You boil the potatoes in water with a little salt so they will not break up. You mash them thoroughly. You mix them well with cheese and salt. You beat the egg whites. Then you add the two spoonfuls of flour to the egg yolks, add these to the egg whites, and keep beating them. You coat the potato patties in this and fry them.

Beatriz *y la Abuelita* Cleotilde

Beatriz recalls the long walks to the market accompanying her grandmother.[7] They were long walks, mostly because *la abuelita* Cleotilde walked so slowly. As the youngest child, born after her mother was working full time outside the house, Beatriz was pretty much raised by her grandmother. She fondly remembers helping *la abuelita* prepare food in the patio: how she taught her to wash, trim, and ring out the *romeritos* that they would buy from a local vendor at the market or that somebody brought them from the *chinampas.* Today, she says, she feels tremendous pleasure in helping her mother in the kitchen, doing those same things that her grandmother taught her.[8] She loves it when Señora Rosa tells her that she does something just like *la abuelita* Cleotilde or when her brother Camilo tells her she should have been named Cleotilde.

Conversation with *Compadre* Benjamín

Señora Rosa's kitchen is a propitious place for conversation with any one of her many regular guests. Sitting at her table after sharing a meal, at the conclusion of his regular Sunday visit, her *compadre* Benjamín invites me to join him and his co-workers and associates as they prepare the meal for the upcoming feast.[9] They will be hosts for a day honoring the Virgen de Xaltocán (see February 26, 2001, entry in Chapter One). Like many native Xochimilcas, he takes great pride in the town's traditions and loves to discuss them. Today he is anxious to share his perspectives on the changes he has observed and laments: "Ya el callejón cambió, ya hay mucha gente extraña" (The *callejón* has changed, there are many strangers here now). Don Benjamín says that the neighborhood, like all of Xochimilco, is now full of people from other states (such as Jalisco and Michoacán) who come to Mexico City looking for "work and progress." With no luck in the city, they end up in Xochimilco instead, many of them working as day laborers on the *chinampas.* Yet, despite the changes which he enumerates for me and discusses in detail, he insists, like everybody else, that Xochimilco's traditions will go on forever. He uses the examples of the Virgen de Xaltocán and the Niñopa to illustrate his point.

Don Benjamín's chief complaint is that people are not treated equally in the barrio anymore. People are no longer all served the same way at fiestas, and not all are invited to participate. He is offended that he did not receive one of the formal printed invitations for a recent fiesta hosted by his niece.[10] Alcohol is another example, he says. Now some people are served a glass, while others are given an entire bottle to share with the people at their table. This is something new. The inequality with which people are treated is also evident in the *itacate*, and not only in the distinctions from person to person. When you left a party you used to be given huge quantities to take home (quarts and pounds), but at the last fiesta he attended he was given a very small *itacate*, "apenas para taparse la muela" (barely enough to fill your molar).

This reflects the social stratification that has always been part of the traditional fiestas, but it is at least in part related to the increasing number of people attending. The *compadre* says that only thirty people or so used to come to a fiesta, whereas now you can expect a thousand or more. On one hand, this change generates a sense of pride in the growing prestige and recognition of local traditions. On the other hand, it creates new social tensions as hosts struggle to keep the number of participants manageable and to attend to them without offending anyone. That is impossible, of course, and necessarily leads people to redraw the lines around their community networks and associations amidst a constant redefinition of "outsiders" and alliances.

This is particularly complicated because the more recent wave of immigration to this area is not the first; in fact many of the barrio's greatest defenders of tradition are precisely those who have arrived from beyond the Federal District in the last fifty years. The *sacristán* of the neighborhood chapel pointed out this phenomenon, which I had already observed in Ocotepec and Tetecala. In many cases this type of participation helps develop a tentative space of legitimacy for newcomers within their adopted community. At the same time, it helps them maintain a link to their more rural and indigenous roots, where food offerings and annual celebrations of saints and other holy images are a key part of their faith and the agricultural calendar. This is certainly a piece of the puzzle in understanding attachment to place through food celebrations and the persistence of rural traditions in increasingly urban peripheries such as Ocotepec and Xochimilco.

To complicate things even further, not only are there too many people in Xochimilco, Don Benjamín complains, but many of them invite guests from Mexico City. The volume of people at the fiestas also means that most people buy disposable dishes and cups made of paper, plastic, and Styrofoam now, he grumbles. They used to pool resources with neighbors and family members to come up with enough clay plates and mugs for a celebration.

Another relatively new development is that pulque is disappearing among the young. In only the last ten years, the *compadre* says, five *pulquerías* closed in the immediate vicinity of the neighborhood. But that is not the only change. Pulque used to be of excellent quality, several people have told me: you gave it to a new mother and within three days "tenía más leche que una vaca suiza" (she had more milk than a Swiss cow). Before, the pulque was always white or natural flavored. Now it is "cured" in many flavors, such as tomato, celery, lemon with salt, oats with cinnamon, pineapple, alfalfa, and even Nescafé.

Finally, Don Benjamín complains that the *chinampas* are changing and no longer yield flowers and vegetables as they used to—thanks in part to the sewage from Mexico City dumped in the canals. This comment is followed by the common complaint that food tastes like chemicals now and the exaggerated statement that chickens now grow in three days, with the help of hormones, electricity, and chemicals. Like most people here, he blames the loss of the role of the *chinampas* in everyday life in part on the overuse of pesticides and fertilizer in recent years. Don Benjamín also mentions another factor: now young Xochimilcas tend to choose to become professionals—especially doctors and teachers.[11] They have abandoned the *chinampas*.[12] The *compadre* himself was the first in his family to leave agriculture behind as a way of life. He says that he did not want to be a campesino like his father and grandfather and that as a child he hated getting up before dawn and working past dark in the damp every day to help his family scrape by. At the age of ten he quit the fields and went to work in a *telar* (weaving establishment) in town, making the shawls that still dominate the gendered landscape today. He worked from 6 a.m. to 10 p.m. for sixty pesos (less than a few dollars) a week. That was the year he bought his first pair of shoes, half a century ago.

Don Benjamín tells his children, one of whom is a lawyer, that folks have it easy these days: "¡Ahora que nacieron ustedes ya estaba la mesa puesta!" (When you were born, the table was already set!).

"Juntos pero no revueltos"

Señora Rosa was so relieved finally to get back to her kitchen after nearly thirty years of a salaried job outside that she moved in and made it clear to all that it was her kitchen. Nobody can cook there but her, as several of her now adult children—some living at home—complained to me. Jesús skipped this hurdle by building his wife a kitchen right next to his mother's. Thus another one of Señora Rosa's favorite refrains: "Juntos pero no revueltos" (Together but not all mixed up).

Señora Rosa is proud of the boundaries that keep each woman in her own kitchen and allow her daughter-in-law and son some autonomy and privacy in a crowded house. This reduces some of the tension between mother-in-law and daughter-in-law that reaches new levels in this crowded and intermarried neighborhood with so much history—and sometimes bad blood—in common. In this small area, Señora Rosa granted her son the space his wife needed to raise their family. While she, the grandmother, carried the babies in her rebozo and fed them and bathed them many a day, only rarely did Jesús come to his mother's kitchen to borrow salsa or tortillas. The kitchen boundaries were so clear that Señora Rosa did not use Raquel's refrigerator or telephone, even though she did not have either herself.

So important is the influence of the mother-in-law in the kitchen that Beatriz, Señora Rosa's youngest daughter, preferred to have her young family share a bedroom with her mother rather than to live in her in-laws' house in their own private room. There she would have to eat in her husband's mother's kitchen, which she does not wish to do. Señora Rosa is proud of the clear victory that she has scored in keeping Beatriz, Antonio, and their two small children in her house. The message is clear: we might be poor but we are proper and we know how to manage household politics—women's spatial politics in the kitchen.

"Gracias a Dios"

In Xochimilco, among older people in particular, there is tremendous reverence surrounding food consumption as well as food preparation. Food—both the more sacred and symbolic tamales or tortillas and the basic *quelites* (greens) or cauliflowers that are part of everyday meals—is always treated with respect. This is reflected in many kitchen sayings like "Hoy comemos, mañana veremos" (Today we eat, tomorrow we'll see). In a context of ongoing economic uncertainty and the deterioration of the local environment, Señora Rosa and other women with whom I have been sharing food preparation, meals, and conversations trust in God to provide tomorrow's meals.

"Gracias," I always say to Señora Rosa after I finish eating at her table. "Gracias a Dios" (Thanks be to God) is the inevitable response, which she repeats to the many children, grandchildren, nieces, nephews, *comadres*, and *compadres* who eat at her table every week. Never is a hungry person turned away. One by one, each person gets up from one of the long benches on either side of the table after eating. As they pass Rosa's place at the head of the table—not sitting, but standing at the stove—they say "gracias," often kissing her hand as they do so. One after the other, they receive the same response: "Gracias a Dios."

Linda

Linda is a middle-aged woman with several grown children, grandchildren, and a sick husband. She frets over him and cares for him and is always working, rushed, and stressed. It was difficult to interview her despite our long acquaintance. Perhaps to compensate for my many visits to her home when she was too busy to receive me, she shared plenty of recipes with me, some of which are included here.

Linda's daughter Ana was a friend of mine when I lived in the neighborhood. Linda is the only woman of her age (fifty-six) who speaks to me in the informal register, treating me more like a daughter than a guest. She has always been kind and generous, freely explaining cooking tidbits that she thinks will be useful to me. Now she lets me in on kitchen secrets which she complains her own family and *comadres* refuse to share with her. Even the baker in the barrio refused to teach her his recipes, she tells me, though she offered to pay him for a course.

Linda loves to cook. She prides herself on not being limited by antiquated cooking traditions and on having educated her family to move beyond them and considers herself a modern and innovative woman. She likes to experiment with new recipes from television programs and magazines, as well as from other women when they are willing to share them.

Nonetheless, Linda too has cultural boundaries that set limits on the degree and type of experimentation allowed in the kitchen. She tells me that once she was asked to rate a *posole* (hominy soup) that her in-laws made in the nearby town of Ajusco. She could not give it more than a six out of ten because it had aromatic herbs (*hierbas de olor*). "*Posole* does not go with herbs," she exclaims. "It is just not right."

El "Quehacer de la Mujer"

Linda tells me about *el quehacer de la mujer* (women's work):

> *¡Son puras carreras! Tengo mucho quehacer. Ahora los pobres pajaritos*
> *los quiero sacar al sol. Soy lenta y pierdo mucho tiempo. Todos los días es*
> *apúrate, apúrate. Ya a darles de comer, ya a recoger a la nieta, ya vete al*
> *mandado, a cocinar, a lavar, a barrer, ya otra vez a darles de comer, ya vete a*
> *vender, luego otra vez a cobrar.*[13] *Son puras carreras. Luego tengo que ayudar*
> *a mi esposo y siento que pierdo tiempo y nunca voy a acabar mi quehacer.* (It
> is always a rush! I have a lot to do. Right now I want to take these poor birds
> out into the sun. I am slow and I lose so much time. Every day it is hurry up,
> hurry up! Now feed them, now go pick up the granddaughter, now go buy
> groceries, go cook, wash, sweep, and then feed them again, now go sell, then
> go collect the money. It is always a rush. Then I have to help my husband and
> I feel like I lose time and that I will never finish my chores.)

Finding Time to Talk to Linda

I walk to the very end of the *callejón* to visit Linda. She answers the door
looking exhausted, perspiring heavily. Her apron is on, her hands are dirty.
It is 10:30 a.m. Like Señora Rosa's, Linda's days start early in the morning
and usually end after midnight. We chat for thirty minutes at her gate. This
is a bad time to talk, because she is sweeping her patio, getting ready to
make today's meal. She is not going to the market today. One of her daughters brought her fresh groceries, as she often does. Señora Linda takes care
of her granddaughter, joining the procession of mothers and grandmothers
who walk out of the *callejón* to take the children to and from the nearby
elementary school. She asks me to come another day a little later, preferably
after the midday meal. Sundays are best, she says.

Linda invites me to join her family for a special Mass for the Niñopa this
Saturday; one of her daughter's in-laws will have the baby Jesus figure for
the day and is hosting a meal. I will not miss the opportunity—I hear they
will be killing nine pigs and serving *carnitas* with nopales in the street.
Regardless, I will keep trying to get a chance to speak with Linda when she
is willing to give me some time out of her busy schedule and multiple family commitments. Small windows of opportunity do arise, though it seems
the most fruitful interactions occur when we meet at the evening rosaries
for the Niñopa in the neighborhood. There we always have a moment to

exchange a few words as we stand in line to kiss the infant or to collect our cup of *atole* and ration of sweet bread or tamales.

One day I call from Cuernavaca to try to set up a time to interview Linda. She is out, her husband tells me, but should be back in a short time. She went for milk at one of the dairy stables in the *callejón* and is surely chatting with a *comadre* ("Nomás fue por la leche pero seguro que está comadreando"), he says.

Linda's Narrative

I have lived in the *callejón* for thirty years, but I am from the barrio of San Juan.[14] I love my house in the back of the *callejón*. I have a garden; I live at the edge of the canal; I have animals and birds. I live surrounded by dairy stables, pigs, and chickens. This is a beautiful, quiet place. I like it because early in the morning I can hear the birds sing. And you hear the people going out to the *chinampas* to work. No cars can get in here [the alleys are too narrow] and the air is clean. There is a lot of security and tranquillity despite all the new people who have come now. And the water from the faucet is clean—in other neighborhoods it smells bad. Here you can drink it without boiling it. The canals are polluted, though—all over Xochimilco.

For me personally, nature is something so beautiful—not everyone is lucky enough to enjoy it, to live it. Not everybody likes it either. I had a tenant who did not like it. Maybe it is because I am from the *campo* (country), but ever since I was little I would come home from school and ask my grandfather to take me to the *chinampas*. And I would flop down on my belly and put my hands in the water and see the fish from the canoe. When my daughters were little, we used to borrow a canoe, and my mother would take us—she rowed—to look for a *chinampa*.[15] I think nature is a beautiful thing.

Things are not the same anymore. The water is polluted, and you cannot cultivate the land the same way. But people have jobs now and live better, since the *campo* does not always provide a good harvest—it floods or freezes and you are left waiting, empty-handed. But the changes in the *chinampas* do not affect the food, because we do not eat food only from here but from what they bring. They bring tomatoes from Cuautla and from the states: Puebla, Guanajuato, Aguascalientes. Now you can go to the central market in Mexico City and find what we used to grow here.

My grandfather used to cook for us, as my grandmother was a vendor in the Jamaica market in the city. Here the custom was that the man worked the land and the woman was a market vendor. She would take the *chiquihuite*, like a big basket, full of vegetables to sell. Before, my grandfather would take my grandmother by canoe all night to sell at the market, then he would return home to work the *campo*. It took all night. It was tough. Later, when the *góndola* [she is referring to an uncovered train] came, we would go wait for her and take her food to eat. She was hungry when she arrived, but she first had to go to the Xochimilco market to buy whatever *el abuelo* did not grow, so she could take it to sell the next day.

Life was beautiful here years ago. We used charcoal and *molcajete*. We cooked tomatoes with pork meat, with *verdolagas* (common purslane, *Portulaca oleracea*). That is the stew my grandfather taught me and my sister how to make, since my grandmother was a vendor. My grandfather would buy beef and make a soup with tomato, onion, cilantro, and *chilacayotes* (another type of squash). There are two types of squash, you know. The round one that grows in the milpa at the time of the *elote* (sweet corn) and the long one that sells more. The *chilacayote* only comes out in rainy season—July and August. Now with the cold it freezes and dies.

My aunt and my mother were teachers. My aunt always liked to live and eat well. She taught us how to eat things like paella and shrimp. The trick is you have to be ingenious to find a way not to eat the same thing all the time. We made a gratin with broccoli or *chayotes* for instance. That is not customary here. The meal always includes dry soup or pasta soup.[16] We do not have beans every day in this house, but soup, yes. The soup can be vegetable, cooked with a chicken back for flavor. That all depends on how you accustom your children. As children, we always had soup.

There are different food customs, depending on people's economic position. Some people like to eat well. Others have the customs of their ancestors—they eat very little meat. They eat more fava beans and things like that. They do not cook new things that the television shows. One woman I know, for instance, cooks only vegetables—such as *quintoniles* (*Amaranthus hybridus*). She does not like new changes, she keeps the traditions (*guarda las tradiciones*). Not me: I change them. Here in Xochimilco people use lard, even if they buy it at the market.[17] Not us: we use oil, even though I have a sister-in-law who raises pigs.[18]

Food Traditions

Linda tells me that there are different food traditions from one barrio to the next in Xochimilco. When her sister was widowed, Linda suggested that the family prepare *pepitas de chile* as is customary in this barrio, but the neighbors from the next barrio got very upset. When her husband's grandparents died in the nearby town of Tepepan, Linda told her in-laws that they should not cook meat for the wake because that showed a lack of respect for the dead. They laughed at her.

The definition of the word *sazón* is literally seasoning, but in fact it signifies much more. It seems to be key to understanding the role of kitchens, women, and people's attachment to place through food. I explored my informant's views of the meaning of the word after the men who were cooking for the Virgen de Xaltocán justified their need for women to cook the rice for their meal with the simple and apparently self-evident affirmation that "only women have *sazón*." Linda tells me that *sazón* is simply the way someone cooks to give food the right flavor. It explains why having a recipe is not enough to prepare a tasty dish. "Aside from the recipe," Linda says, "each person has her own *sazón* . . . it is not the same. But still people do not want to share their recipes!" According to Linda, even when people say they will show you a recipe, they find a way to get rid of you before putting in the final secret ingredient.

Linda Speaks about Recipes

Food is satisfaction—both cooking and eating. Because you have to know how to make it. One of my *comadres* that cooks very well will not say how she does it. She makes a delicious dish in peanut sauce, and I do not know if she uses ancho or guajillo chile. She lies to me: she says it is one thing and it is not. She makes a great yellow rice, and she says it is because of the butter, but it is not true. It is silly really, because it really depends on your *sazón*.[19] *Sazón* is how you cook. For instance, when making beans, you have to sauté the onion just right. Or when making soup with pasta, you have to let the pasta brown just right and then fry the tomato a bit—always stirring and stirring—you have to let the tomato cook well before adding water or it tastes raw.

We make something here called "washed beans"—*frijoles lavados*. You wash them and cook them with lard or oil and onion. Some people wash them before mashing them and refrying them, and others do not. But in order for them to cook quickly there is a secret that nobody will tell: you add a little *tequesquite* to the beans to boil them. Some season them without washing them first; others wash them, but the flavor changes. For mole, one secret is that you have to burn the oil a little first.

A dish in peanut sauce is good for any fiesta, such as a birthday or a ninth day (at the end of the nine days of funeral ceremonies). You take the seeds out of the dried chile (ancho chile) because it gives a different flavor. You save both the seeds and the veins to use in a different dish later. Then you toast the peanuts in oil or lard, and you add the ancho chile whole, garlic, clove, peppercorns, cinnamon, and four toasted tortillas for each half pound of peanuts, and onion. You take this to the mill to grind. Then you season it and add chicken broth. It is very good with pork meat, especially the backbone. Dishes with almonds (*almendrado*) are prepared the same way, but with almonds instead of peanuts and with a little bit of tomato.

No cualquier persona da sus recetas. Muchas son egoístas. Tengo una cuñada que hace un pollo al naranja con arroz amarillo. Me meto en la cocina y le digo: "Comadre, ¿no me da la receta?" Y comadre nada, y no le saco la receta (Not just anybody will share their recipes. Many people are selfish. I have a sister-in-law who makes chicken with orange that she serves with yellow rice. I go into her kitchen and ask her: "*Comadre*, will you give me the recipe?" But *comadre* nothing; I cannot get the recipe out of her).

Doña Teodora, *la Abuelita*

Doña Teodora is full of stories and memories and happy to find someone with whom to share them. Like many widows, she lives in a multigenerational household where other women take care of food preparation on a daily basis. I met with her during my neighbor Doña Ofelia's party. She was happy for the opportunity to cook for a special event. Both because I interviewed her after the tamales were in the pot and because of her relative lack of responsibilities due to her age, that conversation took place in a very relaxed, unhurried setting.

La maestra (respectful title for "teacher") Ofelia Lozano invited me to this fiesta months ago, insisting that I write it on my calendar right then so that I would not forget. My son Juan, the mole connoisseur, also encouraged me. He had been at a birthday party at her place recently and raved for days about her delicious mole. Ever since retiring as a schoolteacher, Ofelia had been celebrating the day of the Virgen del Carmen with due pomp and circumstance: formal invitations, mole, music, and even poetry proclaiming the virtues of Xochimilco. Today (July 16, 2001) a painting of the Virgin dating to 1664 that has been in Ofelia's family for five generations has been brought out into the house-lot garden for the fiesta. But the most important item in her possession is the title to the land on which we celebrate, dating to 1864, framed, and hanging on the wall inside the house. The land has been in her family for seven generations, Ofelia says proudly. In fact, her grandmother was born just across the canal in what became my house fifteen years ago.

The fiesta is attended by family, neighbors, and special guests, including poets, young dancers, singers, and a priest—all from Xochimilco. I am primarily interested in the 82-year-old woman who sits solemnly in the smoke kitchen at the back of the house-lot garden, watching over the huge pots of mole, rice, and tamales. Juana Teodora González, better known as Doña Teodora in the barrio, is the expert who has been called in to make the rice and to ensure that the meal meets everybody's expectations. These are by far the best mole, rice, and bean tamales I have ever tasted.

I spend several hours sitting by Doña Teodora and the multiple hearths in the back of the house-lot garden. She stirs the mole and checks on the rice and tamales now and then, but most of the work is over. The younger women who helped her cook are running around dealing with last-minute details. Most guests walk back to the smoke kitchen to greet the *abuelita* with respect and affection before sitting down at the tables that have been set up in the yard. Besides her reputation as an excellent cook, this woman seems to be related by blood, marriage, or kinship to nearly everybody who joins the party.

Sitting in the smoke of the burning firewood, Doña Teodora is at first suspicious but soon relaxes and seems happy about the company and conversation. She shares her memories, becoming nostalgic and tearful as she tells stories about the changes she has lived through and the people and food that she has loved. Beginning with a discussion of chiles, "picosísimos, sabrosotes" (very spicy, very tasty), our talk includes intimate details about recipes and sex.

The in-depth interview was facilitated by my being a special guest of Ofelia's and arriving with Señora Rosa's family. It also helped that I have a history in the neighborhood, and Doña Teodora has recollections of my family. It was truly a golden opportunity to get the perspective of a representative of the older generation of *cocineras* without whom food traditions and fiestas in Xochimilco could not take place. "Aquí me quieren mucho; me llaman por venir [*sic*] a hacer el arroz" (They love me a lot here; they call me to come make the rice), Doña Teodora tells me.[20]

Doña Teodora's Narrative

Nosotros en Xochimilco estamos acostumbrados a las fiestecitas, nuestro arroz, nuestros frijoles y nuestros tamales (We in Xochimilco are accustomed to our little fiestas, our rice, our beans, and our tamales), she begins.

For meat tamales, with corn dough, you put the corn on to boil with lime, you wash it, take it to the mill, and you end up with corn meal that is like a fine powder. You beat that with lard and Royal (baking powder). We used to use a bit of *tequesquite,* which is salt of the earth. But now we use Royal, which I think is carbonate. It is a chemical, isn't it? Then you use tomato, cooked, and cumin, and that is it. You grind the cumin with the green chiles. And when the dough is all beaten, you take a spoon like the one we eat with. One spoonful of dough in the husk. And you add chiles, already ground. Tomato, with cumin, with chiles and tomato. You put it in the husk and then wrap it like this.

Whoever wants to can tie ears on the handles, and if not, just take a handful of salt and make the sign of the cross. That is the belief. It is not the same as the ears. For example, whoever sets out the pot, if it is a large pot, has to tie a strip of corn husk from the same tamales. Just a belief, in case a child comes by crying or something like that. Salt is for the same thing. That is for meat tamales. Now bean tamales, they really get angry. The dough just falls apart, it gets mushy. Bean tamales are very delicate. Meat tamales can be fixed, but not bean tamales. Who knows why.

Antes comíamos puro máiz [*sic*] (We used to eat only corn).[21] Good corn, good beans born here. But what we used to eat about fifty years ago, while we still grow it, it does not taste the same anymore. The earth is good, and it gives good corn, pretty corn, tasty. Beans too. Everything we used to plant. But now it has no taste. Not the corn, not the beans. Neither one has any taste. Everything, everything. *Sí se come, porque es de comerse* (We eat it, because it is for eating). But the taste it used to have is gone. I should know, with the years I have! I am eighty-two. I got married in 1940, and I was twenty then. That is why I say that I know, and it no longer has any taste. The taste of the tortilla is not the same either! Even if it is from *nixtamal*, made by hand. Well, we make it with *la maquinita* (tortilla press). You put the tortilla on the *comal*; and when you go to turn it, it breaks. *Ya no es igual. Está como pellejoso* (It is not the same; it's sort of flaky).

Se llevaron el agua (They took the water). [It is impossible to speak about Xochimilco to most locals over the age of about thirty without hearing a reference to the transcendental event that provoked a series of traumatic changes in the community: when Mexico City took their water, only to re-turn some of it as wastewater years later, after the campesinos had become salaried workers and no longer wanted to work the land (Canabal Cristiani et al. 1992).] *Pues ya no cultivan como antes. Porque, como hubo un tiempo que se secó aquí Xochimilco. Se llevaron el agua—la ciudad metió las tube-rías para llevarse el agua y los hombres que trabajaban aquí sus tierras pas-aron a abandonar sus tierras. Se los llevaron. Se fueron a trabajar a México y se acostumbraron ahí. "Tráigame el dinero," pues ya. Porque nuestra agua no nos falta, porque nosotros teníamos manantiales y de esos manantiales les damos y tenemos. Y tenemos nosotros, y a nosotros no nos debe faltar agua porque tenemos nuestros manantiales* (They do not sow like they used to. Because there was a time that Xochimilco dried up. They took the wa-ter—the city put pipes in to take the water, and the men who worked the land went and abandoned their land. They took them. They went to work in Mexico [City] and became accustomed to it there. "Bring me the money," well, that's it. Because we never ran short on water, we had springs and from those springs there is enough to give and still have some. And we have our water, and we should never run out of water because we have our springs).

"Nosotros Que Somos Pobres"

For day to day, we are used to drinking our cinnamon tea or spearmint tea, chamomile, or tea from a plant that you find in the water called *amozote*. Just ask anyone one day and they will tell you which one is *amozote*. It is from the canals, right at the edge of the *chinampas*. The people with money drank coffee. Those that did not, well, we did not drink coffee. *Nosotros que somos pobres* (We who are poor). The ones with money drank milk. And now, well, since we have CONASUPO (Compañía Nacional de Subsisten-cias Populares), we have milk.[22] And from that we make corn *atole*. White or cinnamon. Plain. There is another *atole* they make, but with chile, called *chileatole.* For lunch (brunch), if there is rice left over from the day before, you heat it up, you eat it, you serve beans. If there is mole left over, you refry the mole—everything left over from the day before you reheat. If there are leftovers, that is what you have; otherwise, you make *chilaquiles* (a breakfast dish made of old tortillas, salsa, and sometimes cheese or cream), with a bit of chicken broth or whatever there is. Or a taco: you go to the market, you get pork rind, avocado, cheese. *De comer, un caldito, el entomatado de tomate o jitomate con carne de puerco* (For the main meal, you make a soup, pork meat in tomatillos or red tomatoes).

"El Mole de Aquí"

Every place is different. Before, with my grandparents, the typical mole here used to be pure pasilla chiles. The sweet kind. That is what we used to call it, "sweet pasilla," but it was not sweet. The other pasilla is hot. You can work with that too and also make mole. Now they use whatever they want . . . some do not want to eat pasilla anymore. They use mulato chiles. It is another generation now, and they have changed. They think it is tastier. And it is tasty, the mulato. But it's not like the pasilla. And it is cheaper, they give it at more comfortable prices. The mulato chile is cheaper than pasilla now. For the *olores* of the mole you use sesame, you use chocolate. Yes, we used to use the bitter chocolate, a chocolate that we almost never get around here anymore (from Oaxaca). They look like this: skinny little bars, like a little book. You used chocolate for mole, but bitter chocolate. I used Ybarra brand chocolate. You add chocolate and sesame. You add walnuts, almonds. If not, just walnuts and peanuts. But I do not use peanuts because it makes people sick. You add one banana: for about half a pound of mole, one sweet, ripe plantain. We used to use—well, I do not use any of that anymore—we used to use orange rind. You would let it dry and then you would brown it. And four tortillas for half a pound. You add raisins. And bread. Rolls, cut into slices. Fresh rolls, but you let them dry and then browned them like the tortillas. In lard. We always used lard. Now it is different. *Así es el mole de aquí* (That's how the mole from here is).

El Entomatado

The *entomatado* (dish cooked in tomato sauce) is something we eat a lot here. You boil the tomato with green chile peppers. The green one, the *tomate* (tomatillo), not the *jitomate* that is red. If it is for seven people or eight, use half a pound of tomato, three-fourths of a pound. If they know how to eat—because sometimes they want seconds—you use four or five pounds. You boil the *tomates;* put water on to boil and when it is hot, you add the *tomate.* Otherwise it falls apart. And you add its chiles; and even if it boils, it will not fall apart. If you want it hot, at least ten chiles. Green ones (serranos), or *chiles de árbol* even, if you want it hot. Then you let it cool. If you have a blender, blend it there. I do that; I add water and salt, onion, and garlic. Cold, cold water. *Tomate,* green chile, and you add squash. When that is cooked, the meat cooks. You put lard or oil in the pan and fry the meat until it is well fried on one side and then the other. Then you put it in the chile sauce and leave it there a while until it seasons, the chile and the meat. And the broth from cooking the meat too. But you add garlic to the chile. With garlic and onion. And you let it simmer. Then you add the squash. Then when the squash is soft it is good.

With *jitomate* it is the same thing, except with *jitomate* you use potatoes. With pork or chicken, as you like. But if it is *jitomate,* it is with potatoes. And if it is with pasilla chile with pork, you add nopales, potatoes, and pork. And do not forget the onion and garlic. *Chimapaxtle* is what the grandparents called pasilla chile. And the grandparents did it like this, they beat it by hand, and what was left over and they could not beat, they put it in the *molcajete* and ground it there. And just a little bit ground, they put it in the stew and it was delicious. It tasted different than with a blender. *Da una cosa rica. Pero ahora eso ya no se hace* (It yields something delicious. But we do not do that anymore).

"Nomás a Veces un Antojito"

Well, let's see. We were not used to dinner here. Just sometimes, but not because we were accustomed. Now we are. If there is no milk, there is bread or cookies. But this is a different time. But when it was us, maybe a little *tamal* of sweet corn. My grandparents had a little *comalito,* and they would make *atole* and give us a *gordita* with lard that they took off the *comal.* And "have your *atole,*" they would say.

No cenábamos. No más a veces un antojito. Las personas que tenían más centavitos, pues sí lo hacían, pero las personas que no, no. No tomaban eso (We did not eat dinner. Sometimes just a little tidbit. People with a little more cash, they did, but people without did not. They didn't have dinner). And we did not have a *merienda* (snack), as they say now. Now people have a *merienda. Atole* and tamales. We did not call it a *merienda*, just an *antojito* sometimes. People with more money, they did, but not us. We did not have that.

El Doctor

We had a doctor, when I had my kids, and he would tell me: "Woman, do not eat tamales because you get fat and your children are born too big. Eat less." "Oh, doctor, but I am hungry!" I would tell him. "Well, do not eat too much." And I was always fat. "Do not eat too much because tamales make you gain weight." That is what the doctor would say. When he would see my kids so big and fat . . . "You see, your kids are fat." "*Doctor, están sanos, están buenos. No les falta nada a mis hijos. Están buenos*" (Doctor, they are healthy, they are good. My children are not lacking for anything. They are good).[23]

Hombres y Tierras

Well, and you live here? Are you the mother of the blondies? And your husband? Real short he is. And now? You living here now? You were the blondie that was living with him? You are, aren't you? Now that I saw you, "I know you." And now that I saw you, I said: "I know that young woman, I know her."

I got married in 1940. My husband is from Doctor Leonardo Navarro's family, the man who sold you your house. He is from here. Who knows where he is now. I lost my husband after thirty years of marriage—he died. He left all my three children married already. But I said, he was not a husband, he was a treasure for me.[24] In the thirty years until today, I still cry for him. He would go to work, because he had two shifts; he worked here in the Plaza, in the National Palace. *Era un hombre bueno* (he was a good man); I do not compare him with anybody. When I lost him, I cried day and night. And I went looking for him, so you get an idea: I cried for him in the cemetery and would call his name.

But when he lived, he would tell me: "Come on, dummy, enjoy it now, because any day you will lose me. Let's go out!" "And your children?" I would ask him. "Leave them with my mother; let's go out!" "But we'd have to come and take care of our children." "Let's go!" We would go and leave them with my mother-in-law. And we'd come back. And my kids, they were getting big by now. "Hey, where did you go out? You left us!" "What? Were you lacking anything?" their father would ask them. "What do you need? What is wrong?" He took care of everything. He worked two shifts.

Before, *trabajaba la tierra* (he worked the land). But as I said, the dry period came, and he left the land and never returned to it. He planted many flowers that are not even sold anymore. Nobody even plants them anymore. Nobody nowadays, nobody plants those flowers. All that he planted. But that is finished now. The lands are empty now. There is nobody to plant them now. They are empty.

My grandsons work our *chinampas* now.[25] The offspring of my oldest daughter. Because their dad was a *chinampero.* He died already too.

"Las Tradiciones en la Comida"

Well, in fact, *las tradiciones en la comida no han cambiado* (food traditions have not changed). The grandfathers ate, in this case, criollo fish we called it—criollo fish with *tomate.* Fish with *tomate,* in *tomate* sauce, but that we call *miximole.* Well, we do. Because from Xochimilco to San Gregorio, we call it *miximole.* It is the same dish, with cilantro and fish. *Tlapique* is something else: it is fish cooked by steam in a corn husk. With epazote, *tomate,* and onion. And eaten with black beans. But boiled separately; or with a fava soup with *chilacayotes.* And cilantro. That has not changed; just about most people eat it. It is very common. But *miximole* is [a term] used for fish, frogs, *ajolotes* (axolotls), or freshwater shrimp. Not all at once, just one of those.

It is not soup, it is a stew, thick. And all of them go well with nopales. If you like nopales, nopales; if not, not. You should not serve it fallen apart. The fish has to be in one piece. *Tiene su punto. Si es un batidillo ya no es comida, es batidillo* (It has to be done exactly right. If it is all mushed up it is not food, it is mush).

There is also *coatatapas,* which is a dish of dry black beans ground on the metate. And you cook them in their own broth like beans. And *chopamole:* that is chopped tomato, onion, squash, chile, garlic, and pork meat. *Sazonado* (seasoned). And many also put nopales in or *xoconostle* (nopal fruit). With epazote. We still eat that, many people do. That is fast food. Then there is *chinmapaxtle:* a sauce made of pasilla with pork chops or backbone or head. That sauce takes green tomatillos. Not much, just three of four little tomatoes. It gives it a special sweet and sour taste. You can add nopales to it too.

Then there is *picadillo,* with chopped squash and tomato. And kernels of corn. And squash blossoms. No meat: it's squash, tomatoes, corn kernels, and squash blossoms—and cheese.

"Pa'los Muertos y pa'los Vivos"

Nosotros ponemos ofrenda de muertos, pero hay personas que ya no ponen; solamente ponen un pancito, el agua. Lo mínimo es el pan y el agua. Pan, agua, y la vela. El pancito. Y nosotros no: tamales, bizcocho, plátano, naranja, su dulce, su mole, su pollo. Sus tamales, su calabaza. Sus camotes. Su copa, su cigarro. Cerillos. ¡Y la mesota grandota! (We put up an offering for the dead, but there are people who do not do that anymore; they just put out some bread and water. That is the minimum: bread and water. Bread, water, and a candle. A small bread. But not us: tamales, cookies, bananas, oranges, their *dulce* [pumpkin cooked in brown sugar and cinnamon], their mole, their chicken. Their tamales, their squash. Their sweet potatoes. Their drink [alcohol], their cigarette. Matches. And a big table!).[26]

Get me a little *tamal* for this young woman to taste! [Doña Teodora yells to another woman.] But give her a little bit of mole too. They are better with mole.

Yes, this is how we make mole. With banana. This is how we make tamales. It is good, isn't it? It starts out the same, but we add a little avocado leaf. You will have to try another one.

As I was saying, that offering, we distribute it among our children, among our *compadres.* You come to the house and we give you your plate: an orange, a little roll, a banana. And then you take your basket with its bananas, oranges, little rolls. You take your basket. *Pa'los muertos y pa'los vivos* (For the dead and for the living). Covered with a napkin. Just as you brought it they give it back to you. *Bueno, antes.* (Well, that was before).

Women of Ocotepec

"We Used to Have a Lot of Pigs"

In the two preceding chapters, we have heard from women of different ages and perspectives. Here we enter into dialogue with four women in Ocotepec. Again, though María Teresa, Isidra, Dolores, and María Soledad are not representative of women in any community, their words shed light on other women's experiences and kitchenspaces in my region of study. As in the rest of the narrative, the journey is as much a part of the story as the destination.

We begin with a closer look at María Teresa's kitchenspace. She was the woman in charge of the meal for all the barrios on May 3 in Ocotepec (Chapter Two) and was introduced to me by her cousin, an old family acquaintance. She is a recently returned Ocotepec native, and her father is one of the few remaining *abuelos* to plant corn in the family milpa. María Teresa and her family were very generous and helpful to me; her willingness to serve as a guinea pig as I tried out my participative mapping methodology and recorded my first full interview was critical to the findings presented in this book.

We continue with Doña Isidra and Doña Dolores, both of whom appeared briefly in "A Taste of Three Places" at the beginning of the book. I met Isidra during the Day of the Dead ceremonies the previous November. Her home was open to visitors, and I was among the strangers served *atole* and tamales from the offering for her deceased mother. In my follow-up visit, she was leaving to help her friend Dolores make tamales and invited me to tag along. The scene I encountered in the outdoor smoke kitchen of Dolores was so emblematic of Ocotepec that I include it here.

I close with María Soledad, an unmarried woman with no children. Like Esmeralda in Tetecala, she is not particularly happy with her responsibility for cooking the everyday meals for her extended family. Like most people in my research communities, María Soledad is identified by others primarily as a member of her family, in her case, "the daughter of Domingo Díaz." She is also recognized and well loved as a teacher in the local preschool.

Because of this and her father's prominent role as a spokesperson for local traditions in Ocotepec, we hear from him in this chapter as well. Don Domingo Díaz provides a musician's perspective on the importance of food in community celebrations; my interview with him illustrates the difficulty that I had throughout my fieldwork in getting men to consider the validity of discussing women's role in food preparation. This section provides a useful contrast between his more public voice as a spokesperson for Ocotepec and María Soledad's equally clear voice from inside the house, as well as their gendered and generational differences.

María Soledad is a classic representative of the unsung heroines to whom I seek to bring attention in this work. She, like all of the women in this section, contributes her time and energy to preparing food on a daily basis. Indeed it is her sister Susana, and not María Soledad, who has achieved recognition for her kitchen skills because of her participation in community celebrations. It is Susana who purportedly inherited the special food preparation knowledges of the elder women of the family.

María Teresa

Symbolically, one of the two entrances to María Teresa's house looks very traditional, the other fully modern. The entrance closest to the center of town is through a huge gate behind Ocotepec's soccer field; it is just a block from the barrio chapel and leads straight into the *abuelo*'s cornfield. Entering from this side, the first thing that hits you is the smell of earth and the view of the cornfield, no matter what stage it is in at the time. The front entrance to the house is a little red gate on a new street that dead-ends shortly thereafter. This side faces away from town and toward the city. On the edge of the barrio de Santa Cruz, about five long blocks away, this newer sector of Ocotepec backs into the highway underpass that leads straight into the Paseo del Conquistador in Cuernavaca. As you approach the house from this side, the first thing you see is a sign on the wall by the door announcing that the family is Catholic and venerates the Virgin Mary. Not uncommon in this region, the sign aims to keep proselytizing evangelicals at bay. The message begins: "Hermano protestante" (Protestant brother).

While María Teresa's family is from Ocotepec, she says that she was born in Cuernavaca. This is clearly separate from Ocotepec in her mind, although the place where she was born, near the once famous Casino de la Selva, was until recently the boundary of Ocotepec lands. She was living in the city of Toluca with her husband and children until her mother became ill and she returned to take care of her. When her mother passed away, María Teresa and her family moved back permanently so they could be close to her elderly father—*el abuelo*. The members of her family are in a tentative position between insider and outsider. Their role in hosting the main meal of Ocotepec (*la comida de todos los barrios*) on May 3 offered an opportunity to affirm their belonging and integrate themselves more fully into the community.

Family unity and love are foremost values for María Teresa's family, and the theme runs through her food. When I arrive for her interview, I am treated to an affectionate reception as she insists on braiding my hair before we start. Apparently I strike her as in need of care. Eventually she has to get back to washing her chicken in the stone washbasin just outside the indoor kitchen. As I interview her from my seat at her kitchen table, she moves on to making *mole verde* in a huge *cazuela de barro* that looks out of place on top of her small gas stove. María Teresa cooks in clay pots every day. She also uses a microwave oven to heat the tortillas in the final rush after everyone sits down at her table, which allows her to join them rather than continue to stand over the griddle throughout the meal.

I am grateful to María Teresa for the hospitality. Because she has a foot in Ocotepec and another in Toluca, where her husband comes from, I know that she has more perspective on local culture than do residents who have not lived outside the community. She was willing to let me test my methodology on her, allowing me to tape-record our interview and obliging my request for her to draw a map of her kitchen. Before I depart on this extended visit, I ask her daughter, a student at the nearby state university, if she would help me interview the *tía* who was in charge of the food at the fiesta on May 3. Overhearing my request, her father chuckles at the very idea and says it would be impossible: "¡Es que aquí son otras costumbres!" (It is just that here the customs are different!).

I am reminded that it is often difficult or impossible to interview folks, even if you have a special relationship. This response was much like Linda's in Xochimilco (when she refused to introduce me to her sister-in-law and explained that people in the barrio "do not lend themselves to that") and Doña Josefina's early declaration that she would not cooperate with my study. People in Ocotepec, as in Xochimilco and to a lesser extent Tetecala, are often suspicious and resentful of outsiders.

María Teresa's Narrative

*La comida es un punto de reunión y de unión. Todos nos reunimos, comenta-
mos, platicamos y estamos comiendo. La cocinera es muy importante en
esto. Pues sin cocinera no habría comida, y no estaría tan bien preparada.
Tal vez los hombres pudieran guisarse, o algo, pero como que las mujeres le
ponemos nuestro toque especial. Más que nada, la cocina requiere de tiempo y calma. Porque no se puede hacer las cosas a la carrera. Pues, la comida
lleva mucho tiempo, quita mucho tiempo la comida* (The meal is a meeting place and point of union. We all gather together, engage in discussion,
chat, and we are eating. The cook is very important in this. Without the
cook there would be no meals, and the food would not be so well prepared.
Maybe the men could cook for themselves or something, but it is as if we
women give it our special touch. More than anything, the kitchen requires
time and calm. Because you cannot do things in a rush. Well, meals take a
lot of time, meals steal a lot of time).

Food tastes better with happiness and love. I mean, you cook with dedi-
cation, with pleasure that it will come out very tasty. I am pleased when
they all savor and like my food. Of course, for it to be tasty you must have
good *sazón,* that is, before adding the liquid to what you are preparing, you
have to let it season well. Even if you are angry it might still come out OK—
because you have the touch—but nobody will savor it. Well, with tamales
and mole, those do not come out right if there is bile: the tamales will not
cook, and the mole sours, it curdles. They will not eat it.

People should be in the kitchen with pleasure, all of the people in the
kitchen. Because eating is supposed to be a pleasure. So if there is somebody
who is cooking all upset, then that is why the food resents that (*por eso la
comida resiente*). It should be something that you savor. And not that we all
become angry. Otherwise, maybe the family would become disunited.

I always make the sign of the cross over my food, so that it will suffice
and taste good. You make the sign of the cross with the salt, and then you
add it. If you add meat, you make the sign of the cross again.

El Abuelo y la Milpa

On one occasion in early June when I visit María Teresa, her father is getting ready to plant his cornfield. An altar to San Isidro Labrador (patron saint of agriculture), complete with flowers and candles, stands behind him. A *morral* (a traditional woven cotton bag) hangs from her father's shoulder, full of the blue corn seed that he selected from his last crop, now ready for sowing. "With two *cuartillos* of corn, I plant 1,200 meters," he tells me as he starts to poke a hole in the dirt with his bare toes. One side of the field is for blue corn, the other for white. A hired man with a pair of mules plows in the background. Don Julián Romero Ávila is visibly moved. He is ready to begin the ritual of planting his corn.

The old man (*el abuelo*) has more land, but this is where he lives and where he plants the most now. Every year he harvests corn, squash, and *cempazuchitl* (marigold), the flower of the dead. María Teresa has chiles in the ground outside her kitchen as well, and lots of plants in old cans and pots.

"Our pueblo has a certain aroma," María Teresa told me when I asked her to describe Ocotepec. "Aquí nos huele a tierra húmeda" (It smells like damp earth to us here). Local food has a certain flavor and aroma as well. The city of Cuernavaca and the town of Ocotepec have both grown so that they are coming together at the seams. One noticeable difference between them, however, besides the cornfields (which are fast disappearing), is the food. According to María Teresa, local food is not only more *condimentado* (spicy) but more filling and satisfying. "En el centro la comida ni te satisface ni te llena; ahí está la diferencia con la modernidad" (Downtown food neither satisfies not fills you up; that is the difference with modernity).

The church bells toll just as Don Julián begins to plant his corn. He stops, looking up from the ground. "Who would have guessed?" he muses. An elderly man and woman, both friends of his, have died on the same day. The cycle of life and death seems to hang over the newly turned earth.

Learning in the Kitchen

María Teresa learned to cook by watching her mother, her aunts, and her women neighbors. She, in turn, has taught her children to cook. Her daughter knows how to make meatballs, *chilaquiles*, enchiladas, rice, and chiles rellenos—she gives me a partial list. Her son, she says, knows enough to survive—if only how to cook eggs with chile peppers and beans. He is the one who helps her with the tedious process of making chiles rellenos. More importantly, the kitchen is a place where María Teresa transmits her values about life in general. "En la comida, yo les enseño a mis hijos que no deben humillar a una persona que es campesina, porque gracias a ellos tenemos qué comer" (With the meal, I teach my children that they should not humiliate a campesino, because it is thanks to them that we have food to eat).

María Teresa is making *mole verde* as we talk. She insists on my staying for dinner and on giving me the recipe so I can make it for my family later.

> Cook the chicken pieces in broth. In a blender, mix five *tomates* (tomatillos) and ten serrano chiles with a piece of onion, garlic, and cilantro. Then season a bit of onion in oil in a *cazuela de barro*. Add half a pound of ground pumpkin seed and stir a minute so it is coated with the oil. Immediately stir in the salsa and stir nonstop until it thickens, about five minutes. Then add the pieces of chicken with a tiny bit of its broth. Serve with hot tortillas.

"The same person must stir until she finishes," she warns me. "But the traditional *mole verde* in Ocotepec used to be made with pasilla chiles, not green serrano chiles."

When I ask María Teresa to draw a map of her kitchen for me, she hesitates and asks: "Which of the two? *¿La de diario o la cocina de humo?*" (The one for everyday cooking? Or the smoke kitchen for fiestas?). She draws both, beginning with the one in which we are sitting. "Bring me a pencil, I am going to make an experiment," she calls to her daughter, giggling. Despite her initial reticence, she enjoys drawing and includes many details indicative of her pride and pleasure in her kitchen—the flowers on the table, the ruffled curtains, the pots—signing her masterpiece when it is complete. Halfway through, she draws a line down the middle of the paper and sketches the huge clay pots for mole with the firewood piled up alongside. Every house in Ocotepec has a smoke kitchen, she insists. Knowing that the huge new houses being built all around the outskirts of the town do not, I wonder if this would not be a clear indicator of a local family, versus one from Mexico City or Cuernavaca that had recently bought land and built a house atop a cornfield.

"Cocina de Humo"

OLLA P/FRIJOLES
CAZUELA CON MOLE
PICHANCHA
LEÑA

"Cocina Moderna
Normal."

ZABADERO
TUBO DE AGUA
VENTANA
VENTANA
MAQUINITA MOLEJETE
TORTILLA MAQUINA
AGUA DOLCE

María Teresa Romero
Ocotepec, Mor.
Año 2001.

"Sin Cocinera No Hay Nada"

María Teresa is surprised when I ask her what would happen if there were no women cooking. She replies that there would be no love and unity in the household. It would bring chaos in the community. Celebrations would not involve children if women were not cooking; they would be drinking affairs for men only.

> *Pues no habría nada, porque sin cocinera no hay nada. Por ejemplo, con hombres hubiera habido bebida, porque va y se compra; el vino va y se compra. Pero si no hay cocineras no hay comida.* (There would be nothing, because without the cook there is nothing. For example, with men there would have been drinks, because you can buy alcohol, you can go to the store and buy alcohol. But without women cooking there is no meal.)

María Teresa tells me about the changes that have taken place:

> *Antes el pueblo era muy campesino, y de eso vivían, del campo. Comían o vendían. Pero ahora la juventud ya empezó a estudiar—no quiere trabajar.*

Facing page: **María Teresa's map of her "modern" and "smoke" kitchens**

María Teresa's *cazuelas moleras* in her smoke kitchen (see also her map)

Además la tierra ya es para vivienda, ya somos muchos. No hay donde vivir. Casi dondequiera hay casas—y son nuevas. (Before, the whole town lived off the land. They all ate and sold their products, but now young people have started going to school—they do not want to work. Besides, now the land is for housing, now there are many of us. There is no place to live. Almost wherever you look there are houses—and they are new.)

Doña Isidra and Doña Dolores

At the end of October and beginning of November the monarch butterflies return to Mexico after a long migration south on tattered wings. Blooming *cempazuchitl* blankets the countryside with orange and gold. It is the time when many communities in central Mexico await the souls that return from different spatial realms of the dead to visit their loved ones in the world of the living. Most people in Mexico prepare an offering on the eve of the celebration of the Day of the Dead on November 2. But the geography and calendar of the pilgrimages carried out by the dead are more complex in Ocotepec and traditionally in many other towns as well. Different days are reserved for different categories of ghosts. Children, for instance, are received on October 31 with appropriate foods—not too spicy—and with toys on their altar. Other days are set aside for receiving the ghosts of people who died by drowning, in violent accidents, or in other ways. Each type of ghost presumably returns from a different spatial realm associated with each type of death.

People in Ocotepec traditionally receive returning souls with altars laden with fruit, bread, tamales, mole, and even cigarettes, pulque, or other pleasures presumably denied the departed in the afterlife. While the custom is not limited to this town, the townspeople's effort to share their traditions with outside visitors is extraordinary. They open their homes not only to family and friends but to unknown guests, sharing food and drink with all of them after the otherworldly visitors have partaken of their essence.

When a person has died within the year, the family may set up a full-bodied altar (*de cuerpo entero*) that includes a representation of the form of the deceased, complete with personal items such as a hat or shirt and a mask. Some altars are truly lavish, but all are at the very least adorned with flowers, candles, a glass of water, and a special bread that is baked only at this time—the famous *pan de muertos* (bread of the dead), with crossbones and colored sugar. Often the *ofrenda* includes the ritual tamales accompanied with mole and the alcohol favored by the deceased. Children's altars offer candy, toys, tiny versions of the *pan de muertos,* and miniature portions of food.

Visiting Isidra's Home on the Eve of the Day of the Dead

Día de los Muertos in Ocotepec provides an opportunity for meeting local people inside their homes, so I visited several *ofrendas,* guided by pathways of *cempazuchitl* petals, glowing candles, and the smell of flowers and burning copal incense on the evening of November 1. The sound of fireworks exploding everywhere and children squealing with delight made it clear that the occasion was one of celebration, despite the otherwise somber mood and relative silence. Everywhere I went, I was given a *tamal, pan de muertos,* or both and a cup of *atole, ponche,* or black coffee. *Ponche* is a hot fruit punch traditionally made in the Christmas season and for wakes and for the extensive celebrations surrounding the Day of the Dead. In Ocotepec the recipe includes guayaba, apple, sugarcane, cinnamon, raisins, and sometimes pineapple. In several homes the hosts offered me a shot of rum for my *ponche:* "¿Quiere piquete?" (Would you like it spiked?).

One home I visited was honoring the death of an elderly woman: her rebozo (traditional woven shawl) was draped over the shape of a body on a long table covered with food and flowers. I was granted permission to take a few pictures and promised to return with copies. It was Doña Isidra's home.

Doña Isidra Takes Me to Meet Her Friend Dolores

My visit began with a trip to Isidra's house: I wanted to give her the photograph I had taken of her mother's *ofrenda* in November. When she was absolutely sure I was not trying to sell her the picture, she finally opened her gate and let me in. I sat at the kitchen table, chatting with her for a while, with the television blaring behind the curtain that separated that room from the rest of the house. Isidra had little time to sit, as she was on her way out to help a friend make tamales that day. She invited me along, arguing that her friend Dolores was better qualified to speak about Ocotepec than she was, because she herself was brought here from Puebla as a child.

Dolores affirms her ancestral roots in Ocotepec: "Yo sí soy de Ocotepec, desde mis abuelos" (I *am* from Ocotepec, since my grandparents). Isidra's friend is even more bashful than she is; but her presence emboldens Isidra, and the two together eventually appear more comfortable with me. It turns out to be a fruitful morning.

Dolores has been making tortillas and selling them on a daily basis for over fifty years, ever since she was a little girl. On occasion—today, for instance—she also makes tamales on request, by special order. She is standing behind her *comal* when we arrive, kneading her masa on the *molcajete* under a roofed but otherwise outdoor kitchen. Isidra gets right to work on finishing the green salsa that they will use in the tamales, which her friend has already begun. She brings a spoonful out for Dolores to taste and approve. Clearly happy to share something about which she feels some authority, she gives me a tip and a different recipe for green salsa: "A la salsa se le pone comino—no muchata [*sic*], poquito. Si se le pone mucho, hace daño, si se le pone poco, ni sabe" (Add cumin to the salsa: not too much, not too little. Too much makes people sick, too little and you can't taste it).

The tamales take one hour to steam, Isidra says. "You put the *tejolote* [the hand of the metate] on top of them to help the masa cook correctly"—yet another ritual meant to guard the tamales from evil and assure their success. "Está viva la masa" (The dough is alive), she tells me. "Si estamos discutiendo, absorbe lo malo. El tejolote es para cualquier cosa" (If we argue, it absorbs the discord [the evil]. The *tejolote* is just in case).

Dolores talks about the many changes that she has witnessed in Ocotepec, while continuing to make tortillas, gingerly placing one after the other on her *comal*. She turns them over nimbly and removes them with her fingertips at just the right moment. Isidra brings me a plate of salt so that I can enjoy a few right off the *comal*.

> *Antes se molía aquí la masa. Ahora se lleva al molino. Se hacían tortillas en casa tres veces al día. Antes la mujer no trabajaba, trabajaba en casa. Ahora los matrimonios los dos salen a la calle a trabajar. Los jóvenes comen huevos o comen en la calle—a taquear.* (We used to grind the masa here. Now we take it to the mill. We made tortillas at home three times a day. Before, women did not work, they worked at home. Today, with married couples, both the man and the woman work outside the home. Young people eat eggs or go out to eat tacos on the street.)

Despite these changes, Isidra and Dolores agree that the basic diet at home has not changed. It consists of the same *sopa, guisado y frijoles* (soup, stew, and beans) that their parents and grandparents ate. In fact *sopa, guisado y frijoles* is the phrase that people I interviewed often used to refer to everyday food. It seemed to reassure everyone that everything was still the same, regardless of the changes they described.

People still bring her their dried tortillas and food scraps for her pigs, Dolores tells me. But now she has only one pig, she chuckles as she corrects herself and stresses the singular: *un marrano.* One big change: while there used to be a large cornfield just beyond her stove in the house-lot garden, that space is now mostly under construction and has been reduced to almost nothing.[1]

As if to conclude, Isidra interjects: "Nobody makes tortillas anymore." I ask Dolores: "Aren't you making tortillas right now?" For many years women in this community have survived by making tortillas, precisely because there have always been women—of the middle and upper classes—who do not. In more recent decades, however, even the poorer women who make up the majority in my three research communities are able to buy inexpensive subsidized tortillas at the *tortillería.* Most are happy to do so, despite the complaints about their quality, texture, and taste.

"La Ciudad Nos Está Tragando"

While Dolores has adjusted to changing circumstances and purchases her corn today rather than growing it, she is sad and uncomfortable with the changes in land use in her immediate home and community and with the swelling population. "Sembré unos elotes para el antojo, para tener maíz fresco" (I planted a few cornstalks for the cravings, to have fresh corn). She says she cannot live without seeing corn.

> *No estamos bien. Ocotepec es un pueblo, pero al rato se convierte en ciudad. La ciudad nos está tragando. Hay menos cosecha y más gente. Ya no hay campesinos. El gobierno no les quiere ayudar. El banco no perdona: exige aunque el campesino cosechó o no cosechó. Y el campesino perdió.* (We are not doing well. Ocotepec is a town, but soon it will turn into a city. The city is swallowing us. There is less harvest and more people. There are no campesinos left. The government does not want to help them. The bank is unforgiving: it demands payment whether the campesino harvested or not. And the campesino has already lost.)

When I leave, a young girl with the last name of Díaz escorts me past the furiously barking dogs that guard the entrance to the property. I ask her if she is related to Don Domingo Díaz at the other end of town. He is her uncle. Knowing of his family's respect for tradition, I ask her: "Do you make tortillas by hand?" "Yes," she answers.

María Soledad, the Daughter of Domingo Díaz

María Soledad Díaz Ríos, thirty-six years old, is a preschool teacher. She is enthusiastic and interested in my research. Her sister Susana is the one called upon to make mole for fiestas. As the only unmarried daughter, however, it is María Soledad who cooks for the extended family every day, including her sister's children. Not surprisingly, she says that she does not like to cook, especially when she comes home from work tired and hungry and has to come up with a meal in a hurry that the children will eat. Nonetheless, María Soledad loves to experiment with new recipes. She especially enjoys preparing desserts on weekends, when she is relieved of kitchen duty for a day or two because her sister is cooking the family meals.

María Soledad tells me: "Your mood is important in the kitchen. One time I came home all stressed out—I had lots of work at school—and I decided to make rice. So I started making the rice and everything and I left it browning. Just for a minute. Well, then I forgot all about the rice!" She laughs. "I burned it! It is like I was in such a hurry coming home from school that I wanted to cook something fast, I wanted everything ready quickly. But that is how things go when you are not in the right mood or you are angry. Then my father says: 'Boy, were you mad!' 'Why?' I ask him. 'Because the salsa came out spicy!'"

María Soledad laughs when I ask her how important the cook is for the community. "¡Sin cocinera no hubiera fiesta!" (Without the *cocinera* there would be no fiesta!). While the older women recognized for their mole are dying out, the tradition continues, with younger women taking their place, she says.

All Roads Lead to Domingo Díaz

On a visit to the local chapel before Christmas, the recently arrived priest made it very clear that he did not want to speak to me about Ocotepec. Instead he gave me the name of Domingo Díaz, saying that he was the person who knew the most about local Christmas customs (*las costumbres navideñas*) and who had the oldest religious images in town.[2] I went straight over to the house of Domingo Díaz in the barrio of Santa Cruz. While he was not home, I did meet his daughter Susana, who invited me to a Posada they were preparing and later told her father of my visit.

Months later (March 26), after having no luck finding a person I was looking for in the barrio of Los Ramos, I wander back again to the Díaz home in the barrio of Santa Cruz. This time a different daughter opens the wooden gate. She calls her father for me. Don Domingo receives me immediately, leading me through a large central courtyard to one of four small adobe houses on the edges of the property. We sit in a room with a tiny window. One wall is covered with portraits of deceased family members, the other with images of religious figures. Two of this man's children and one son-in-law were killed in highway accidents, surely one of the costs of "progress" coming to Ocotepec in the form of the two highways which slice through it. One splits the town in half right at the church, leaving two barrios on one side and two on the other. The toll road from Mexico City to Acapulco serves as a physical barrier between the town of Ocotepec and the city of Cuernavaca.

Don Domingo sits down at a small square table where he has been transcribing sheet music with a quill pen, making copies for younger band members who have not yet learned their parts for the upcoming Easter celebrations. Having completed over fifty pages already, he still has at least that many more remaining. Clearly a photocopy is not acceptable to this man, whose time and patience are equal to his respect for tradition.

Clearing his desk, Don Domingo invites me to open my notebook and take all the notes I want. Unlike the women with whom I speak in kitchens, he is evidently accustomed to interviews and to representing his community. Yet while he is not shy about my note taking, he tells me repeatedly that I do not need to write anything down, that he has it all written down for me already. Eventually, after delivering the oral version of the tale, he gets up and brings me a little book about local Christmas traditions which he had published in 1995 with support from the state government (Díaz 1995). "There," he says triumphantly, "it is all right there."

Of course it is not all there. The book contains only two pages on the history of Christmas traditions and his own *imágenes* and none of the "insignificant" details from everyday life in which I am interested, which permeate his story. True to the oral version, however, the book tells the saga of how the relics that his family is responsible for were hidden during the revolution of 1910 in the Cuernavaca cathedral. Don Domingo's uncle of the same name inherited them after the previous owner—who had died during the revolution—did not pick them up and the man's family no longer wanted to take responsibility for them. The priest who was in charge of the state cathedral, who was from Tepoztlán, gave them to the uncle, arguing that someone from Ocotepec, the town of the original owner, should take them.

Don Domingo, born on the same day as his uncle, August 7, inherited the man's name and his responsibility for keeping *las tradiciones* going. The Posadas have been in his family's hands since 1920. The women in his family have been making the traditional mole and tamales for even longer. In those days, he says, the town had few people, nothing like today. The *chiquihuite* would still be full of candy at the end of the night. "¡No se terminaba la colación!" (The Christmas candy never ran out!).

It is impossible to convince this 73-year-old male spokesperson for local tradition of my interest in kitchenspace, though Don Domingo agrees that food is essential to the celebrations of which he speaks. Nonetheless, his life's story and perspectives provide an important social and historical context for what I see and hear in kitchens today.

Don Domingo's wife died three years ago, and he is sad and lonely despite being surrounded by family and continuing to be active in the community. "It is not the same for people who live alone their entire life," he says, "but we would have been married forty-seven years this year, and I still cry for her every night." He complains that his children do not let him have a new *compañera* (female companion), out of fear that a new woman will want part of the land that is their inheritance. "They do not have to worry," he assures me, "because I have already built them each a house and divided the property." Don Domingo insists that he could leave them alone with their land, but they will not hear of it. He could start all over again, he seems to be thinking aloud, though he admits it would be tiring to build yet another adobe house and is not sure if he could do so anymore at his age.

Reminiscing, Don Domingo tells me that neither he nor his wife knew anything at all when they were young (he married at the age of twenty-four) but that together they learned to move ahead in life: "Between the two of us we learned to progress." He starting praying at age twenty-one, he says, referring to his role in leading the rosary at community events. His involvement with the church was in part the reason why he inherited the *imágenes*.

"My wife did not know anything besides how to make tortillas and sell them in town," Don Domingo says. She, like many other women of her generation and some today, brought in some income by making and selling tortillas. She sold fruit from their land as well.

Don Domingo's wife learned to sew in a course that was offered in nearby Cuernavaca, the same one that Doña Emilia mentioned during the Fifth Friday celebration in Los Ramos. He tells me that his wife was the best in the class, cutting the cloth in minutes and finishing her sewing before anyone else. Heads turned when they heard her machine whirring. In forty-two minutes the dress was made from start to finish, beginning with her drawing the pattern. "She beat them all!" he says proudly. She began by sewing aprons and clothes for their six children. Then one day a neighbor asked her for help making a dress for a *fiesta de quinceaños*, and soon she was sewing for a living. Her sewing machine sits in one corner of the room where we talk.

Don Domingo learned to play trumpet while still in school and was eventually invited to join the state band. He recalls his hesitation to abandon his cornfield and his embarrassment at not having money to buy shoes, which he needed to be presentable for the job. His father-in-law encouraged him and provided crucial support, agreeing to help with the harvest of whatever he sowed. "Mi suegro me animó, me ayudó. Me dijo: 'Es una cosa segura' (My father-in law encouraged me and helped me. He told me: 'It is a sure thing')—not like *el campo*."

Planting seems to be even more difficult today, according to Don Domingo:

> *Ya no hay donde sembrar, con la venta de terrenos y la construcción de carreteras. Hace como treinta años para acá ha cambiado mucho. Vino gente de afuera a vivir acá y nos robaron mucho en las noches. Todo pasaron a destruir.* (There is no place to plant anymore, with so much land sold and the construction of the highways. Much has changed in the last thirty years. People from other places have come to live here and robbed us a lot in the night. They destroyed everything.)

Don Domingo prefers to rent the land that he does have—what used to be his cornfield—to a man who pays him by the month to stack junk cars on it. He says that is better than people robbing him of his work. "It is one of the most difficult situations, when you plant and then at harvest time you go and there is nothing there."

Don Domingo used to plant only corn, but then he and his wife had the idea of planting half of his field with *cempazuchitl* to sell for the Days of the Dead. When the flowers were in bloom, he went to gather part of them for the altars of the *muertos chiquitos*, the souls of the dead children that are received on the first day. He planned to bring in the rest of the harvest the next morning. "Al día siguiente no había nada. Ahí se me quitó las ganas de sembrar" (The next day there was nothing. Right there I lost the desire to work the land). The remainder of Don Domingo's crop had been stolen in the night. "Better to rent out the land and to buy my corn and squash with the money I get for it," he concludes.

And yet, despite the changes in the land, Don Domingo assures me that young people are keeping traditions alive: "My daughters make mole; my nieces are learning also: they watch and they make tamales too."

Why is this so important? I ask Don Domingo, still trying to get him to address women's work in kitchens. Why do women work so hard to prepare food for the fiestas? "The people who invite us musicians are happy we come. It moves their heart; they feel that Jesus is with them. It is for the honor of supporting the tradition." Apparently it is a pleasure, an honor, and an opportunity to visit with people.

But what about everyday eating in his house, within the family? I ask. "We eat lots of meat now," Don Domingo says, "mostly chicken, pork, or beef. And always *sopa, de arroz o de pasta*" (rice, referred to as dry soup, or pasta in tomato and chicken broth, called wet soup). "And tortillas?" I ask. "Yes," he says, "but tortillas in many different ways, not just for tacos but in *picaditas* [like *sopes*] or quesadillas, for instance." He says that members of his family often buy masa at the *molino* and make their own. When his children do not have to work—on a weekend or a holiday—they like to share a big mid-morning meal in their common house-lot garden. "We sweep and water early in the morning, pull out the *comal,* and the tank of gas or the charcoal, and start making meat or *sopes.* And that's it. In the afternoon we all go back to our own houses."

As I leave the house, I see a familiar sight, a countertop covered with old tortillas spread out on top, drying. I wonder where the chickens or pigs are that will be eating them.

"¡Aquí es el Mole, Esa Es la Tradición!"

While María Soledad's description of Ocotepec's food traditions matches what several other women have told me, I am initially interested in her perspective on this because of the role that her family plays in community affairs. "Más que nada aquí en Ocotepec son sus fiestas . . . preparan la comida más típica de aquí, el mole. Aquí es el mole, esa es la tradición" (Ocotepec is known for its fiestas . . . and mole is the typical dish. Here it is mole, that is the tradition).

On May 3, the date of the annual fiesta in María Soledad's barrio, the women in her family prepare mole. They invite friends and *compadres* "y a toda persona que guste venir a la fiesta" (and anybody who wants to come to the fiesta). After hearing her detailed description of the various *mayordomos* who commit to hosting particular meals, I ask María Soledad how many different families participate as *mayordomos*. She counts aloud—breakfast, *comida, comida* for the *chinelos,* for the musicians, for the fireworks crew for two whole days—and concludes that approximately ten households are involved with the food alone.

María Soledad's Narrative

There must be approximately ten houses that have the responsibility of *mayordomo*. Besides that there is everything else—the flowers, candles, music, fireworks. That is just for the food. And in addition to that there are all of us who do not have a specific responsibility, but because we are from the barrio we have to prepare a special meal and invite others. Since it is only our barrio that makes food [for that particular celebration], we invite people from the other barrios . . . people from Ocotepec or people from downtown [Cuernavaca] who know our customs. And they all come. That is just for the fiesta on May 3, the one that is our barrio's fiesta. Then there is the big fiesta on August 6, the town's celebration. There are even more people then. The whole town participates, starting on August 2. After eating, we send them [guests] home with a plate or basket of food, their *itacate*. "Here you go, for your lunch or dinner." Like a token of appreciation for their having participated or something.

The mole in Ocotepec is not sweet, because we do not use chocolate or banana. We use cacao. The seed, that is, toasted and ground together with the almonds and the raisins. We use raisins, but not much, so it will not be sweet. Mole is what is typical here in Ocotepec. So some might complain: "Hey, this mole is store-bought!" In other words, they know the flavor! The one that is purchased tastes sweet sometimes or too spicy. But not the mole from here.

More than anything, what gives mole its flavor is the condiments. If you do not use enough, the ones that are the mole condiments, then "hey, the mole is missing such and such an herb." Or "it needs more almonds." In other words, you can taste it. Or if it is too spicy, they say: "You did not take the veins out of the chiles right." Because you have to devein the chiles for the mole not to be too hot.

The mole in Tepoztlán is different, because in Tepoztlán they use fewer condiments. It has less condiments and it tastes more like chiles than like mole. It is different in each place and even between different people. For instance, here, we might say: *Híjoles, este mole lo preparó tal señora* (Wow, this mole was prepared by such and such lady). Because it is her *sazón.* You can taste it. For instance, the people who visit us here will say: "You have your mother's *sazón,* that is how she prepared it." *Sazón* is the flavor. I think things have *sazón* depending on whether you use enough salt or not enough. Or if it did not boil right. Maybe we are ready to serve it but no, it still tastes too much like chiles. It does not taste right. Or it tastes like water. Then you simmer it a little longer so it loses that taste. *No es de la receta, ya es de uno* (It is not from the recipe, it is from yourself). It is the way our parents or our mother taught us to cook, and then it is just your way.

Here the tradition is that if we have a big expense, we invite people, such as family members, to help us prepare the meal. Before we used to say: "Let's go see such and such a lady; she is old and knows how to prepare the food." But we hardly do that anymore because the people are almost all dying off now. But the tradition continues. Well, at least in our case, my mother prepared a delicious mole. And my sister Susana inherited it. Sometimes my aunt comes looking for her: "I want you to prepare my mole." And she does go, she lends herself for preparing the mole. Because you have to cook everything, the condiments and everything.

Changes

In a curious turn of phrase, María Soledad describes how Ocotepec is "almost becoming a city already" ("Ya casi va siendo ciudad"). Things are not like they used to be anymore. "Before this was all cultivated land. Now people do not plant anymore, there is almost no place left to plant in anymore."

Before, María Soledad says, many people earned their living by gathering and selling firewood from the towns' communal lands. This has changed now that most women prefer gas stoves to firewood for cooking most of the time, though firewood is still used for fiestas.

> Firewood is still used, but few people buy it anymore. Almost never. If we buy it, it is for a fiesta, to cook outdoors. It is not a little bit of food that we make, it is a whole lot! They are giant pots, and things cook faster with firewood than with gas. And it tastes different. We do not use enamel-coated or aluminum pots here. We use clay pots, the big ones, the *cazuelas moleras*.

> The mole has sesame seeds even now. Though people use fewer and fewer condiments, they are still an important part of the mole. Before, we used the condiments, including sesame seeds, cocoa beans, seeds (*semillitas*),[3] peanuts. We still do, but in lesser quantities. Now it tastes more like chiles than anything. And of course the condiments are more expensive too now, so we do not use so many anymore.

"Antes Teníamos Muchos Puercos"

In Ocotepec, as in Tetecala and Xochimilco, increasing urbanization has been accompanied by an intolerance for animal smells. "Everything bothers us nowadays," María Soledad complains. Although members of her family always had many pigs in a pen in the yard, now they have none, because it bothers the neighbors. She laments that they have no more pigs, not only because the pigs were good to eat but because now she has to throw away all the food scraps that they used to eat.

> *Puercos, antes teníamos muchos puercos. Pero la cosa es que como a los vecinos les molesta el olor y todo eso. Antes no les molestaba el olor y toda la gente tenía, pero ahora ya nos molesta todo. Es la misma gente, pero ya son hijos, y como que ya no quieren tener animales. Y pues yo digo que un animalito, por ejemplo un marrano, pues si tenemos su chiquero, ¿no? Y era ayuda porque a veces el desperdicio, lo que sale de la comida, en lugar de dársela al marranito que es algo que después se vende o se mata y sirve para comer, pues a la basura. Entonces ya no juntamos el desperdicio. Las tortillas que*

quedaban mucho, ya en lugar de juntarla, a la basura. Y pues es desperdicio,
¿no? Es desperdicio. Pues nosotros siempre habíamos tenido marranos, siem-
pre, siempre. Ahora a veces se los damos a los perros, pero los perros a veces
de tanto ya no quieren, o hay comida que no les gusta y el marrano se come
todo. Todo. (Pigs, we used to have lots of pigs. But the thing is that the smell
and all that bothers the neighbors. Before, the smell did not bother them and
everyone had pigs, but now everything bothers us. It is the same people, but
now their children, and it is like they do not want animals anymore. And I
say, well, a little animal, a pig, for example, I mean, we have their pen, don't
we? And it was a help because now the food scraps that we used to give the
piggies that are something you sell or kill and serve at the table, now they go
to waste. So now we do not gather the waste. The tortillas that we always had
so many left, instead of gathering them, they go in the trash. And they are
scraps, aren't they? I mean, they are scraps. Well, we always had pigs; always,
always. Now we sometimes give the scraps to the dogs, but sometimes from
getting too many, they just do not want them. And besides, there is some
food they do not even like, and the pigs eat everything. Everything.)

María Soledad's Kitchenspace

When I ask María Soledad to draw her kitchen, she hesitates and asks: "¿La
cocina, la del diario?" (The kitchen, the everyday kitchen?). Despite her initial reticence, she does eventually map both the everyday and the *leña* (firewood) kitchen, which she describes in more detail.

"Aquí está mi parrilla, mi fogón, aquí puse mi estufa, y este es mi trastero"
(Here is my grill, my hearth, here I put my stove, and here is the rack for
my dishes). María Soledad refers to her metate and her blender, one indoors
and one outside. "Para moler, está afuera, por el lavadero, está en el patio"
(For grinding, it is outdoors, by the sink, in the patio). She uses the metate
to grind beans when she makes the *tlaxcales* (described below) for the days
of the dead, after first cooking them with *tequesquite.* When she makes
tortillas at home, she uses the metate to knead the dough, arguing that it
is just the right shape: "Lo ocupo para la masa, para tortilla. Para amasar.
Porque es un espacio más como para recargarse encima. Por la forma. Sí.
Por la forma y para recargarse, y se amasa bien la masa" (I use it for the
dough, for tortillas. To knead the dough. Because it is one more space to
lean on. Because of its shape. Yes, because of its shape and to lean on, and it
serves well for kneading the dough).

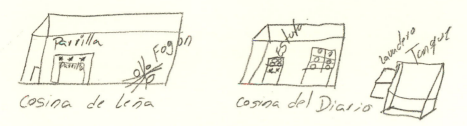

María Soledad's map of her "firewood" and "everyday" kitchens

The metate is in the smoke kitchen; the blender is indoors. While the outdoor kitchen is in the house-lot garden, it has a roof and can be closed fully, which she says is important when you make a lot of food for a fiesta, so the animals do not get in.

Three different herbs grow in the garden: spearmint, epazote, and chamomile. Besides the pigs, the family once had many chickens.

> According to the beliefs, since the chickens belonged to my mother and my mother passed away, they say that everything that was hers is lost. And she is the one who used to feed them. But still, when she died, we still fed them. We took care of them, but they were hers. But, no, they say that no: "Everything your mother left, if she left cooking pots, everything is going to break." And yes, it is true, because the enamel pots she left are getting holes in them. And one morning the chickens were all dead. The only one left is that hen running around there. But we only have one.

Clay pots have many traditional beliefs associated with them. Significantly, they provide a link to loved ones in the world of the dead as well as to people in this world. María Soledad tells me that there is a saying that if you need to see a person in a hurry you yell the name into a pot and the person will come right away. "In other words," she explains, "you give the pot the name of the person you urgently need to see. Yell it into the pot, and the person arrives."

María Soledad Talks about *Tlaxcales* and the Dead

The special food I remember my mother making that we all loved and that you can hardly find anymore is the *tlaxcales*. You make them during the Days of the Dead, that is when the corn is just right. Only older people know how to make them anymore. They are like tortillas but thicker. Or sort of like a type of *enfrijolada* (fried tortilla coated with refried beans) but instead of cooking them in a pan, you grill them on a *comal*.

They are made of corn that is about to become *mazorca* (dry, on the cob)—that is, neither too soft nor too hard. You grind it. You take it to the mill to grind it and you mix it with sugar and that's it. Some *tlaxcales* have special beans and sugar too—then the *tlaxcales* come out sweet. They have a wonderful smell. They are nothing like what they sell in the market. Those we made at home. Because it was pure corn. Now they mix a bit of flour in them because if you do not know how to make them, they break. Nobody knows how to make them anymore.

The custom here is that a week after November 1, of the Days of the Dead, you put them on the altar because that is when the souls depart. You put out the *tlaxcales* or tamales made of sweet corn for the children. So that is how you send the children off, with their coffee or their *atole*, as you like. The next day, a week after November 2, you make meat tamales for the grown-up ghosts. With chile sauce. To send them off, it is their food for the road. Here we do that after the Days of the Dead, because they leave. After being with us for a week—the children arrive on the first of the month and they leave on the eighth. On the ninth the adults leave.

Supposedly, our belief is that [if we do not leave food out for the dead] they will not have anything to eat on their journey. So nothing happens, but the custom that we have is that you have to set the food out for them.

The custom is to have the *ofrenda* ready by noon on November 1 or 2, before the souls return to their earthly home. If at that time everything is not ready yet—because you have to serve the mole, the boiled chayotes,[4] the bread for the dead, the bananas, apples, and everything. So if at that time all the food is not ready yet, at least you set out a glass of water, tortillas, and a little plate with salt.[5] So they can have a glass of water while the food is being prepared—since they arrive tired from the journey; so they can have a glass of water and rest. And you lay out their *petate* (traditional woven mat). If it is a new offering, in other words if it is a death from that year, then it has to be a new *petate*. If not, then any *petate* is fine.

María Soledad Describes How to Prepare Tortillas and Beans

Everyone will tell you that tortillas made of *nixtamal* and over a firewood stove and beans cooked in the traditional clay pot (*frijoles de olla*) are much tastier. Of course tortillas made at home are much better than the ones sold in *tortillerías*.

More than anything, if the dough is from *nixtamal* and all, the tortillas taste sweet. They are sweet, they have a different taste. *Porque en la tortillería hasta las compra uno y saben a crudo* (Because the ones in the *tortillerías*, you buy them and they even taste raw).

The ones [beans] in the pot, even the flavor is different, but especially they come out lighter in color (*güeros*). If you put them in an enamel pot or aluminum, they come out dark (*prietos*). We have observed that. I do not know if it is because we have always used clay pots, but one time we came home and "Oh no, we have to get the beans ready for a certain time," and we put them in an aluminum pan for them to cook faster. Then they come out darker, and you can taste it too—as if they were forced to cook! So they do have a different flavor.

Cooking Every Day

María Soledad describes a situation that many women cooking for families the world over would recognize: she has to find a way to feed hungry but finicky children by using her creativity to make a variety of dishes with the same basic ingredients. She says that the cook is important—even if she is "not really a cook"—but "just doing the cooking."

"The cook has to know how to make the menu a little interesting even if she uses more or less the same ingredients," María Soledad tells me; "otherwise people will not eat it. Chicken soup, for instance. Sometimes we are in a hurry and just to be quick we wash the chicken and into the water. And sometimes we are just tired of it: chicken soup every day!" She imitates the voices of her nieces and nephews: "¡Ay! ¿¡Otra vez vamos a comer otro pollo!? ¡Ay, pollo! Pero en caldo no. No" (Oh! Chicken again? Not again! Yuck, chicken. Not in soup again. No). She adds:

> *Pues, un guisado. Entonces, pues hay que estarle variando. Entonces yo digo que sí es importante la cocinera. ¡Y aunque no sea cocinera! Hay que estar— "Ay, ¿qué vamos a comer? ¿Hoy qué vamos a comer?" No, pues hay que cambiarle a otra cosa. Hay que darle variedad.* (OK, a stew. But you have to be varying things. So I say the cook is important. And even if she is not a cook! You have to be putting up with "What are we going to eat today? What's cooking?" No, you have to change things. You have to provide variety.)

Now we eat more meat than vegetables. Before, we were satisfied with some beans and an egg. Now it's: "What, this is food?" Like we want something more. And before, that was not so. Whatever there was was fine: vegetables, fried or boiled squash, or something in tomato sauce. But not now. Now we want more meat.

Like most women I interviewed, María Soledad did not consider herself a *cocinera* or think she knew "how to cook." Instead she and others like her just think that they know "how to prepare food" or make a pot of rice—in other words, the work without the status. Very few women are considered *cocineras* by their communities or their families, sometimes not even those who know the mole recipe and are called on to make sure that a special event is properly celebrated.

I do not have children. Those that eat here are from my nieces and father. My sister works in the afternoon, so the five days of the week I cook, and on Saturdays and Sundays they are hers. Yes, I am the everyday cook, even though I work everyday myself. It is quite a feat (*Es una hazaña*).

"¡No Me Gusta Cocinar!"

Like several other women I met who were responsible for preparing food every day in addition to working outside the home, María Soledad does not like to cook when she comes home from work tired and hungry. While she particularly dislikes making chiles rellenos and other complicated recipes that her family sometimes demands, she does enjoy trying out new recipes and experimenting with desserts on weekends, when her sister takes over in the kitchen. Describing the never-ending chores in the kitchen, she says she is grateful that at least her family does not eat dinner but rather the traditional *merienda* (snack).

¡No me gusta cocinar! Aparte que no tenemos el tiempo, se me hace como que—"¡híjoles cocinar!" ¡Apenas acabé de hacer el almuerzo y pensar de qué vas a hacer de comer! ¡Y, por fortuna, no cenamos! Hay comidas laboriosas, que dicen, por ejemplo: "¡Ay, vamos a hacer chiles rellenos! ¡Yo quiero comer chiles rellenos!" Bien laboriosos, estar cociendo los chiles, pelándolos, rellenándolos. ¡Nos gusta comerlos, pero no nos gusta hacerlos! Aparte de que la comida sea laboriosa, lo que no me gusta es cocinar con hambre. Que yo quiera hacerlo rápido para comer o llega uno cansado del trabajo y "órale, vamos a comer algo sencillo"—rápido, guiso y a comer. No, pues "yo ya tengo

hambre." Bueno, al menos en mi trabajo como no nos dejan comer nada. Yo entro desde antes de las nueve y llegó a la casa como a la una. Y en lugar de comer algo—¡a la cocina a preparar la comida! ¡Eso sí da coraje, cocinar con hambre, y que sea la comida laboriosa, pues peor tantito! (I do not like to cook. Besides not having the time, it just seems like—"ugh, cooking!" I just finished with brunch and to think about what I have to prepare for the mid-day meal! And, luckily, we do not have dinner! There are some very laborious meals. They will say, for instance: "Let's make chiles rellenos. I want to eat chiles rellenos!" Very labor intensive to be grilling the chiles, peeling them, stuffing them. We like to eat them, but we do not like to make them! Besides the meal being laborious, what I don't like is cooking when I'm hungry. If I want to make something quick for the meal, or I get home tired from work and "all right, let's eat something simple" and quick, I cook, and we eat. Well, but "I am already really hungry." In my work at least, we are not allowed to eat anything. I go in before nine and come home around one. And instead of eating something—it's go to the kitchen to cook! That makes you mad, cooking while you are hungry. And if it's a laborious meal, it's even worse!)

FOOD FOR THOUGHT

This book is both an ethnography of women's everyday lives in three semi-urban communities in central Mexico (Xochimilco, Ocotepec, and Tetecala) and an innovative approach to gendered spaces of social and cultural reproduction. It explores the lifeworld of ordinary women in a region where many spend much of their time and energy in kitchenspace and have tremendous—though little recognized—social impact. Kitchenspace is a site of adaptation and innovation where gendered subjects work within the parameters of cultural boundaries to accommodate changes in the natural and social landscapes. It is a privileged and gendered site of cultural and social reproduction. Territoriality and hierarchies within kitchenspace reflect its vital importance for the reproduction of social relations within and beyond the household, its value as a living cultural archive and laboratory, and its role as a source of power for many women in this region of study. Kitchenspace in Xochimilco, Ocotepec, and Tetecala is a place from which to taste the environments to which the towns are linked (through markets and local food production) and observe the social reality in which they are immersed. It is vital to the individual and collective experience.

In this region, kitchenspace is unequivocally gendered, constructed as feminine through women's activities and power therein, their narratives, and aesthetics. It is a space in which gendered and embodied knowledge is selectively transmitted to younger generations and where children are literally fed the traditions and beliefs of older generations through quasi-sacramental food rites that make up the fabric of everyday life. It is at once the center of the household and—at times of traditional celebrations—the center of community life. Here reciprocity networks are strengthened as women transmit everything from recipes to organizational forms from one generation to the next. Because of the essential role that women's cooking practices play in establishing alliances and maintaining such networks, kitchenspace is a site of social reproduction. For the same reason, kitchenspace in this region can be semipublic and ritual space. Kitchenspace facilitates cultural reproduction as women keep alive, reinvent, and transmit ways of doing and being to new generations. Given the dynamic characteristics of kitchens-pace and its essential function in humankind's physical survival, it is a rich area in which to explore strategies of cultural adaptation and innovation.

The examples from my fieldwork testify to the profound cultural importance of kitchenspace in central Mexico. Although women's roles in kitchenspace may share some characteristics in different parts of the world or within one culture region—in this case the responsibility of preparing meals for the household on a daily basis and participating in community life via food preparation—my data indicate that these are mediated by the geographic specificity of their particular location. In addition to always revealing the economic status of a particular household and often the climate and vegetation of its geographic location, kitchenspace reflects factors such as ethnicity, religious practices, and generational differences. A sensitive observer of culture can find, in the persistence of food traditions, locally specific manifestations of attachment to place and women who are experts at adapting to change. Future studies of kitchenspace in other regions will also provide unique perspectives on the changing relationship between society and the natural environment, including its manifestation in gendered spaces and relationships.

This book brings attention to the often neglected and gendered spaces of everyday life and to women's role in food preparation for traditional celebrations in central Mexico, where their contributions have usually been taken for granted. Many painful and pressing social issues affecting women and men have surfaced in this context, including poverty (and the resulting migration to and from my research communities), domestic violence, alcoholism, and changes in land tenure and livelihoods. These deserve focused attention and analysis that is beyond the scope of this book (but see, for example, Dwyer and Bruce 1988; Eber 1995; McClusky 2001; Watanabe 1992). In this final chapter I revisit the notion of kitchenspace as gendered space, discuss several dualities, and consider gendered knowledge and women's role as creative agents.

Gendered Spaces

The kitchenspaces in which I spent a year in central Mexico were primarily inhabited by the women who cooked in them from three to ten hours a day. Men came, waited to be served, ate, and left: fathers, brothers, husbands, sons, nephews, uncles, *compadres,* neighbors. They spoke little, never interrupted the woman of the kitchen, and left their dishes on the table. The young woman whose behavior challenged this arrangement in Tetecala was described in the worst terms—not only did she not cook her husband's breakfast before running out of the house to go to class, but she left her dishes on the table "como un hombre" (like a man). A refuge to some, a jail to others, kitchenspace is strictly gendered social space.

Feminist scholars have long deconstructed the nature/culture binary that associates women with nature and men with culture (Massey 1995; Ortner 1974). This chapter considers another binary that has also been of interest to feminists, the domestic/public dichotomy (Lamphere 2001). Throughout this work I have used the word "nature" in the broadest possible sense to refer to the use and interpretation of natural elements rooted in a Mesoamerican cosmovision. My focus on women in kitchenspace is not grounded in any "natural" ability or biologically determined predisposition for food preparation but rather in gender roles that are socially constructed and reflect a specific cultural and social context. To avoid creating the impression that either "nature" or "women" is a homogeneous category, this book includes women of different communities, from different generations, with different perspectives. The case of men returning from working the *chinampas* in Xochimilco to prepare food for the children while their wives went to market to sell their products is also an example of the social construction of gender roles in kitchenspace.

Food preparation spaces are indeed gendered social spaces, which in part explains the lack of attention they have received. As I peeled tamarind, cleaned chiles, or soaked corn husks during my year of fieldwork, I often wondered if women would ever permit a male researcher—regardless of his national origin or ethnicity—to join them in such activities. At the same time, many female researchers have chosen to avoid kitchenspace for a variety of reasons. Yet, precisely because of its spatial segregation in my region of work, gender is a necessary element in any study of nature/society relations. This is particularly so in central Mexico, given the strict gender lines in the Mesoamerican cosmovision.

Women's organization orders space and sets the rhythm in kitchenspace, as with Rosalinda's *grupo femenil* (women's group) from her church in Ocotepec or the *comadres* who gather throughout central Mexico when it is time to make tamales. When people come together in the house-lot garden at times of celebration, one end of the area—surrounding the hearth—fills with women talking, laughing, and even drinking and dancing as they cook; the other end fills with men talking and drinking among themselves; in the middle is mixed space with men and women, boys and girls, sitting at the tables.

Nowhere are the gender lines clearer than in relation to meat and corn. The taboos surrounding gender roles in hunting and agriculture reflect a complex interplay between culture and social life. In her study of a Mexican village where outmigration of men did not result in a feminization of agriculture, Cora Govers (1997) concludes that taboos rooted in gender roles and cosmology were a key factor. While some foods (such as *carnitas* or *barbacoa*) that involve slaughter and are cooked outdoors are generally prepared by men, the majority of food preparation in Mexico is in the hands of women, especially traditional foods involving corn. Never did I observe or hear of any men grinding, kneading, or shaping corn dough—not for tortillas, *memelas, sopes, gorditas,* or any other *antojito mexicano* that women prepare at home and on street corners and markets throughout the region. The very idea of men preparing tamales proved laughable to the women I spoke with. This gender line is linked to women's socially prescribed role as nurturers in central Mexico and the almost sacred reverence and tenderness that people express toward the grain that is at the center of the Mesomerican cosmovision and diet: corn.

In contrast, men can be found cooking and selling *tacos de cabeza* (literally, "head tacos") and *tacos al pastor,* both made of meat, on street corners and markets throughout Mexico. In my research sites, men were responsible for slaughtering cattle and pork, even when the pigs were raised by women. When Antonio's uncle butchered the *abuelita*'s sow in preparation for the house blessing for the Niñopa celebration in Xochimilco (January 20, 2001, in Chapter One), the gendering of space was crystal clear. The slaughter transformed the house-lot garden into male space temporarily, with the young men in the front close to the blood, and the young girls nervously huddled together in the back. The *abuela* who had raised the sow was even farther away, sobbing in her room as the animal she had raised squealed for a few very long minutes until its life came to an end.

Interestingly, in the United States and other countries, outdoor cooking space (usually in the backyard) is often the only place where men can prepare food without challenging established gender roles. In my course on Food, Cuisine, and Kitchenspace at the University of Texas, I had over a hundred students investigate gendered spaces in their home kitchens and found that this was overwhelmingly the case. There were exceptions, particularly in cases of divorce when kids lived with their father or visited him in their stepmother's house. The garage also surfaced as an extension of male kitchenspace, with a freezer to hold meat from hunting, for instance. In many cases students reported that the only male space in the indoor kitchen was the refrigerator, in particular for access to beer and whatever was needed for grilling meat. Clearly the house-lot garden is an important place to explore the ongoing negotiation of changing gender roles in various cultural settings.

How is kitchenspace constituted as feminine? Besides the ornamental plants and decorative use of wall space, the many concave receptacles used for food preparation or storage and found throughout kitchenspace create an overwhelmingly feminine landscape. Women's words, as well as men's relative silence, fill kitchenspace with gendered narratives and (together with women's physical occupancy) mark it as gendered territory. Kitchenspace not only is constituted as feminine but also serves to reinforce parameters of the "feminine." With changing social and economic landscapes, painful adjustments take place as some young women depart from traditional gender roles and seek further education or employment outside the home. Others—young and old—shoulder an increasing share of the household and community burden as they try to meet cultural expectations that are increasingly out of reach in Mexico's continuously deteriorating economic environment.

Nostalgic for a past when the woman at the hearth typically spent hours boiling *nixtamal* and making fresh tortillas, many criticized the lack of flavor and inappropriate consistency of tortillas sold at the *tortillerías.* Esmeralda's father may have been the most vocal, but he certainly was not the only one to rail against the imported transgenic "animal" corn flooding Mexican markets. This resistance to changes in the grain that is the very basis of Mesoamerican culture reflects angst about society's changing relationship with nature as well as the increasing anti-U.S. rhetoric and anger with the Mexican government's agricultural policies. Together, they fuel a powerful discourse against "lazy women," blaming them for structural changes that set the parameters for their options in kitchenspace.

"La cocina es muy laboriosa" (The kitchen is hard work), every one of my informants remarked at one time or another. Food preparation in my research communities seems like a never-ending activity, both from day to day and with the fiesta cycle. It is often back-breaking work. The women I interviewed who were responsible for preparing family meals were busy all day: going to the market, sweeping the house-lot garden, cooking, serving, and washing dishes. As Linda in Xochimilco said: "¡Todos los días es apúrate, apúrate!" (It is always hurry up, hurry up!).

Beyond the usual undervalued and often hidden nature of female and "domestic" labor, many traditional Mexican dishes like mole and chiles rellenos are particularly tedious. Women's most common response to my question "What is your least favorite task in the kitchen?" was "Beating the egg whites for the chiles rellenos." While this dish is not customary for community celebrations, it is a favorite for special family celebrations like birthdays. These and other labor-intensive favorites require hours if not days of work, perhaps explaining why their preparation is often a ritual involving cooperation between women. It is the social aspects of the fiesta system, and the diversion it provides from everyday work, that prompted Beverly Chiñas (1973: 78) to suggest that its decline in the Zapotec region of Mexico would be "especially tragic for the women." Food preparation for large community celebrations throughout central and southern Mexico requires stamina and prolonged physical effort. For February 2 in Xochimilco, the day of the Niñopa, breakfast included seven large pots of *atole* that a group of women began preparing at dawn, stirring for hours after their backs hurt. Because their strategic role is carried out largely hidden from view, I came to see women in kitchenspace as the *retaguardia* (rearguard).

Despite the central role of food in family and community life, women in Xochimilco, Ocotepec, and Tetecala blushed when I asked about the importance of their role as *cocineras.* Few received compliments in the home; the value of their work became evident only if they fell ill and were unable to prepare meals. Several women told me that the only way they knew that people liked their food was when they asked for a second helping. Despite the taxing nature of kitchenwork, and the lack of recognition, most women I spoke with derived a sense of satisfaction from their contribution to the family or community. They were proud of their resourcefulness and ability to make ends meet and feed the family even in dire economic circumstances. Many were happy to bring pleasure through food to those they loved and confident that their service to community through their work in kitchenspace was important.

Women are perhaps more likely to receive recognition in community celebrations that showcase their skills, though the collective work of several women primarily brings honor to the hostess or woman in charge. Older women with recipes, cooking skills, and knowledge of traditions have a role to play here and are held in esteem by the community. Doña Teodora (Chapter Five), a great-grandmother with few responsibilities left in a household with four generations of women, was proud when her neighbors called her to prepare the rice for the fiesta. Indeed the benefits of the fiesta system seem to accrue to women with age, perhaps a factor that contributes at least in part to the shortage of young women working in the fiesta food preparations. Rarely are women recognized for their heroic feats in kitchenspace by national and international media, however, as in the case of the national and European TV crews that interviewed the women who prepared the *atole* for the Niñopa celebrations in 2001.

Independently of the cultural and social importance of food preparation in my research sites, many women are ambivalent or resentful about their role in kitchenspace. Women of younger generations often feel trapped by the roles imposed on them in the kitchen and the lack of opportunities outside the home and are eager to escape from the kitchen—and not just for the daily run to the market or the *tortillería*. Economic and social factors affect women's lack of opportunities outside the home. In Xochimilco, Ocotepec, and Tetecala salaried jobs were hard to find and decent pay practically nonexistent, but women also complained that jealous husbands, overprotective fathers, and sexual harassment kept them from working outside the home. I spoke with one woman who cleaned the house of a wealthier neighbor in order to pay for her children's school uniforms and supplies; she kept that secret from her husband, certain that he would not allow it and afraid of his temper and the beating she would receive if he found out.

Esmeralda in Tetecala dreamed of escaping the tedious work in the kitchen and the strict limits that her family imposed on her life. Indeed she went back to the state university to study law. María Soledad in Ocotepec, also in charge of cooking for her extended family, resented the hours in the kitchen—particularly difficult after a hard day's work outside the house. Some women, however, were eager to retire from work outside the home to

The *cocineras* with television crews

a full-time occupation cooking for their extended family. Señora Rosa in Xochimilco could not wait to quit her salaried job after over thirty years of working in the city so that she could take over the kitchen in her house.

Kitchenspace is not just gendered space in my research communities; it is maternal space, almost a symbolic womb. Full of the nourishing liquids such as the soups, *aguas de frutas* (fresh fruit drinks), and *atoles* that are regular fare, it is womblike in various senses. In this most intimate space of the home, even the outdoor portion is often spatially located in its center or at least surrounded by things that appear to provide a protective barrier, such as the chicken coop, wash basin, and bathrooms. Without a doubt, mothering and kitchenspace are linked in this region. Both are associated with nourishment and nurturing. Given the importance of fertility for agricultural societies, and the devoted worship of the Virgin Mary in Mexico, it should come as no surprise that the maternal figure is prominent in most Mexican kitchens.

The normative function of kitchenspace based on essentialist notions of women as nurturers became clear throughout my research. As early as 1949 Simone de Beauvoir (1973: 301) raised the issue of sex vs. gender or biology vs. social construction with her famous statement that "one is not born a woman, but, rather, becomes one." The focus of this book is on a gendered and socially constructed space for nurturing social relations. In neither household nor community space is this role necessarily linked to biological motherhood. There is no question that men in my research sites are generally denied a nurturing role in kitchenspace. But while *cocinera* connotes mother and mothering, the opposite is not necessarily true. In both fiesta and everyday kitchenspaces, only one woman is in charge. As in the case of Esmeralda and María Soledad, and indeed Señora Rosa's kitchen before her retirement, it is often not the mother but an unwed sister who is in charge of cooking for the extended family.

Many times I heard women say that the secret to making satisfying food is the love that the cook puts into her efforts. The cook must show reverence and respect for the food itself. While the idea of cooking with love is not unique to Mexico, its present form in these sites is grounded in Mesoamerican prehispanic culture. When cooking with corn and making tamales, the sacred food *par excellence*, people must be especially careful to observe certain rituals that reflect traditional beliefs. On February 2 in Xochimilco and other communities in the region the corn seeds that are to be planted before the impending rains are taken to church to be blessed, together with young children and Niño Dios figures. Many people in Ocotepec will not sell corn in the evening because it is "sleeping."[1] Women also treat tamales and mole as if they were infants in need of nurturing.

In a curious manifestation of embodiment, the idea that cooks must be happy and free of discord while preparing tamales or cooking everyday fare persists in my research communities. Women claim that their stews turn out too spicy or burn if they are in a bad mood or otherwise ill-disposed toward cooking. They tie ears made of corn husks onto the handles of the pot to protect the tamales from "hearing" arguments or being affected by any ill will, chaos, or other disruption while they cook. Women in Ocotepec go the extent of dancing around the pot if necessary to "make the tamales happy."

The precise ritual surrounding particular dishes may vary slightly from one barrio or community to the next, but all unmistakably communicate the delicate and sacred nature of the task entrusted to *las cocineras*. The same woman who begins to stack tamales in the pot or stir the mole must complete the task. In either case the pot must be blessed beforehand by making the sign of the cross over the top or for tamales (in Xochimilco, for instance) by placing chiles or nails bound together to make a cross at the bottom. The cook must stay near the pot until she is finished serving, meaning that she might work all day and into the night. Women take on the responsibility of caring for the mole at a fiesta with the same seriousness and pride with which they would raise a child—their own or somebody else's—and tremendous respect for the sacredness of food and tradition.

The parallels between the strong mother figure and the earth or *la naturaleza* (nature) are important in understanding the socially constructed and gendered role of women in the kitchen and the almost magical powers associated with this space in central Mexico. The association of women with nature in Western thought is based to a great extent on women's biological role in human reproduction. Although the *cocinera* clearly fulfills a social and not a biological function, and food preparation is irrefutably a cultural act, gender roles in my region of work make it almost impossible to disassociate the *cocina* from the maternal. In Xochimilco, the community with the greatest agricultural heritage of the three, the multiplicity of Virgin Mary and baby Jesus figures in popular celebrations is more than suggestive of the importance of fertility.

Quinceañera

The symbolic celebration of fertility in these fiestas as well as in the *fiesta de quinceaños* is linked to an agricultural tradition and a representation of nature as nurturer. The popularity of seeds as snacks or in dishes such as mole or *pipián* and (together with flowers, which are also eaten in various dishes) as decoration throughout the region alludes to their symbolic importance. At the same time, the multiple religious figures reflect the concern with twins and dualities that is central to prehispanic Mesoamerican tradition.

Pregnancy and human fertility are valued in my region, as is fertility of the soil. Childlessness elicits pity and sadness; children are often treated as sacred fruits of the earth, like the corn itself. It is no coincidence that the corn-blessing ceremony takes place on the day of the Niñopa celebration: the day of the Presentation of Jesus at the Temple and the same day that children and baby Jesus figures are taken to church for a blessing.

Narratives of the flesh and body aesthetics in my region stand in contrast to the anorexic ideal promoted by the media and the fashion industry in the United States and other developed countries. Perhaps reflecting the long history of poverty, being thin suggests hunger and misery, while being plump suggests happiness, health, and satisfaction. Doña Teodora (Chapter Five) recalled with amusement how her doctor told her to stop eating tamales when she was pregnant and to put her children on a diet because they were too fat. Her response: "No les falta nada a mis hijos. Están buenos" (My sons are not lacking anything, they are good). "Están buenos" does not mean they are "fine" (*bien*) or "good" as in "well-behaved." *Bueno* in this case means good as in good to eat, like plump little tamales. Regardless of the authority granted to the male-dominated medical establishment in other spaces, kitchenspace is not such an area. Throughout my years in Xochimilco I was struck that Señora Rosa (Chapter Five) and many of my other neighbors who had gall bladder, cholesterol, or diabetes problems refused to follow the doctor's orders when it came to eliminating mole, *carnitas,* and other spicy and greasy foods from their diet.

Traditional gender roles in Mexico provide women with a certain degree of power as long as they assume a maternal role and stay within the parameters of kitchenspace. That role is not necessarily constrained to the family kitchen, as I hope Part One has shown. Most women I asked about men's role in the kitchen seemed to consider cooking a survival skill and said that they had taught or would teach their son, in case his wife or future wife (the expectation was that he would grow up to marry and have a family) became

Twin virgins, Fiesta de la Virgen de Xaltocán on a *chinampa*

ill or died and he had to take care of his children himself. I did learn of a couple of men who were single parents and cooked for their children. Their case was always introduced to me with scorn for the women who had abandoned them, regardless of the reason for their departure. People seemed to consider a man taking responsibility for food preparation a temporary situation until he found another woman to take over. Men's paternal irresponsibility—perhaps in part sustained by the very gendered networks that give women power in the home and reduce men's role there to one of relative impotence—was a recurring theme in kitchenspace, however, and seemed to be expected if not acceptable.

Power and Gendered Territory

Feminists sometimes assume that women's liberation or empowerment depends on men sharing responsibilities in the kitchen and women leaving this space for a salary outside the home. Echoing Virginia Woolf (1989, originally published in 1929), one of my neighbors who had inherited her family's land in Xochimilco had this to say when she heard that I was studying women: "La salvación de la mujer es que perciba su propio salario" (Woman's salvation is that she earn her own salary).[2] Certainly many women today—some of them working outside the home—demand that men help out in the kitchen. It is important to acknowledge the value and extent of unpaid female labor in the home and community around the world and the common *doble* or *triple jornada* (double or triple workday).[3] It is just as important, however, to recognize that kitchenspace in central Mexico is a source of power for many women. It often provides women—especially older women—with a meaningful role in family and community life, which women with successful professional lives (and especially elderly women) elsewhere often lack (Christie 2006). In addition, kitchenspace in Xochimilco, Ocotepec, and Tetecala, as in many semirural communities in central Mexico, does not isolate women in their homes but instead connects them to vital gendered social networks and allows them to play an important role in their communities.

Women in my research communities were often extremely territorial about their kitchens and recipes, even in relation to their own daughters and granddaughters. In his classic work *Human Territoriality,* Robert Sack (1986: 19) defines territoriality as "the attempt by an individual or group to affect, influence, or control people, phenomena, and relationships by delimiting and asserting control over a geographic area." Human territoriality, he notes, is in no sense biologically rooted but is rather a strategy "entirely within the context of human motivations and goals" (1986: 21). While political geographers have generally focused on spaces outside the home in their studies of territoriality, Sack includes home and work spaces in his analysis. Curiously, he draws on the kitchen to illustrate the use of spatial strategies, though his focus is on child-rearing and not on food preparation.

Despite their complaints about younger women not knowing how to cook and men being useless around the house, older women were often in part to blame. Discussions with young women revealed their frustration at being kept out of the secrets of the kitchen until the *abuelita* of the house was ready to pass them on. Young women complained to me that even when they did help in the kitchen they did not necessarily learn the family recipes. When I introduced my research to women, they always assumed that I wanted their recipes. I assured them that I did not and stressed that I was interested in the other "ingredients" that formed part of kitchenspace and in their perspectives. In the end, many went to great lengths to provide me with evidence of their generosity and goodwill by sharing family recipes and remarking on the importance of this act. Of course I did take down recipes when they were offered, because they were valuable ethnographic data and I hoped to try them at home and because I would have appeared ungrateful had I not.

Kitchenspace is always one woman's territory, regardless of the number of women working there. From my observation over the years, it is evident that many women in Mexico find in food preparation an effective mechanism for nurturing and dominating members of their households. Weismantel (1998: 26) refers to "a specifically feminine sort of political power" within "the domain of the kitchen" where a woman "exerts control over her subordinates: mother over children, mother-in-law over daughter-in-law" and is "answerable only to her husband, who considers cooking to be outside his domain." When an older woman in my research communities takes over the kitchen either after years of working outside the home or upon replacing the previous *abuela,* she reasserts her position as head of the household in charge of the distribution of resources. Nobody questions a *mayordoma* when she tells the women helping prepare the meal for the community how they should proceed (whether to leave the chile seeds in or take them out, for instance). In a society where women's power is rooted in their role as mothers and nurturers, it should be no surprise that older women are reticent to give up their territory in the kitchen, or their sons for that matter, to a younger woman.

Never is women's territoriality in the kitchen more evident than when a younger woman shares a house with her mother-in-law. When Señora Rosa pointed out the small kitchen that her son had built for his wife in what used to be the other half of her own, she implied that it was key to keeping the peace in her home. Even with a separate kitchen or house, however, the younger woman's battle for the husband's preference in the kitchen is lost from the beginning. He will always compare her cooking to his mother's and find it inferior. Given the combination of sensual pleasure and motherly nurturing in kitchenspace, the bonds between mother and son sometimes take on an almost incestuous quality at the table.

Women's power in my region of work arises because relationships are maintained in part through feeding others. The miracle of survival that takes place on a daily basis in many central Mexican kitchens should not be underestimated. The collective preparation of food for community celebrations also strengthens women's reciprocity networks and support systems and provides women with a powerful role in maintaining community cohesion. At the same time, however, the multitiered menus (for common people on one hand and special guests on the other) reflect and reinforce the hierarchy in a traditionally stratified society.

While feminist scholars protest the lack of women's power in "public spaces" in Latin American societies, where men appear to make all the decisions, most men in Mexico will readily concede that women "run the show" in their home, despite appearances to the contrary. In my communities at least, the seat of that power is in kitchenspace, where a woman makes decisions about the household economy and determines the portions and distribution of the food she has prepared. As an extension of this role, she is responsible for maintaining the household's status in the community and supporting the community or barrio by formally participating in the fiesta system either as *mayordoma* or by accepting a *comisión* to help another woman in this role. If, as Daphne Spain (1992: 61) claims, power within kinship networks is a measure of women's status and women's ability to influence people outside the immediate family is a demonstration of participation in the public sphere, then kitchenspace in central Mexico is powerful gendered space. Clearly this is one cultural context in which the domestic/public dichotomy does not fit.[4] Unfortunately, as long as scholars look for women's participation and power in places where they are not found and ignore the less visible, accessible, or "desirable" (according to the scholars' bias) places where they are, research is more likely to reflect scholars' own ideological positions and turf battles than the reality of different women's lives and spaces (Christie 2006). This is all the more reason to heed calls for increasing "embodied diversity within feminist geography and the discipline as a whole" (Dias and Blecha 2007: 4).

Dualities

I chose to organize this book around the dual physical, temporal, and social spaces of kitchenspace, using a twofold approach to being in kitchenspace in Part One and Part Two. I associated fiestas and community life with outdoor kitchenspace and everyday life and the household unit with indoor kitchenspace. Yet there are important overlaps between the two—or rather six—spaces; an either/or approach not only simplifies but obscures their

Dualities in kitchenspace

Kitchenspace	Dualities	Overlap
Physical Space	Indoor/Outdoor	House-Lot Garden
Temporal	Everyday/Fiesta	Cosmovision based on agricultural calendar
		Festive cycle
		Stockpiling and preparing food in advance
		Offerings for the saints and the dead
		Promesas (commitments) for future celebrations
		Fertility, seeds of the future
Social Space	Household/Community Private/Public	Reciprocity networks and *comadrazgo*
		Multigenerational households
		Tías, abuelas

complexity. In contrast to the clear male/female dichotomy in the gendered space discussed above, it may be helpful to consider some aspects of kitchenspace in terms of dualities.

I have discussed how the false dichotomy between nature and culture can impede an understanding of people's experience of the natural environment in different cultural and geographical contexts. What might be considered mutually exclusive categories in one cultural experience—such as indoor and outdoor, everyday life and celebratory occasions, household and community, and even work and pleasure—are not necessarily so in others. Just as life and death are not opposites from the perspective of a Nahuatl cultural tradition but rather part of a never-ending cycle, it would be misleading to imply that the pairs of terms above are mutually exclusive. In my region of study, it is often impossible to draw a line marking where the "kitchen" ends and the "yard" begins; instead we find that kitchenspace spills over into and includes the house-lot garden. I have shown that this spatial overlap in the house-lot garden is a fertile place to explore nature/society relations. It is also in this space that kitchenspace becomes community or public space.

On the material plane, society's relationship with the natural environment is evident in the many elements from nature (and culture) found there, such as the firewood, clay pots, water, metates and *molcajetes* made of volcanic rock, and even the rocks and ornamental plants serving an aesthetic purpose. At the same time, nature/culture is also present in the cosmovision passed down from the elders to younger generations, often reflected in the rituals of everyday life and religious/agricultural fiestas and life-cycle celebrations, with food preparation playing a central role in both.

The house-lot garden is important in my sites as a source of fresh food, though perhaps more in terms of cultural values and sense of place than in terms of the material reality of physical reproduction. More often than not, the house-lot garden provided the households I visited with some fresh fruit on a seasonal basis. The exact type of fruit trees varied from place to place, with lemons and plums everywhere, peaches and figs in Xochimilco, avocados in Ocotepec, and the hotter-climate mangos, soursops, guavas, and papayas in Tetecala, and much more. Women also usually grew herbs and chiles there for cooking and medicinal use, almost always including *ruda*, which is used to cure various maladies caused by *aires* (spirits, air), such as earaches. Growing vegetables in the house-lot garden was rare in my research communities, perhaps because people often had access to other land for planting (or were accustomed to having such access even if they no longer did) and also because of the small animals that women raise there.

When there were chickens or pigs in the house-lot garden they were generally in women's care, raised for special events or to help stretch the family budget. Not every household had a pig or chicken in the house-lot garden or harvested fruit or herbs there. But enough households in each community did—or were connected with someone who did—that the taste of fresh food and a sense of immediate connection with living food were part of the collective experience.

Reuse and recycling are part of the kitchenspace landscape: tortillas carefully separated and laid out to dry are a common sight. Most of my informants did not like to eat day-old tortillas unless they appeared transformed into *chilaquiles,* enchiladas, or other such spicy dishes commonly served for breakfast, lunch, or dinner. Thus stale tortillas were often destined for small animals somewhere in the barrio if not in the house-lot garden.

` Another key duality in kitchenspace besides the physical is the temporal. In my fieldwork and previous living experience in Xochimilco I found that celebrations punctuated the yearly calendar with such frequency as to be part of the texture of daily life. The line between everyday life and fiesta is particularly blurry in Xochimilco, where there is more than one fiesta on most days and the fireworks that announce them are heard beyond the host barrio. Many celebrations are so lavish as to require extensive planning and preparation in kitchenspace, sometimes preceding the event by years. The list of future *mayordomos* for the Niñopa extends over thirty years into the future, and each *mayordomo* selects who will host the Posadas at Christmas at least a decade in advance. The list is legendary and goes to the core of interbarrio relations and competition in Xochimilco, given the prestige that the Niñopa bestows on the members of a host family and their barrio. Like the *abuela*'s mole recipe, the list of future *mayordomos* is guarded almost as zealously as the Niñopa.[5] While this is perhaps the most extreme illustration of the temporal reach of these celebrations, the pig raised in a house-lot garden to be sacrificed at the *fiesta de quinceaños* or the fiesta for the Virgen de Xaltocán several months away is not altogether different, although on a smaller scale.

Scholars of Mesoamerican cultural traditions have written extensively on the integration of ritual celebrations into everyday life in the indigenous cosmovision (Broda and Báez-Jorge 2001). In Xochimilco and Ocotepec in particular, elements of Nahuatl cosmovision seem to be very much alive and palpable in the fiestas. What scholars have usually neglected is the central role of kitchenspace and women in these ritual celebrations. Tetecala, though it has different ethnic roots and identity, is still very much an agrarian society with indigenous roots. It too has many celebrations revolving around the same agricultural cycles and fertility rituals that form the basis of collective fiestas in my other two sites.

Miguel Morayta, the historian at the Morelos School of Anthropology and History who has produced television documentaries on Ocotepec's traditional fiestas, stresses that fiestas are part of daily life, from the preparations to the reheating of leftovers the following day ("La fiesta es de lo cotidiano—desde la preparativa hasta el recalentado").[6]

Rituals surrounding death and performed with food also link the here and now to the space and time beyond and illustrate the cyclical nature of life and death. Even the rituals surrounding a person's funeral might extend years into the future: the regional version of Catholic tradition includes the obligatory nine-day celebration that is often repeated year after year in a cyclical fiesta in memory of the deceased. When I first arrived in Xochimilco looking for a place to live in 1986, I was greeted by a group of women at the end of the *callejón* who were cooking in honor of a man who had died the year before. The anniversary of his death was again celebrated during my fieldwork in 2001, as it was every year.

In Xochimilco the mourning party is traditionally invited back to share a meal of *frijoles adobados.* One informant told me that people typically respond to that invitation with the comment: "Pasó a trabajar el difuntito" (The deceased has gone on to work). The implication is that the departed soul is already working on behalf of the living, as evidenced by the generous sharing of the prescribed meal of *frijoles.*[7] The departed are also honored with their favorite foods on the Day of the Dead in early November or, at the very least, with a candle, bread or fruit, and water.

These food rituals connecting the living with the dead are changing in many households due to a variety of factors, among them the success of evangelical Protestant groups that have been gaining converts in recent years. Yet kitchenspace appears to be a site of cultural resistance. One woman described what I call the new phenomenon of "homeless dead." She explained that she had increased the portions of food on her father's altar

Ofrenda de muertos (Offering for the dead)

in order to provide for his deceased friends whose families had converted and no longer "kept the custom." Otherwise, she feared, their ghosts would be left wandering the streets.

Another woman expressed her resistance to the idea that people should no longer set out an *ofrenda* for the dead in these terms:

> *Si nos quitan nuestros muertos, si nos dicen que no pongamos nada para nuestros muertos porque los muertos no vienen, que no hay espíritus, nos dejan vacíos, nos quitan nuestra fe.* (If they take our dead away from us, if they tell us not to put anything [food] out because the dead are not coming, that there are no spirits, they leave us empty, they take away our faith.)[8]

While many people in Tetecala did not put up altars for the dead, they were never short on stories of ghosts roaming the community.

The proper execution of rituals surrounding the dead is anchored in the cultural and gendered boundaries in kitchenspace. With members of the community contributing coffee, sugar, other food, and perhaps alcohol to a wake, household members traditionally do not suffer a death in the family alone but rather spend a week of mourning sharing food and drink in the company of others. During the year when I undertook my fieldwork, a university researcher in Cuernavaca suffered a terrible tragedy: the death of her son in a car accident. It seemed to me a second tragedy that she lacked a cultural tradition of collective mourning to support her in the initial stages of mourning—like the one I had shared several times when I lived in Xochimilco.

Just as celebrating life-cycle passages including marriage and baptism is a top priority for even the poorest families in my region of work, many consider the appropriate celebration of the dead essential. One elderly woman in Tetecala said she had no problem with people in her community becoming Protestant except for the change in burial customs. She was still sad that without the church bells to announce the death of a woman who had always generously provided her with beans and canned food in times of need she had missed the funeral and the opportunity (and obligation) to help send the woman off properly to the other world. Another woman who told me that she was too poor to participate in fiestas nonetheless found it indispensable to have a collection of cups with which to offer coffee at a wake.

If the distinction between yesterday and tomorrow, everyday and fiesta, or indoor and outdoor is not absolute, neither is the distinction between family and community. In each of my sites, it was not uncommon for people to raise children who were not biologically theirs or even related by blood but whose parents had died, were ill, or had emigrated to the United States.

In all three of my communities, the bonds established through this process of *compadrazgo* and *comadrazgo* are sometimes greater than the bonds with blood relatives and are key to the social dynamics. In his article on the home, David Stea (1995: 187) points out that "family" has a very different meaning in Mexico than in the United States.

> The *familia* is extended beyond grandparents, uncles, aunts, and cousins in many parts of Latin America, through first, the system of *compadrazgo*, the incorporation into the *familia* of another set of godparents at each of many ceremonies, and second, the incorporation of *cuates* (literally twins), or best friends. The resulting enormous conglomerate is an "insurance umbrella" encompassing nearly everything of importance to traditional rural Mexicans: members of such extended families live close-by and often constitute entire neighborhoods. But the importance of the *familia* to *urban* Mexicans is not markedly less.

The respect for the elderly that is part of the regional culture also results in a broad web of relations. People in Xochimilco addressed all elderly women as *abuelitas* out of respect. *Tías* (aunts) and *abuelas* (grandmothers) were part of a family's extended social network but not always part of the biological family. Women who came together to prepare food for a celebration were sometimes generically referred to as *las tías* in Xochimilco and Ocotepec. Notwithstanding the loss of many community members to outmigration, people in my communities were often surrounded by family and usually had plenty of blood cousins, uncles and aunts, and grandparents in their barrio or community, if not in the immediate household. All these factors provide individuals with multiple networks in the community and beyond through their various family and kin members or representatives.

Women's gendered activity in weaving barrios and communities together through fiesta food preparation indisputably takes kitchenspace beyond the private space of the home. It is not correct to characterize the collective space created simply as public space, however, given its sacred and ritualistic nature and restriction of those who are welcome to participate: only people who are considered part of the hosts' extensive reciprocity network. At the root of these collective celebrations is the sense of a shared identity (including religious identity) and the idea that the group must act in unity to meet future challenges. Key to survival—which historically required a successful harvest—are links to the other world that are maintained through sacred food preparation rituals.

Meals for fiestas celebrating the town or barrio's patron saint, like the food offerings placed on the altars of the dead in November, are intended to solicit divine intervention on behalf of the living. The realizations of *promesas*, like the meal that Doña Andrea prepares for the Virgen de Coatetelco year after year and the rosaries for the Niñopa that conclude with a communion of food and drink every evening, represent the embodied performance of faith. Thus gendered activity in kitchenspace extends a group's reciprocity network to the divine realm, officially represented by a Catholic holy figure whose treatment like a living being or twin presence is more characteristic of Mesoamerican cosmovision than of the Catholic church. Significantly, the kitchenspaces supporting the celebrations are not located in the public square or church courtyard but in the gendered space of the house-lot garden in women's territory.

Kitchenspace: Tradition and Modernity

When I asked María Teresa to draw her kitchen, she brought the dual nature of kitchenspace to my attention. "Which kitchen, the indoor or the outdoor kitchen? The everyday or the fiesta kitchen?" she asked. As discussed above, the two usually coexisted; despite some overlap, each was associated with different social functions. In her drawing she labeled one a "modern, normal kitchen" and one a "smoke kitchen." Other women used similar terms to describe their kitchenspaces, always including either the word "modern" or "traditional" for one of the two parts of this dual space and a word connoting its opposite for the other. It appeared that people saw a dichotomy between the traditional and the modern in kitchenspace; the distance between the two was established through food preparation and preferences. Furthermore, this ideological divide was clearly associated with rural (traditional) vs. urban (modern) elements.

Traditional/rural elements were associated to a lesser extent with indigenous traditions, though none of the women I interviewed considered themselves indigenous (even when their parents or grandparents spoke Nahuatl). Elders in such cases were sometimes referred to as *los de antes* (the ones from before) in apparent contrast to the current, more modern people and reflecting a linear concept of inevitable progression toward the modern. In regard to the fiesta cycle, residents of Ocotepec and Xochimilco proudly referred to *nuestras tradiciones* (our traditions), while several people from Tetecala pointed me to the nearby town of Coatetelco for what they considered traditional fiestas very far from their own customs. Because religious fiestas were considered celebrations of Catholic saints and holy figures, people never referred to them as indigenous and indeed explicitly distanced themselves from what might be considered pagan elements, stressing their belief in one god or the Virgin Mary.

The word *moderno* was frequently used by people in my sites, sometimes pejoratively (as when referring to women's haircuts or loss of traditional values such as respect for elders) and sometimes in the positive sense (as when referring to an easier life and more stable income). This positive sense often implied depending on a salary and not on an uncertain harvest, though the ongoing economic crisis and all too frequent devaluations of the peso seemed to negate the potential advantages of an increasing insertion into the capitalist system. The use of the words *moderno* and *tradicional* in

María Teresa's drawing provides a clue to the contradictory and complex nature of kitchenspace.[9] It is no secret that Mexico's attempts to modernize its economy in the last few decades have not improved the standard of living for the majority of the population. They have been accompanied by a destruction of traditional livelihoods throughout the country, with campesinos in particular bearing the brunt of the costs. The ambivalence surrounding increasing opportunities amid increasing inequalities is palpable among ordinary people in kitchenspace.

Food preparation for fiestas usually took place in the *cocina de humo* (smoke kitchen), also called the *cocina de fiesta,* which was always separate from the main structure and often fully out of doors. It might have four walls, a roof for shade, or no permanent protection from the weather at all. With few exceptions, houses had both outdoor and indoor kitchenspaces. The majority of women with kitchens that were at least partially indoors still carried out part of their everyday food preparation activities outdoors, particularly those involving water or fire. Many women used the hearth in the house-lot garden to make tortillas on a periodic—if not daily—basis and for steaming tamales or *mixiotes* for special occasions. The gas stove was often (though not always) indoors, and the firewood stove was often (though not always) outdoors. The majority of homes also had a portable outdoor stove called an *anafre* or *bracero,* usually fueled with charcoal or attached to a small tank of gas. The *anafre* might take the place of the traditional smoke kitchen in some homes, though more often it complemented it. It also allowed women to cook or reheat food for sale at the market or on the street.

A traditional hearth was present in most of the households I visited and is clearly a carrier of cultural tradition in my sites. It is so central that it practically defines and constitutes kitchenspace, or at least traditional kitchenspace. All of my informants used the Nahuatl word *tlicuil* or *clecuil* to refer to their firewood hearth. When I asked what the word meant, they would inevitably refer to *las tres piedras* (the three stones) where the *abuelitos* cooked their meals. Esmeralda's family constructed what she referred to jokingly as a *tlicuil moderno* (modern *tlicuil*—a seeming contradiction in terms), a triple and permanent hearth made of cement where members of her family boiled large quantities of corn for their mill.

The *tlicuil* is a permanent fixture in kitchenspace. I found that women make use of different materials, including cinderblocks and tractor tires (as in the case of the squatter in Tetecala in "A Taste of Three Places"), to construct it when necessary and use firewood, charcoal, scrap wood, or even old furniture as fuel. The hearth's use has remained practically the same—primarily grilling and steaming corn-based traditional foods—and it has kept its Nahuatl name, despite the multiple adaptations and variety of cooking contraptions that I came across in my informants' house-lot gardens. The stove, modern or traditional, seems to mark the social center or "heart" of the home and the fiesta in my communities.

Another traditional item present in most of the kitchens I visited is the ancient metate or three-legged grinding stone made of volcanic rock. The metate is used to grind things such as corn, beans, cocoa, and pumpkin seeds. Laden with symbolic meaning and long a pillar of Mesoamerican culture, like the *tlicuil,* it continues to have center stage in many kitchens. Handed down in the family from one woman to another, the metate, like the mole recipe, is treated like a family heirloom and is the subject of extensive folklore. More than one informant told me a story of her mother accepting marriage on the condition that her husband carry the heavy metate to her new residence, even if it was several days away on foot.

The metate's use has shifted in the last century, with increasing access to labor-saving technology. Women's labor in transforming seeds into ritual foods such as mole or *nixtamal* into tortillas was once an indispensable contribution to family survival and community celebrations throughout Mexico. It still is in many isolated rural communities, including parts of each of my sites. With electric mills a stone's throw away from the majority of the houses in the communities where I worked, most women were happy to leave the hard work of the metate in the past and either took their *nixtamal* to grind at the nearby *molino* or purchased hot tortillas every day at the *tortillería.* Several women with whom I spoke still used the metate to grind cooked beans for *tamales de frijol* or cocoa for *atole champurrado.* Even women who did not use their metates expressed a strong emotional attachment; they associated the metate with their mothers and grandmothers and often refused to let their married sons or daughters take it out of their house.

I was struck by the common use of the metate by women who made fresh tortillas but did not grind their corn by hand. Their assertion that it was the best place to lean on to knead the corn dough seems to be extremely symbolic, an affirmation of the ongoing cultural importance of food preparation traditions, particularly those associated with corn. Upper-class homes in Coyoacán in Mexico City often had a metate with a little clay Indian woman sitting on top, a further clue as to its symbolic significance and association with tradition or *lo mexicano*. In addition to the traditional metate and *molcajete* (also made of volcanic rock and with three "feet" though rounder in shape and used primarily for salsas), every indoor kitchen with electricity that I saw had a blender that was used almost daily.[10]

In addition to the many traditional elements and materials in kitchenspace, many "modern" and reused containers and materials (such as scrap metal for a *comal*) are utilized for storage and cooking. *Barbacoa*, a common food for celebrations where a large number of people will be eating, is almost always made in huge used oil drums rather than buried in the ground according to ancient custom. Beef is the most common meat used today. While cattle were introduced to the Americas by the Spaniards, the traditional maguey plant is still used to wrap the chile-soaked beef. The same drums—or others made of plastic—are also used to store water. Plastic bags are regularly used to cover rice cooking in clay pots. I did not find a single house-lot garden without recycled kitchen containers such as cans or pots holding decorative plants; together with the caged bird, *plantas de adorno* (ornamental plants) are part of women's aesthetic experience and the material culture of kitchenspace.

Despite the whole gamut of easily accessible and inexpensive modern materials used in cooking, traditional pots and cooking techniques based on grinding and steaming have remained at the center, particularly when preparing large quantities for a celebration. A notable exception is the large aluminum pot with a rack in the bottom used to steam tamales, which is inexpensive and more readily accessible than the traditional clay pot with a smaller top that was used previously. Older women complained, however, that the newer aluminum pots on the market were of lower quality than the first ones they had bought several decades ago.

Many dishes considered traditional in Mexico have not lost their status or appeal in modern times, while others representing success and European or U.S. tastes have become popular among groups that did not consume them before (see Weismantel 1998 for an extensive discussion of a similar situation in the Andean region). While it is nowhere near as popular or inexpensive as traditional Mexican treats, fast food representing the United States is sometimes consumed as something novel or exotic.[11] With many families suffering a continued loss in their standard of living, corn and beans remain standbys despite the higher social status of rice and meat. Increasingly, the trend in my communities is for women to serve *carnitas* instead of mole or even pork in green salsa in order to stretch the budget further in large celebrations.

Kitchenspace generally reveals people's economic situation. People sometimes eat and drink one thing at home, however, but eat or drink something considered higher in status in public. With professionals replacing campesinos, pulque is losing ground to Brandy Presidente or other bottled alcoholic beverages in Xochimilco and Ocotepec. In Tetecala, known historically for its distillery, cane alcohol has long been the tradition. It became less popular after a number of people died about five years ago in a tragic and notorious case of alcohol poisoning. They all drank liquor from the same local distillery (now closed), which had used the wrong type of alcohol. Many of the victims were men who drank together at a friend's wake. Esmeralda's father was there with them but was spared because, as a Jehovah's Witness, he did not drink. Some people say the dead man wanted to take his friends with him to the other world.

I frequently heard affirmations revealing people's strong and emotional identification with their community based on what they considered to be local culinary traditions or *comida típica* (typical food). When I asked about food customs, people would enthusiastically respond: "Aquí es el mole" (Here it is mole) or "Lo nuestro es el mole" (What's ours is mole) or "Aquí puros frijolitos" (Here only beans) or "Lo típico son los tlapiques" (Fish tamales are typical here). Tortillas are so integral to the culture in my region that they were almost never mentioned, though they accompanied or were the basis of every meal.

In fact, what is considered traditional food in Mexico today is based on a combination of native ingredients such as corn, cacao, chiles, and beans and products from around the world, including the cheese, onions, and pork products that arrived with the Spanish conquest (Butzer 1995). Nothing represents the fusion of two agricultural and culinary traditions better than the popular breakfast, a *torta de tamal* (corn *tamal* in a wheat roll). Traditional fiestas are as much a product of *mestizaje*—a mixture of Spanish and Indian elements—as is the rich mole sauce that many consider the quintessential Mexican dish. Mole ingredients only came together as a result of the Columbian Exchange. Its chiles, chocolate, and tomato are of

Mexican origin. The almonds, raisins, and garlic were brought by the Span-iards but are Arabic in origin, and the spices (pepper, cinnamon, and cloves) are from the Orient (Benítez 2004: 85).

It appears that the same ongoing and painful social transitions and eco-nomic crises that rob campesinos of their way of life without offering an alternative and dignified means of survival are expressed in the emotion-ally charged ambivalence toward the flavors of *el campo* (the countryside).[12] Mole and beans, though both mentioned as examples of local traditions, are a world apart. The first is a symbol of luxury and increasingly priced out of reach of community celebrations (though still important in weddings and served to special guests). Beans, in contrast, are the old standby—as reflect-ed in the common phrase "frijoles aunque sea" (beans at least), used when people wanted to express that they were not going to go hungry though their food was scarce. Beans have been a staple in Mexico for thousands of years and are increasingly rejected by younger generations (who prefer red meat), to the horror of their elders, who see this as a sign of disrespect for food and life.

Kitchenspace appears to provide a refuge for culture, allowing the re-production and reinvention of "lo nuestro" (what's ours) or core elements of collective identity. Mexico's complex and incomplete process of *mestizaje*, with its confusion, pain, and racism, plays out in people's relationship with food. The shortage of Spanish women in New Spain in the sixteenth cen-tury assured that indigenous women were the ones who raised new genera-tions of Mexican mestizo children in their kitchens, training their tastes in the process. Ironically, indigenous women and women from Mexico's rural areas working as domestic servants have continued to raise and feed the children of the lighter-skinned Mexican middle and upper classes to this day, facilitating an ongoing connection with "typical" Mexican food that is associated at the same time with the tenderness of childhood and with the lower classes, campesinos, and indigenous groups.

Despite its cultural significance, the house-lot garden is losing ground to overcrowding, construction, and changing values and lifestyles in semi-urban communities near Mexico City, such as Xochimilco and Ocotepec. Even in Tetecala, new neighbors from the city (or, as one of my informants said, the "modern" children of the old neighbors) complained about the smell of pigs. As I completed my fieldwork, Esmeralda's family faced a legal battle with neighbors who were attempting to introduce a city ordinance on this issue. The ordinance did not pass, but it illustrates the tension between urban and rural lifestyles that exists in all three of my sites. Curiously, these same people for whom animals in the house-lot garden are intolerable swell the ranks of the community feasts. Even as the physical space that forms the basis of these celebrations shrinks, the social space and nostalgia for what has been lost seem to grow. At the same time, the steady income that comes from salaried jobs linked to the city, industry, or seasonal migration has facilitated the celebration of an agricultural life that is slipping away.

Gendered Knowledge: Cultural Resistance, Adaptation, and Innovation

In her brilliant defense of women's right to education, Mexico's seventeenth-century genius Sor Juana Inés de la Cruz wrote—tongue in cheek—about the difficulty she had in obeying orders from her superiors and abstaining from intellectual activities, given her work in the convent kitchen. "¿Qué podemos saber las mujeres sino filosofías de la cocina?" (What can we women know besides kitchen philosophies?) (de la Cruz 1989 [1695]: 838). Mentioning several of the "natural secrets [she] discovered while cooking" (de la Cruz 1989 [1695]: 838), she describes several chemical interactions on the stove. If Aristotle had cooked, she asserts, he would have written much more than he did.

Kitchenspace is at once a cultural archive and a laboratory. It is a place where women nurture and educate children, transmitting recipes, organizational forms, food preferences, and a particular vision of life from one generation to the next. *La cocinera* must know how to obtain what she needs in the kitchen, how to adapt a recipe when the ingredients of choice (or even the ideal amount of time) are not available, and how to combine things to achieve the desired product and flavor. In a place with elaborate culinary traditions such as Mexico, she must also know when it is culturally appropriate to offer certain dishes and what she should or should not serve with them. This knowledge is handed down from one woman to another, though each must use her own intelligence and creativity to adapt to constantly changing circumstances.

Food preparation in central Mexico requires the cook to perform a balancing act between tradition and innovation. Women's adaptive strategies are essential in kitchenspace, where *la cocinera* is always adjusting her menus and recipes based on availability of ingredients, cookware, and fuel, not to mention changes in her own life cycle and schedule and in the demands of people around her. Despite these changes and others in food-gathering and preparation spaces, a certain cultural resistance imposes limits in terms of taste and food rituals, whether for everyday meals or for fiestas (Christie 2002). In Xochimilco and Ocotepec, despite changing ingredients, bean tamales are still made with a "belly button." As in Tetecala and many other communities in central Mexico, baking powder has replaced other additives as a rising agent and lard is used to make the tamales "suavecitos y sabrosos" (soft and tasty). Yet tamales are undoubtedly still essential for ritual celebrations.

Esmeralda included ingenuity as a key characteristic of a *cocinera*, together with patience and curiosity. She must draw upon these qualities to substitute for missing ingredients. "Si no tienes lo necesario, tienes que ingeniártelas para reemplazarlo con algo que le de el mismo sabor" (If you do not have what you need, you have to use your ingenuity to replace some of the ingredients with something that will give it the same flavor). It is significant that the objective is not to innovate but to achieve the same flavor—or as close to it as possible. Innovation and creativity are valued in the context of achieving traditional products and celebrating traditional fiestas in ever-changing circumstances, not in the creation of new flavors or hybrid dishes.

From the vantage point of a *cocinera* who sells delicious chiles rellenos and other typical foods in the market, Esmeralda says: "¡Acá los mexicanos somos muy exigentes en el sabor! ¡En otras partes con que sea nutritivo, aquí que sea sabroso!" (We Mexicans are very demanding with our tastes! In other parts, as long as it is nutritious; here it has to taste good!).

It is impossible to deny the weight of custom and social pressure in the kitchen sometimes exercised by individuals with relative power vis-à-vis the woman cooking, such as her husband, father, *abuela,* or mother-in-law. But to conclude that the *cocinera* has no power is to ignore the dialectic that exists between supply and demand and women's protagonism in the ongoing process of negotiation, adaptation, and innovation in kitchenspace. In effect, it too "erases history" (Sundberg 1999).

Food traditions are not the product of cultural inertia. Traditional cuisine in Xochimilco, Ocotepec, and Tetecala exists thanks to the women who—with able hands, ingenuity, and work—have reinvented it time and time again despite ongoing challenges and while respecting cultural boundaries. If many families in these towns and communities maintain food traditions in spite of ongoing changes in the social and natural environment, it is because the subjects responsible for their reproduction have been able to adapt, keeping the indispensable aspects while changing the nonessential.[13]

Kitchenspace in Xochimilco, Ocotepec, and Tetecala is a site of cultural resistance because it is where the special dishes for fiestas and the traditional elements of everyday food are prepared, both of which nurture cultural identity. The house-lot garden where the fiesta kitchen is usually located is a space for the reproduction of traditional forms of gendered forms of organization and reciprocity networks.

My use of the word "resistance" differs from that of J. C. Scott (1985, 1990) when he speaks of the opposition, at times subtle, of weak individuals against dominant ones. Yet, like Scott, I am referring to a resistance that forms part of everyday life and is expressed by individuals in spaces that are little visible or recognized. Cultural resistance is not the act of one individual against another and does not require a political conscience or motivation. To the contrary, culture in the experience and spaces of everyday living forms a part of collective identity and behavior to such an extent that it is invisible to those inside the group—unless it becomes notably threatened by outside forces. In such a case, as when my informants complained about the opposition of evangelical sects to their food preparation customs and their fiestas, we can speak of a conscious resistance against something or someone in particular.

Sherry Ortner (1995) argues that many well-known studies on the subject of resistance are limited by their lack of ethnographic perspective. Resistance, she says, is much more than opposition or reaction to domination and can be creative and transforming. In my region, kitchenspace is a site of cultural resistance not because it is a museum where we can observe the past in relic form but rather because we can find in it a certain continuity with the past that reflects a group's relationship with the larger society and environment, even when economic and ideological structures have transformed the spaces of everyday life. This cultural resistance resonates with Catharine Good Eshelman's approach (2001b), even though my research sites differ greatly from hers. Working with an indigenous community in Guerrero, she sees in their use of ritual food the Nahuatl tenacity to maintain their own life project in the face of opposition from modernity and a globalizing, industrial economy.

On one hand, the folk Catholic tradition of fiestas provides Xochimilco and Ocotepec with a mechanism to forge strategic alliances with wealthier city residents. On the other hand, the agriculture and rural attitudes that they still retain are strengthened by the rural migrants that overflow into their communities after migrating to the capital in search of work. It remains to be seen what impact the privatization of land and loss of traditional land tenure will have in Mexico's more "traditional" communities, given the basis of cooperative social relations for religious fiestas and *compadrazgo* (Ingham 1986: 47) and the function that fiestas play in "reaffirm[ing] rights in communal lands and neighborhood structures" (Beezley et al. 1994: xx). What is certain is that women will continue to carry inordinate responsibility from kitchenspace for these and other celebrations with food at their center.

Living Culture

In his prologue to the *Nahua Cookbook of Morelos*, José Antonio MacGregor discusses the contradictory nature and importance of food and eating, going so far as to call eating "one of the most significant and transcendental practices" (Hernández Cortés 1999: 11). It is, he says, at once "a basic need for the survival of man" and "at the center of all cultural life."

"Food is history, class struggle, globalization, and daily interaction between tradition and modernity synthesized in a *tamal de ayocote* and a MacDonald's [*sic*] hamburger. Unclear and contradictory interaction: *tlacoyos* alongside a Coca-Cola, and *mixiotes* accompanied with Sabritas [chips]" (Hernández Cortés 1999: 12).

Addressing the "important archive of human knowledge" that "finds its center in how man eats" and in obvious reference to agriculture, MacGregor looks at "how society relates to nature through the definition of ecosystems that have different meaning and management for each people in terms of the climate and what the environment has to offer, making use of scientific and technical knowledge forged patiently over a long period of time." Eating, he says, "generates significant symbols that give cohesion and a sense of belonging, which permits the construction of identities and 'nurtures the spirit' of man" (Hernández Cortés 1999: 11–12).

It is truly amazing that scholars—feminists among them—can continue to exclude women's contributions to "the archives of knowledge." Many respected books presenting recipes and other cultural aspects of *la cocina mexicana* rarely mention the gendered nature of food preparation spaces or the women who accumulate and transmit cultural and technical knowledge from generation to generation. Except for the occasional figure of a topless Indian woman grinding corn on her metate, references to women or their kitchens are generally sparse in Mexican cookbooks and studies of Mexican food.

Upon the recommendation of several scholars in Mexico, I looked up the original version of a Mexican classic. The *Recetario del maíz,* a collection of recipes based on corn, had just been published in its newest version (Echeverría and Arroyo 2000) as part of the Cocina Indígena y Popular series of the National Council of Culture and Arts. The original 1982 version, published as part of the inauguration of the National Museum of Popular Cultures in Coyoacán with the name *El recetario de maíz,* is known to many as Guillermo Bonfil Batalla's book on corn (1982). The newer version appears to be faithful to the first in all but a few details. One in particular caught my eye: the new edition fails to recognize the 17 men and 101 women who contributed recipes to the original recipe book.

Sobremesa (After Dinner): Final Reflections

Most of us who write articles, books, or dissertations depend on our rational, analytical mode of interaction with our environment for our professional and economic survival. We tend to disregard the importance of bodies and emotions or processes that are not easily measured, counted, or expressed in writing. From many perspectives, it may seem perfectly acceptable to explore the world from behind a desk and rather unusual to do so in a kitchen. These limitations can prevent us from even trying to understand the different ways in which ordinary people in many parts of the world experience their relationship with nature.

If you are a woman in a semiurban community in central Mexico, chances are that you spend a good part of the day gathering and preparing food. You probably grow some edible plants or raise a few animals in your house-lot garden, if only a few herbs for daily meals or common ailments, and a pig or two for an upcoming celebration. You may be acutely aware of what campesinos and campesinas produce in your region and how this is affected by changes in the water or in government policy. You are increasingly familiar with markets in faraway places and how these affect local producers and consumers. What you do not know from seeing, smelling, tasting, and poking your fingers into the fresh products at the market, you learn from talking to the vendors from your own and neighboring communities. You use your senses and your hands both to select ingredients and to transform them into dishes that your family and community find acceptable. This is increasingly difficult with the changes in nature and society affecting you as well as the materials that you have to work with.

Everyone counts on you to make things right in the kitchen, no matter how things are outside or how you feel inside. You find ways to feed the family when things are scarce, perhaps relying on the *gorditas* of corn, lard, and salt that you ate as a child and the seasonally available fruits and vegetables that assure a variety of fresh flavors. Beyond feeding the family, you must provide some sense of continuity with local food traditions even when the environment no longer produces what it once did or "el gasto ya no alcanza" (the budget does not reach anymore). The feasts you work to prepare with other women are often fertility rituals of sorts, marking passages in the agricultural calendar or (as in the *fiestas de quinceaños*) in women's lives.

Your challenge is to keep people satisfied even when the corn is no longer the same—some say it is animal feed trucked in from the United States. Things must taste right even though, more and more, you use gas instead of firewood and enamel-coated pots instead of clay and you feel that you have increasing responsibilities and less time to spend preparing meals. While you know that food cooked in clay tastes better, things cook so much faster in the new pots—and they do not break as easily. When a pot wears out and the man who comes by every month or so cannot patch it anymore, you recycle it in your garden and use it to hold a plant that makes you happy with its presence.

Among the key ingredients in the kitchen are your own intuition, creativity, patience, sense of balance, good humor, and love. Everybody says that it is important to be happy in the kitchen—regardless of whether or not you want to be there—because a cook must prepare her food with love for it to taste good and to nourish and satisfy the people who eat at her table.

Kitchen spillover space: gendered aesthetics in the house-lot garden

Some days it seems that everything is different than when your mother, your grandmother, or your grandfather raised you and taught you how to prepare food. Some days you swear things have not changed at all: people still eat "su sopita, su guisado, sus frijoles. Sus taquitos pues" (their soup, their stew, their beans. Their tacos). And you are still cooking every day.

Notes

Introduction

1. "Physically, a household in Zumbagua consists of a series of one-room buildings around a patio. These rooms always include a kitchen and a storage room, but additional dormitories may be added at need. The word 'kitchen' in itself implies much more than a room in which food is prepared. It is there that meals are made and eaten, male and female heads of household sleep and live, baths are taken, decisions made, wakes held, babies born, and the sick nursed back to health" (Weismantel 1998: 169).

2. The principal and most common day to celebrate the dead is November 2, Día de los Muertos. The Aztec calendar, however, celebrates an entire week, as explained later in the text. That period of multiple celebrations is referred to as Días de los Muertos or simply Muertos.

3. Some, but not all, of the *chinampas* are part of the *ejido*, because there are more *chinampas* than were permitted to be distributed through this system. Thus many people own a *chinampa* that has been in their family for generations (prior to the redistribution of land under the *ejido* system after the Mexican Revolution). *Chinampas* may be sold, rented, or loaned through personal arrangements (Canabal Cristiani et al. 1992). Some people do not cultivate their *chinampa,* while others cultivate several, which they may be renting or borrowing from others.

4. Even through intermarriage, people are not easily accepted; their status is made clear in traditional community spaces where issues affecting the community are discussed and decisions are made.

5. I found several different pronunciations of the name. Miguel Morayta Mendoza (2000) refers to it as Tlanihuili.

6. A *quinceañera* marks a girl's transition into womanhood and coming out in society. It is a very formal, codified event (including music and dance) where the girl wears a special dress, often resembling a wedding gown.

7. This is one of many important issues that surface in kitchenspace that I do not pursue and is a potentially rich area for future research.

8. Surprisingly, Chiñas does not address the role of the increasing numbers of Jehovah's Witnesses in discrediting the fiesta system, though she does discuss increasing converts to evangelical Protestantism elsewhere in the book.

9. Interview with Guillermo Helbling, March 8, 2001.

10. *Journal of Latin American Geography:* http://www.utexas.edu/utpress
/journals/jlag.html; the *Geographical Review:* http://amergeog.org/gr/grhome.html;
Gender, Place and Culture: http://www.tandf.co.uk/journals.

Points of Departure

1. A solid literature on difference by feminist geographers focuses on gendered
landscapes and women's narratives about the landscape (Kolodny 1975, 1984; Monk
1984, 1992; Norwood and Monk 1987).

2. Much of this section appears in my article "Kitchenspace: Gendered Territory in Central Mexico—Savouring the Kitchen," Special Issue on Kitchens (Part 2):
Gender, Place and Culture 13(6) (2006). See the journal's website: http://www.tandf
.co.uk/journals.

3. The garden section of my literature review in this section is taken from my
article in the *Geographical Review* (Christie 2004). See that article for further discussion of the house-lot garden.

4. I found both in this preliminary research and in my principal fieldwork later
that relationship was key to being able to talk to women about the household; hence
I selected research subjects whenever possible based on a prior relationship or at
least introductions by someone with a prior relationship.

Part One

1. Speaking an indigenous tongue at home is underreported throughout Latin
America, a product of the ostracism and racism that plague indigenous peoples.

Chapter One

1. The fiesta of Xaltocán may begin in February or in March, depending on the
liturgical calendar. Each of the barrios in Xochimilco takes a turn bringing the
fiesta—music, fireworks, food, Mass—to the Virgin. During June, July, and August
the Virgin is paraded through the streets of each barrio.

2. Huitzilopochtli is the Aztec god of war, protector of the mother.

3. Xochimilcas refer to the figures in this way, using the word *imagen.* Despite
the emotion and celebration that I observed, several times people pointed out to me
that it was clear to everyone that the figures were only representations of Jesus or
Mary. I believe that this reflected the renewed efforts of the Catholic church to curb
the veneration of relics, which are often the source of criticism by the increasingly
present Protestant churches.

4. Comisión de Rescate Histórico y Cultural Ex-Convento San Juan Bautista,
A.C.

5. This was reported to me by the *sacristán* in an interview at his home on November 26, 2000.

6. For instance, in 2000 a group of young men had their own Christ figure made in honor of one of their fathers who passed away and began their own tradition of carrying him on their backs to Chalma, a favorite pilgrimage site. As fiestas continue to grow and the barrios become more populated, a fragmentation of festivities surrounding some images occasionally occurs, resulting in separate celebrations requiring a special Mass and blessing.

7. Literally, "Bengal lights" (a reference to the origination of gunpowder in Asia).

8. The *estudiantina* is a Spanish tradition involving students with stringed instruments playing in the streets that has been adapted in Mexico.

9. Older women are often called *abuelita* by younger people in Xochimilco out of respect. In the same way, the term *tía* (aunt) is used to address women who are younger or the same age, out of respect. Both terms refer to a kinship network that is based on reciprocity and respect to a great extent, rather than on blood.

10. Hibiscus tea is not uncommon in the United States. "Water" made from hibiscus—whether or not it involves boiling water—is not considered a tea in central Mexico but one of many naturally flavored waters, like *agua de limón* (lemonade).

11. Several different family members told me about when the host couple signed up for the commitment to host the Niñopa. In addition, their names are on the list of future hosts included as an appendix of a master's thesis focusing on the Niñopa (Orta Hernández 1991).

12. Doña Teodora has only fond memories of her husband: she says that he was not her husband but her treasure. See her story in "Kitchenspace Narratives."

13. While the woman who helped me was born in the neighborhood and told me she was from the barrio, I guessed from her dress and behavior that she was not. Others later referred to her as the daughter of some people who had moved into the barrio, stressing that she was not Xochimilca. People from the barrio are generally proud of their origins and take care to distance themselves both from the poor migrants from other parts of the country who find agricultural work on the *chinampas* and from the refugees from Mexico City who move in to escape the pace, price, and pollution of the city to some extent. This attitude exists even as people intermarry with outsiders, who suffer for it and are always aware that they are "not from here" even if they were only born a few blocks away.

14. Xochimilcas so clearly constitute an ethnic group that I was often able to identify a person from Xochimilco in the middle of Mexico City. In general, however, they use the term *indio* in a pejorative sense, as many people do in Mexico when they feel that their status is above that of indigenous people, for whatever reason.

15. Xochimilco is a favorite for tourists not only from Mexico City but from the whole country. The principal activity is a ride in one of the traditional *trajineras*

decorated with flowers (now made of plastic) that take tourists along the canals. The tourists generally travel on different canals than do Xochimilcas who are involved in *chinampa* agriculture use. During their ride, which generally lasts for several hours, the passengers are greeted by mariachis, food vendors, and others who approach the *trajinera* on a similar vessel. The *guías* earn a commission for bringing tourists to the *trajineras* and generally work with specific boat owners with whom they have made previous arrangements.

16. "Over 400 annual festivities are celebrated in this entity, with respect and veneration resulting due to diverse Cultural, Religious, and Political reasons," reads the government flyer (Delegación Xochimilco 2000).

Chapter Two

1. *Pancita* is tripe prepared in a soup. It is a much less expensive meal than mole.

2. *Mexicano* (Mexican) is used to refer to the native Nahuatl tongue. Older people call Spanish *castilla*, for *castellano*.

3. The pig weighed over 250 pounds. While Rosalinda did not raise it, she purchased it from somebody in the neighborhood who did.

4. While buying tortillas at a commercial tortilla factory or *tortillería* may be acceptable for a fiesta in Ocotepec, reheating them is not. Thus, while tortillas are often purchased for the midday meal, handmade tortillas are often still made for dinner.

5. Personal interview at Dr. Cordero Espinosa's home on November 26, 2000.

6. This refers to the road that cuts through the town.

7. The water in which the *nixtamal* is cooked is used for sweeping the house-lot garden as well. While it is said to work miracles in keeping the dust down because of the lime, the practice is clearly rooted in ritual.

Chapter Three

1. See John Ingham's *Mary, Michael, and Lucifer: Folk Catholicism in Central Mexico* (1986) for extensive discussion of the role of clearly inappropriate behavior in such parades in reinforcing appropriate behavior and of elements such as these devils that form part of the fiesta tradition in many other towns in central Mexico.

2. I had originally planned to include Hueyapan (see Judith Friedlander's classic study on ethnic identity, *Being Indian in Hueyapan* [1975]) as one of the sites in my research because of its traditional culture and location near the smoking Popocateptl volcano. The violence from drug-trafficking that plagued the community quickly made me change my mind.

Chapter Four

1. Esmeralda makes tortillas from scratch every day. She uses a tortilla press rather than her hands to shape the tortillas, so they are not considered *de mano* (handmade). Most young women living in the urban part of Tetecala buy hot tortillas at the *tortillería* every day.

2. It seemed to be the case in each home I visited that one woman from each generation received most of the kitchen knowledge, whether at the side of her mother, her grandmother, or another woman.

3. Sometimes in the past Esmeralda's sister who lives across the street or an aunt who comes in to help with the dishes would cook for the family. Esmeralda does most of the everyday cooking now, in part because her cooking is so good and in such demand by her brothers.

4. Nearly all of the women I interviewed said that they gauged people's appreciation of their work in the kitchen by how much they ate or if they had seconds, rather than by any overt recognition.

5. Esmeralda's family members buy big bucketfuls of mole paste from Guerrero to use as a base for mole, though they add fresh ingredients, including both the basics (listed above) and fruit (a typical ingredient in Tetecala), in this case plantain and apple.

6. Women in all of my communities recalled with great sadness a diversity of foodstuffs that had since disappeared.

7. The preference for white or lighter-colored foods, especially corn and beans, was particularly apparent in Tetecala.

8. The discourse against dark-colored food, and the importance of balancing appearance with flavor by combining ingredients, came up over and over again in my three sites, as in the case of hibiscus flower in Xochimilco. In this instance, the only answer I could get to explain the preference for light-colored beans was that with so many flies around you never knew if a fly had gotten into your pot of beans if they were black. Although black beans were most common in Xochimilco and Ocotepec, red or white beans were more often preferred in Tetecala, in the same way that white tortillas were greatly preferred over blue ones. My hunch is that the preference is linked to the ethnic identity: people in Tetecala like to distinguish themselves from the dark-skinned people in the nearby indigenous community of Coatetelco, who are often suspected of ill-will. On one occasion when I asked for blue tortillas at the market, my informant, Doña Eustoquia, explained to the surprised vendor that I liked dark ones, "the ones from Coatetelco."

9. This conversation took place as Esmeralda was selling a combination of two types of beans to a woman, who agreed with her about how to select beans and added a few "extinct" species of beans that she missed to Esmeralda's list. The cause of the "loss" of certain types of beans seems to be rooted in the market, with inex-

pensive beans imported from the United States and Canada sometimes outcompeting local and national varieties.

10. Peanuts are locally grown and are used in a variety of stews in Tetecala. Esmeralda feels that using a blender for salsa is cheating but still uses it to make her work easier, though without her father and brothers knowing it. Like using the hand-press tortilla maker, this is not considered right by some. The rationale is that the flavor is noticeably affected by replacing traditional forms of cooking, including grinding, with newer, more efficient forms.

11. *Tlacoache* is the Nahuatl word for possum.

12. Unlike Xochimilco and Ocotepec, Tetecala shares many cultural elements from hotter climates and Guerrero in particular, such as the salted meat (*cecina*) often brought to market from Iguala, Guerrero, or from Yecapixtla, Morelos.

13. Don José does not consider the tortillas available at the *tortillerías* to be real tortillas, as he does not consider the corn flour sold in supermarkets to be real corn.

14. Don José is referring to the pasteurized, partially vegetable-based cream that is sold in stores in Mexico today.

15. Tetecala has grown over the last few decades in particular, with new migrants from poorer states or poorer areas of Morelos settling on the outskirts of town, building up areas that were previously uninhabited. Don José and others in town who have lost cattle and other animals to theft often blame the newcomers in their town and region and are generally suspicious of them.

16. Esmeralda is referring to our earlier conversation about the *clecuil*, in which she called the hearth where her family boils the *nixtamal* a "modern" *clecuil*.

17. Using animals instead of sticks to plant your crop represented modernity to Doña Eustoquia.

Chapter Five

1. See Good Eshelman (1995) on the Nahuatl concept of work (*tequitl*) and the role of the dead in working with the wind and the rain to support the living.

2. Though they no longer use the two metates, they will not give either one to Señora Rosa's daughter Rosita, who wants it for her house. The metate is no longer useful as it was in the past: several women told me stories of their mothers marrying a man on the condition that he carried her metate to the new hometown. While the metate is still very laden with emotion and connection with the mother for some, in other middle- and upper-class settings it has become a symbol of Mexican roots. In Coyoacán (a district in Mexico City) metates can be found in wealthy people's gardens with statues of Indians on top.

3. Señora Rosa has three sons and two daughters and is proud that they know

how to take care of themselves—but they complain that she does not let them cook in "her" kitchen.

4. One of the noticeable changes in food traditions in Xochimilco is the replacement of fish and vegetables with red meat to a great extent, which is at least partly to blame for the tremendous increase in diabetes among young people there.

5. Unfulfilled desire or longing is considered the cause of many illnesses in this entire region. The dreaded *mal de ojo* (evil eye), for instance, can make a baby become listless or cry a lot and is caused by someone looking at the baby and longing for a child. Unlike the custom in the United States, where it seems to be considered an invasion of personal space to reach out and touch somebody's child, in Xochimilco it is considered dangerous if you look but do not touch the child. Evil is transmitted in a variety of ways. Food may be cursed by the person who prepared it, for example, so people are careful whose food they eat.

6. Like other older women, Señora Rosa is scandalized at young people's lack of respect and taste for traditional foods like mole and frijoles and their preference for meat.

7. Structured interview on February 11, 2001.

8. At age thirty, Beatriz finds the kitchen a welcoming place. She would like to spend more time there, though her mother allows her only a peripheral role.

9. Structured interview on February 22, 2001.

10. Written invitations are not required to attend most traditional fiestas in Xochimilco, though the hosts always distribute a certain number of them to people they consider their most important guests, which serves as an opportunity to show patronage. Invitations are often beautifully handmade and saved as a souvenirs (*recuerdos*). In the case of the Niñopa, they often include a photograph and prayer and become a relic of sorts.

11. Señora Rosa says that one of her superiors at the school where she worked told her that Xochimilco produces so many teachers that you would be hard-pressed to find a public school in the entire Federal District (including and surrounding Mexico City) that did not have at least one teacher from Xochimilco. In fact many of the middle-aged women I interviewed in the *callejón* were teachers; despite the lack of professional opportunities for women in general in Xochimilco—as in many places around the world—education seems to be one area of work considered appropriate for women.

12. Although many Xochimilcas no longer work in agriculture because of what they consider better opportunities, the loss of the traditional landscape and way of life associated with the *chinampas* is very much a painful topic of discussion. It is also important to note that many but not most locals do maintain a traditional lifestyle, though they have had to adjust to a changing market, often benefiting from the growth of Mexico City at the same time as they are hurt by the globalization of

local markets. In some cases younger generations in the *callejón* are returning to the land that their grandfathers worked but their fathers abandoned and approach their work with a combination of traditional knowledge and modern technology.

13. Linda sells lingerie and silver from catalogs door to door with friends and neighbors.

14. Linda's barrio is a five-minute walk away but, like every other barrio, has a distinct personality and is considered by locals to be very much a different place.

15. Rowing is the wrong word: the flat-bottomed canoes (as well as the larger *trajineras* that resemble gondolas) used in the canals by Xochimilcas are moved by pushing off from the bottom of the canal floor with a long pole (poling).

16. *Sopa seca o sopa aguada* (dry or wet soup) in this region refers to the dish served before the main dish (usually rice, pasta, or consommé, "dry" or with broth, with or without cream).

17. As opposed to obtaining it from their own pigs or buying it from a neighbor after a fiesta.

18. When I ask Linda to introduce me to her sister-in-law, she refuses, saying that people here do not lend themselves to interviews ("Aquí la gente no se presta para una entrevista").

19. Linda thinks it is silly for someone not to share a recipe because the recipe itself is not enough in any case, and your *sazón* is not transferable.

20. Because this entire interview was recorded on tape (July 16, 2001), the first-person selections here accurately reflect a way of speaking that is so Xochimilco that I almost feel like I am there. I have chosen to leave some repetitions and idioms in for this reason.

21. Doña Teodora pronounces *máiz* (corn) differently than most, with an accent on the *á* (rather than *maíz*).

22. Doña Teodora is referring to the governmental subsidized milk program for low-income families. Every morning a truck comes to the mouth of the *callejón*, and people line up with their plastic buckets to receive the day's ration of milk.

23. For Doña Teodora, fat has a positive connotation, in direct contrast to the negative connotation in the doctor's usage.

24. Doña Teodora becomes very sentimental and cries as she recalls her husband.

25. Doña Teodora's family is not alone in this pattern in Xochimilco today: grandsons are returning to work their grandfather's land, which their fathers never worked.

26. This story of the respect for the dead and for ancestors is one of many that I heard from informants in central Mexico that seem to combine indigenous and Catholic elements. As Doña Teodora was telling this particular story, a Catholic priest in the yard was saying Mass for the partygoers, his words booming on a loudspeaker in the background juxtaposed with hers.

Chapter Six

1. See "A Taste of Three Places" at the beginning of the book.

2. Although Ocotepec may not have a Niñopa, there is no shortage of religious figures that are treated with the same devotion and respect and are likewise linked to community celebrations.

3. I assume that María Soledad is referring to pumpkin seeds.

4. The tradition is to offer the native spiny chayote squash, which is cooked outdoors over a woodfire for hours.

5. Others have told me that at the very least they need a glass of water and a candle. The candle, which I think María Soledad is forgetting in this conversation as she is focusing on food, is to light their path and help them find their way home. That is the belief in Xochimilco in any case. In Ocotepec the pathways of *cempazuchitl* petals serve the same function and are always accompanied by candles.

Food for Thought

1. As reported to me by Miguel Morayta, Morelos Regional office of the National School of Anthropology and History, March 12, 2001.

2. Interview with la Maestra Ofelia, September 2000, Xochimilco.

3. Development organizations often take advantage of women's commitment to family and community service to further their program goals, ignoring the extent of women's considerable unpaid labor.

4. See the collection of papers on "hybrid" kitchens in *Gender, Place, and Culture* 13(6) (2006).

5. Given this, and how suspicious Xochimilcas are of outsiders in general, I made no attempt to see it. A copy of the list from 1987 that appears in a social anthropology thesis on the Niñopa in Xochimilco (Orta Hernández 1991), however, includes *mayordomos* through the year 2023, including the family that received the Niñopa *mayordomía* during my year of fieldwork.

6. Interview, March 12, 2001.

7. See Good Eshelman (1995) regarding the "work" performed by the dead in the traditional Nahuatl belief system.

8. Interview with Señora Magdalena, October 16, 2002.

9. See the set of themed papers on kitchens in *Gender, Place and Culture* 13(2) (2006) for a discussion of how the discourse of modernity shaped sociospatial relations in kitchenspaces in the twentieth century.

10. See the chapter on the Aztec blender in Jeffrey Pilcher's study of Mexican food and the making of Mexican national identity (1998).

11. One man invited to a wedding in Veracruz was surprised that the family requested that he bring a bucket of Kentucky Fried Chicken from Mexico City to the banquet.

12. See Enrique Ochoa's *Feeding Mexico* (2000) for a look at the political uses of food and the government's intervention in food production and distribution in dealing with the series of crises over the past century in Mexico.

13. See the discussion of tradition as "an interpretive process that embodies continuity and discontinuity" (Handler and Linnekin 1984: 273). Their article includes several examples relevant to my research sites and stresses the symbolic construction of "tradition" as well as the necessary role of creativity in the process.

Glossary

adobo: spicy red sauce made of ground dried chiles, garlic, vinegar, oregano, and other herbs, often used to marinate meat or in *frijoles adobados*

agua fresca (de tamarindo, de limón, de sandía, de jamaica): refreshing drink or "water" like lemonade made of fruit (tamarind, lemon, watermelon) or hibiscus (*jamaica*)

almuerzo: early midday meal (which might typically include eggs, nopales, and beans) around noon that is equivalent to lunch or brunch in the United States; not breakfast, which may be light (see *desayuno*) or nonexistent, or the main meal of the day (see *comida*), eaten around 3 p.m.

anafre or *bracero* (different names for the same thing, depending on the region): small portable outdoor stove, usually fueled with charcoal or attached to a small tank of gas

antojitos: literally, "little whims" (tacos, quesadillas, *gorditas,* etc.), mostly hand-made of corn dough and available in markets and on street corners throughout Mexico

arroz: rice

asistencia (dar la asistencia): contribute your share, take responsibility for a particular cargo

atole: hot, thick drink made of corn (fresh masa, toasted and ground corn, even cornstarch), boiled with flavorings such as cinnamon, fresh fruit, cocoa, brown sugar, or vanilla; *atole champurrado* is made with cocoa, cinnamon, and brown sugar

banderitas de papel picado: traditional paper banners with cut-out designs, which are part of almost every fiesta, along with paper flowers

barbacoa: various meats steamed with chiles, wrapped in the leaf of a century plant (maguey), commonly served at celebrations; the traditional method of steaming in a hole in the ground has been replaced in many places by the use of large recycled oil drums

barrio: roughly equivalent to a neighborhood in the United States; together with the family, it is an important identity marker and social unit around which a community organizes, especially in Xochimilco (with seventeen traditional barrios) and Ocotepec (with four); sometimes interchangeable with *colonia* (which has a higher-class connotation)

barro: clay (as in clay pots used for cooking) or the flavor that people claim it gives the food

bracero: see *anafre*

buscapiés: fireworks that spin on the ground at people's feet

calabaza: traditional squash or pumpkin

calabaza en dulce: pumpkin cooked in brown sugar

campesino: peasant or person who makes a living by working the land (*el campo*)

campo: countryside

cargo: one of a variety of formal responsibilities (usually considered political and religious), including responsibility for special food in a traditional fiesta (see *mayordomo* or *mayordoma*)

carnicería: butcher shop

carnitas: fried pork, often prepared for fiestas when a pig is slaughtered

castillo: "castle" or fireworks tower

cazuela: open-mouthed clay pot placed over a firewood stove or other kind of stove; *cazuelas de barro* (clay pots) are used for mole and rice

cempazuchitl: marigold; known as the flower of the dead, it is used in the celebration of the Day of the Dead

chilaquiles: breakfast dish made of old tortillas, salsa, and perhaps cheese or cream, believed to cure a hangover

chiles rellenos: literally, "stuffed chiles" (often stuffed with cheese or meat with raisins); this is many people's favorite food and most women's least favorite dish to prepare

chinampa: type of intensive wetland agricultural field developed in the Basin of Mexico

chinelos: masked dancers (originally from Morelos), who often accompany processions and take part in many traditional fiestas in central Mexico

chiquihuite: large basket traditionally used to carry produce or corn to market (still used in my sites for storage and for transporting goods)

clecuil or *tlicuil:* firewood hearth (a Nahuatl word)

cocina: kitchen; also means cooking (from *cocinar,* "to cook")

cocina de humo: literally, "smoke kitchen"; traditional kitchenspace away from the main structure of the house where foods such as tortillas and beans or large quantities of food for celebrations (such as tamales and mole) are often prepared

cocol: special bread from Chalma (pilgrimage site) with anise seeds

cohetes: fireworks (see also *buscapiés, castillo, torito*)

comadrazgo or *compadrazgo:* an institution adopted from Spain and the Catholic church, initially associated with sharing the responsibility for raising a child as a godmother (*comadre*) or godfather (*compadre*); today used more broadly: for instance, being the godmother of the tamales or the godmother of the dress for a *fiesta de quinceaños*

comal: disklike griddle made out of clay or metal, used daily in most homes to grill tortillas, quesadillas, and other foods

comida: food; also the main (or only) meal of the day

comisión: assignment or duty (as when women take on a formal role and specific task in the food preparation for a fiesta)

desayuno: breakfast (very light, perhaps just coffee and a tortilla or bread), as opposed to brunch (see *almuerzo*)

elotes: fresh, sweet corn (eaten on the cob, in tamales, or in other ways)

epazote: common herb (*Chenopodium ambrosioides*) used in black beans and other typical dishes and also for its medicinal properties

fiesta del barrio: celebration held for the neighborhood's patron saint

frijoles (singular *frijol*): beans

gorditas: literally, "fat ones": thick, handmade corn dough patties made with salt and lard and often filled with bits of cheese or pork rind patties

güera, güerita (feminine) or *güero* (masculine): blond(e) or blondie, referring to light skin or hair and to light-colored things (such as beans)

itacate: food to take with you, often taken to men working in the fields or given to guests as they leave a fiesta

jitomate: red tomato, as opposed to tomatillo, which has a skin covering the green fruit (see *tomate*)

masa: dough (made from corn) for tamales or tortillas

mayordomo (masculine) or *mayordoma* (feminine): host in a *mayordomía,* a traditional type of sponsorship rooted in indigenous forms of religious-political organization, including sponsorship of a meal (a position of respect and authority); see also *cargo*

meclapil or *tejolote:* pestle or "mano del metate" (hand of the metate), used to grind seeds or to place on top of tamales so that they will cook

memelas: handmade oval corn dough patties like tortillas

merienda: snack, often used to refer to a light meal before bed (such as bread or a *tamal* with coffee, *atole,* or milk)

metate: three-legged grinding stone made of volcanic rock (for grinding corn, beans, cocoa, and seeds)

mixiotes (in Xochimilco): like tamales, but made with meat rather than corn, traditionally wrapped in maguey (century plant) leaves, like *barbacoa,* but most commonly wrapped in corn husks or even tinfoil today

molcajete: stone mortar (for grinding chiles, tomatoes, and other ingredients), still commonly used

mole: thick traditional sauce, the quintessential fiesta food, varying by region and family; green mole (made from ground pumpkin seeds) is much less expensive to prepare than red mole (which includes at least two types of dried chiles and several types of seeds)

molino: mill (for grinding *nixtamal,* chile seeds, beans for tamales, and other ingredients)

nixtamal: corn boiled with lime to soften it, to make into tortillas

nopales: prickly pear cacti (part of the landscape of central Mexico); the young stem segments of the prickly pear, also known as cactus paddles, are eaten almost on a daily basis in my research communities; they are very high in vitamin C and have many medicinal properties

novenario: nine-day collective mourning period, usually accompanied by food, drink, and alcohol

olla de barro: closed-top clay pot for frijoles, coffee, or tamales (see also *barro*)

patrón del pueblo: patron saint of the community

pepitas de chile or *pipián:* traditional smooth sauce made with ground chiles and chile seeds saved from previous meals, somewhat like mole though much more economical and lower in status *piloncillo:* cone of dark sugar, which is cheaper and considered less desirable than refined white sugar (used in traditional dishes such as *calabaza en dulce*)

promesa: literally, "promise": a vow or commitment to contribute something to a particular celebration or holy figure; also used in Ocotepec to refer to a pilgrim from outside the barrio who comes to contribute to a local celebration by fulfilling a promise

quinceañera: celebration of a girl's fifteenth birthday, marking her transition into womanhood and coming out in society (a very formal, codified event, including music and dance); also used to refer to the girl herself (who wears a special dress often resembling a wedding gown); *quinceaños* is often used to refer to the fiesta

recalentado: heated-up leftovers, often served the morning after a fiesta

sazón: special touch; seasoning or flavor

tamales: literally, "carefully wrapped" in Nahuatl: food steamed in corn husks or banana leaves, usually referring to ground corn dough (*masa para tamales*) mixed with some other ingredient (the ritual food of choice for special celebrations)

tejolote: see *meclapil*

tequesquite: mineral substance used in cooking traditional foods such as beans and corn, called "the salt of the earth" by one of my informants

tlapiques: tamales made by wrapping fish in corn husks (seasoned with veins from dried chiles, tomatillos, and epazote) and steaming them, a local specialty in Xochimilco; similar tamales are called *tamales de pescado* (fish tamales) in Coatetelco

tlicuil: see *clecuil*

tomate: tomatillo (with a skin covering the green fruit), as opposed to red tomato (see *jitomate*)

torito: fireworks bull, which is carried on someone's shoulders and spins other fireworks into the crowd (see *buscapiés*)

tortillería: tortilla factory

trajinera: gondola-like vessel used to navigate the canals of Xochimilco, in particular to take tourists around the *chinampas;* a *canoa* is a simpler, smaller vessel used to work and to bring the harvest in

xoconostle: fruit of the nopal, added to dishes such as *mole de olla*

zompantle: red flower of the *colorín* tree; a favorite food of many in Morelos

Bibliography

Abu-Lughod, L. 1991. Writing against Culture. In *Recapturing Anthropology: Working in the Present,* edited by R. G. Fox, 137–162. Santa Fe, NM: School for American Research Press.

———. 1993. *Writing Women's Worlds: Bedouin Stories.* Berkeley: University of California Press.

Agrawal, A. 1997. *Community in Conservation: Beyond Enchantment and Disenchantment.* Gainesville, FL: Conservation and Development Forum Discussion Paper.

Aguirre Beltrán, G. 1991 [1953]. *Formas de gobierno indígena.* Obra Antropológica IV. Mexico City: Fondo de Cultura Económica.

Ahrentzen, S. 1997. The Meaning of Home Workplaces for Women. In *Thresholds in Feminist Geography: Difference, Methodology, Representation,* edited by J. P. Jones, H. Nast, and S. Roberts, 77–92. Oxford: Rowman and Littlefield Publishers.

Almeida Salles, V. 1988. Mujer y grupo doméstico campesino: Notas de trabajo. In *Las mujeres en el campo,* edited by J. Aranda Bezaury, 3–23. Oaxaca, Mexico: Universidad Autónoma Benito Juárez de Oaxaca.

Arizpe S., L. 1989. *La mujer en el desarrollo de México y de América Latina.* Mexico City: UNAM, Centro Regional de Investigaciones Multidisciplinarios.

Ávila Sánchez, H. 1997. Agricultura, urbanización y cambios territoriales en el estado de Morelos. *Geografía y Desarrollo* 14: 53–58.

———, ed. 2005. *Lo urbano-rural, ¿nuevas expresiones territoriales?* Cuernavaca: UNAM, Centro Regional de Investigaciones Multidisciplinarias.

Azuela, M. 1986 [1916]. *Los de abajo: Novela de la revolución mexicana.* Mexico City: Fondo de Cultura Económica.

Barbieri, T. 1984. *Mujeres y vida cotidiana: Estudios exploratorios en sectores medios y obreros de la Ciudad de México.* Secretaría de Educación Pública 80. Mexico City: Fondo de Cultura Económica.

Beezley, W., C. English Martin, and W. E. French, eds. 1994. *Rituals of Rule, Rituals of Resistance: Public Celebrations and Popular Culture in Mexico.* Wilmington, DE: Scholarly Resources.

Behar, R. 1993. *Translated Woman: Crossing the Border with Esperanza's Story.* Austin: University of Texas Press.

Benítez, A. 2004 [1974]. *Pre-Hispanic Cooking.* 9th ed. (bilingual). Biblioteca Interamericana Bilingüe 5. Mexico City: Ediciones Euroamericanas Klauss Thiele.

Bonfil Batalla, G. 1982. *El maíz.* Mexico City: Museo Nacional de Culturas Populares/SEP.

Bordo, S. 1986. The Cartesian Masculinization of Thought. *Signs* 11: 239–256.

Broda, J. 1971. Las fiestas aztecas de los dioses de la lluvia: Una reconstrucción según las fuentes del siglo XVI. *Revista Española de Antropología* 6: 245–327.

———. 1982. Astronomy, Cosmovision, and Ideology in Pre-Hispanic Mesoamerica. In *Ethnoastronomy and Archaeoastronomy in the American Tropics,* edited by A. Aveni and G. Urton, 81–109. Annals of the New York Academy of Science 385. New York: New York Academy of Sciences.

———. 1988. Templo Mayor as Ritual Space. In *The Great Temple of Tenochtitlan: Center and Periphery in the Aztec World,* edited by J. Broda et al., 61–123. Berkeley: University of California Press.

———. 1991a. Cosmovisión y observación de la naturaleza: El ejemplo del culto de los cerros. In *Arqueoastronomía y etnoastronomía en Mesoamérica,* edited by J. Broda et al., 461–500. Mexico City: Universidad Nacional Autónoma de México, Instituto de Investigaciones Históricas.

———. 1991b. The Sacred Landscape of the Aztec Calendar Festivals: Myth, Nature, and Society. In *To Change Place: Aztec Ceremonial Landscapes,* edited by D. Carrasco, 74–120. Boulder: University of Colorado Press.

———. 1993. Astronomical Knowledge, Calendrics, and Sacred Geography in Ancient Mesoamerica. In *Astronomy and Culture,* edited by C. L. N. Ruggles and N. J. Saunders, 253–295. Boulder: University of Colorado Press.

Broda, J., and F. Báez-Jorge. 2001. *Cosmovisión, ritual e identidad de los pueblos indígenas de México.* Mexico City: Consejo Nacional para la Cultura y las Artes.

Buckley, S. 1996. A Guided Tour of the Kitchen: Seven Japanese Domestic Tales. *Environment and Planning D: Society and Space* 14: 441–462.

Butler, J. 1990. *Gender Trouble: Feminism and Subversion of Identity.* London: Routledge.

———. 1993. *Bodies That Matter: On the Discursive Limits of "Sex."* New York: Routledge.

Buttimer, A. 1980. Home, Reach, and Sense of Place. In *The Human Experience of Space and Place,* edited by A. Buttimer and D. Seamon, 166–187. London: Croom Helm.

Butzer, K. W. 1995. Biological Transfer, Agricultural Change, and Environmental Implications of 1492. In Crop Science Society of America, *International Germplasm Transfer: Past and Present,* 3–29. CSSA Special Publication 23. Madison, WI: CSSA.

Canabal Cristiani, B. 1997. *Xochimilco: Una identidad recreada.* Mexico City: Universidad Autónoma Metropolitana, Unidad Xochimilco.

————, ed. 2000. *Agricultura urbana en México*. Mexico City: Red Águila Mexicana de Agricultura Urbana; Red Latinoamericana de Instituciones en Agricultura Urbana-Águila; and Universidad Autónoma Metropolitana, Unidad Xochimilco.

Canabal Cristiani, B., P. A. Torres-Lima, and G. Burela Rueda. 1992. *La ciudad y sus chinampas: El caso de Xochimilco*. Mexico City: Universidad Autónoma Metropolitana, Unidad Xochimilco.

Cancián, F. 1976. *Economía y prestigio en una comunidad maya: El sistema religioso de cargos en Zinacantán*. Mexico City: Instituto Nacional Indigenista y Secretaría de Educación Pública.

Carter, W. 1966. *Crazy February*. Philadelphia: Lippincott.

Chiñas, B. 1973. *The Isthmus Zapotecs: Women's Roles in Cultural Context*. Prospect Heights, IL: Waveland Press.

————. 1987. Women: The Heart of Isthmus Zapotec Ceremonial Exchange. Paper presented at the Women in Exchange Symposium, 86th Annual Meeting, American Anthropological Association, Chicago, November 20–23.

————. 1993. *The Isthmus Zapotecs: A Matrifocal Culture of Mexico*. New York: Harcourt Brace Jovanovich.

Christie, M. E. 2002. Naturaleza y sociedad desde la perspectiva de la cocina tradicional mexicana: Género, adaptación y resistencia. *Journal of Latin American Geography* 1(1): 17–42.

————. 2003. Kitchenspace: Gendered Spaces for Cultural Reproduction, or Nature in the Everyday Lives or Ordinary Women in Central Mexico. Doctoral dissertation, Department of Geography, University of Texas.

————. 2004. Kitchenspace, Fiestas, and Cultural Reproduction in Mexican Houselot Gardens: Rural Spaces in Increasingly Urban Contexts. *Geographical Review* 94(3): 368–390.

————. 2006. Kitchenspace: Gendered Territory in Central Mexico. Savouring the Kitchen. Special Issue on Kitchens (Part 2): *Gender, Place and Culture* 13(6): 653–661.

Cordero Espinoza, S. 2000. El Nazareno de la Asunción Colhuacatzingo. *El Ahuejate* (Xochimilco, Mexico City) 42: 48.

Counihan, C., and P. Esterik, eds. 1997. *Food and Culture: A Reader*. New York: Routledge.

Crossley, P. L. 1999. Sub-irrigation and Temperature Amelioration in Chinampa Agriculture. Ph.D. dissertation, Department of Geography, University of Texas at Austin.

Csordas, T. J., ed. 1994. *Embodiment and Experience: The Existential Ground of Culture and Self*. Cambridge Studies in Medical Anthropology. Cambridge: Cambridge University Press.

Curtin, D. W., and L. Heldke, eds. 1992. *Cooking, Eating, Thinking: Transformative Philosophies of Food*. Bloomington: Indiana University Press.

De Beauvoir, S. 1973. *The Second Sex*. Trans. E. M. Parshley. New York: Vintage.

de Certeau, L. G., and P. Mayol. 1998. *The Practice of Everyday Life: Volume 2, Living and Cooking*. Translated ed. Minneapolis: University of Minnesota Press.

de la Cruz, Sor Juana Inés. 1989 [1695]. *Obras completas*. 7th ed. Mexico City: Editorial Porrúa.

Delegación Xochimilco. 2000. *Xochimilco: Folclore, color y tradición*. Xochimilco, Mexico City: Subdelegación de Desarrollo Social.

Dias, K., and J. Blecha. 2007. Feminism and Social Theory in Geography: An Introduction. *Professional Geographer* 59(1): 1–9.

Díaz, D. 1995. *Cantos y alabanzas: Danza de pastoras*. Ocotepec, Morelos: Dirección General de Culturas Populares, Unidad Morelos.

Domosh, M. 1998. Geography and Gender: Home Again? *Progress in Human Geography* 22(2): 276–282.

Doolittle, W. E., A. Sluyter, E. P. Perramond, P. L. Crossley, and D. P. Lambert. 2002. Feeding a Growing Population on an Increasingly Fragile Planet. In *Latin America in the Twenty-first Century: Challenges and Solutions*, ed. G. Knapp, 45–77. Yearbook (Conference of Latin Americanist Geographers), Vol. 27. Austin: University of Texas Press.

Dwyer, D., and J. Bruce, eds. 1988. *A Home Divided: Women and Income in the Third World*. Stanford, CA: Stanford University Press.

Eber, C. 1995. *Women and Alcohol in a Highland Maya Town: Water of Hope, Water of Sorrow*. Austin: University of Texas Press.

Echeverría, M., and L. E. Arroyo. 2000. *Recetario del maíz*. Cocina Indígena y Popular, 10. Mexico City: Dirección General de Culturas Populares del Consejo Nacional para la Cultura y las Artes.

Ehlers, T. 2000 [1990]. *Silent Looms: Women and Production in a Guatemalan Town*. Revised ed. Austin: University of Texas Press.

Esquivel, L. 1989. *Como agua para chocolate*. Mexico City: Editorial Planeta.

Ezcurra, E. 1990. *De las chinampas a la megalópolis: El medio ambiente en la Cuenca de México*. Mexico City: Fondo de Cultura Económica.

Fernea, E. 1969. *Guests of the Sheik: An Ethnography of an Iraqi Village*. Garden City, NY: Doubleday.

Folbre, N. 1988. The Black Four of Hearts: Toward a New Paradigm of Household Economics. In *A Home Divided: Women and Income in the Third World*, edited by D. Dwyer and J. Bruce, 249–289. Stanford, CA: Stanford University Press.

Friedlander, J. 1975. *Being Indian in Hueyapan: A Study of Forced Identity in Contemporary Mexico*. New York: St. Martin's Press.

Friedmann, J. 1992. *Empowerment: The Politics of Alternative Development*. Cambridge: Blackwell.

Giarracca, N., ed. 2001. ¿Una nueva ruralidad en América Latina? Grupos de Trabajo de CLACSO: Desarrollo Rural. Buenos Aires, Argentina: CLACSO.

González de la Rocha, M. 1986. Los recursos de la pobreza: Familias de bajos ingresos de Guadalajara. Guadalajara: El Colegio de Jalisco/CIESAS/SPP.

Good Eshelman, C. 1995. El trabajo de los muertos en la sierra de Guerrero. Paper presented on August 21, 1995, in the Simposio Latinoamericano: No una, sino muchas muertes, organized by the National School of Anthropology and History, reprinted as Sobretiro de Estudios de la cultura náhuatl, Vol. 26. Mexico City: n.p., 1996.

———. 2001a. El ritual de la reproducción de la cultura: Ceremonias agrícolas, los muertos y la expresión estética entre los Nahuas de Guerrero. In Cosmovisión, ritual e identidad de los pueblos indígenas de México, edited by J. Broda and F. Báez-Jorge, 239–297. Mexico City: Fondo de Cultura Económica.

———. 2001b. Ofrendar, alimentar y nutrir: Los usos de la comida en la vida ritual nahua. Paper presented at the XXVI Mesa Redonda, Sociedad Mexicana de Antropología, Zacatecas, August 3.

Govers, C. 1997. Agriculture, Cosmology and the Gendered Division of Labour in a Totonac Highland Village (Mexico). In Gender and Land Use: Diversity in Environmental Practices, edited by M. de Brujin, I. van Halsema, and H. van den Homberg, 27–47. Amsterdam: Thela Publishers.

Greenberg, L. 1996. You Are What You Eat: Ethnicity and Change in Yucatec Immigrant House-Lots, Quintana Roo, Mexico. Ph.D. dissertation, Department of Geography, University of Wisconsin.

Gujit, I., and M. Kaul Shah, eds. 1998. The Myth of Community: Gender Issues in Participatory Development. Participation in Development Series. London: ITDG Publishing.

Handler, R., and J. Linnekin. 1984. Tradition, Genuine or Spurious. Journal of American Folklore 97(385) (July–September): 273–290.

Haraway, D. 1988. Situated Knowledges: The Science Question in Feminism and the Privilege of Partial Perspective. Feminist Studies 14(3): 575–599.

Harding, S. 1986. The Science Question in Feminism. Ithaca: Cornell University Press.

———. 1991. Whose Science? Whose Knowledge? Thinking from Women's Lives. Ithaca, NY: Cornell University Press.

Hastrup, K. 1990. The Ethnographic Present: A Reinvention. Cultural Anthropology 5(1): 45–61.

Hayden, D. 1981. The Grand Domestic Revolution: A History of Feminist Designs for American Homes, Neighborhoods and Cities. Cambridge, MA: MIT Press.

Heidegger, M. 1971. Poetry, Language, Thought. New York: Harper and Row Publishers.

Hernández Cortés, E. 1999. Recetario nahua de Morelos. Cocina Indígena y Popular, 4. Mexico City: Dirección General de Culturas Populares del Consejo Nacional para la Cultura y las Artes.

Ingham, J. 1986. *Mary, Michael, and Lucifer: Folk Catholicism in Central Mexico.* Austin: University of Texas Press.

Instituto de Seguridad y Seguro Social de los Trabajadores del Estado (ISSSTE). 1985. *Para celebrar.* Volume 4 of *Y la comida se hizo.* Mexico City: Distribuidora CONASUPO, S.A.

Instituto Nacional de Estadística, Geografía e Informática (INEGI). 1995. *Sistema para la consulta de información censal por colonias (SCINCEC).* Cuernavaca: INEGI.

———. 2000a. *XII Censo general de población y vivienda: Tabulados básicos, Distrito Federal.* Mexico City: INEGI.

———. 2000b. *XII Censo general de población y vivienda: Tabulados básicos, Morelos, Tomo I.* Mexico City: INEGI.

Jackson, J. B. 1993. The Past and Present of the Vernacular Garden. In *The Vernacular Garden,* edited by J. D. Hunt and J. Wolschke-Bulmahn, 11–17. Washington, DC: Dumbarton Oaks Research Library and Collection.

Kennedy, D. 1986 [1972]. *The Cuisines of Mexico.* Revised ed. New York: Harper and Row.

Keys, E. 1999. Kaqchikel Gardens: Women, Children, and Multiple Roles of Gardens among the Maya of Highland Guatemala. *Yearbook, Conference of Latin Americanist Geographers* 25: 89–100.

Kimber, C. T. 1966. Dooryard Gardens of Martinique. *Yearbook, Association of Pacific Coast Geographers* 28: 97–118.

Kolodny, A. 1975. *The Lay of the Land: Metaphor as Experience and History in American Life and Letters.* Chapel Hill: University of North Carolina Press.

———. 1984. *The Land before Her: Fantasy and Experience of the American Frontier, 1630–1860.* Chapel Hill: University of North Carolina Press.

Korsbaek, L. 1996. *Introducción al sistema de cargos.* Toluca, Mexico: Universidad Autónoma del Estado de México.

Kwan, M-P. 2007. Affecting Geospatial Technologies: Toward a Feminist Politics of Emotion. *Professional Geographer* 59(1): 22–34.

Lamphere, L. 2001. The Domestic Sphere of Women and the Public World of Men: The Strengths and Limitations of an Anthropological Dichotomy. In *Gender in Cross-Cultural Perspective,* edited by C. Brettell and C. Sargent, 100–119. 3rd ed. Upper Saddle River, NJ: Prentice-Hall.

Lewis, O. 1960. *Tepoztlán: Village in Mexico.* New York: Holt, Rinehart and Winston.

———. 1963. *Life in a Mexican Village: Tepoztlán Restudied.* Urbana: University of Illinois Press.

Longhurst, Robyn. 1995. The Body and Geography. *Gender, Place and Culture* 2(1): 97–105.

———. 1997. (Dis)embodied Geographies. *Progress in Human Geography* 21(4): 486–501.

Losada, H., H. Martínez, J. Vieyra, R. Pealing, J. Cortés, and R. Zabala. 1998. Urban Agriculture in the Metropolitan Zone of Mexico City: Changes over Time in Urban, Suburban and Peri-urban Areas. *Environment and Urbanization* 10(2): 37–54.

Loyd, B. 1975. Woman's Place: Man's Place. *Landscape* 30: 10–13.

———. 1981. Women, Home, and Status. In *Housing and Identity*, edited by J. Duncan, 181–197. London: Croom Helm.

Lupton, E. 1992. *The Bathroom, the Kitchen and the Aesthetics of Waste: A Process of Elimination*. New York: Princeton Architectural Press.

Maldonado Jiménez, D. 2000. *Deidades y espacio ritual en Cuauhnahuac y Hueaxtepec: Tlahuicas y xochimilcas de Morelos (siglos XII–XVI)*. Mexico City: Instituto de Investigaciones Antropológicas, UNAM.

Massey, D. 1995. Masculinity, Dualisms and High Technology. *Transactions of the Institute of British Geographers* 20: 487–499.

Matthee, D. 2004. Towards an Emotional Geography of Eating Practices: An Exploration of the Food Rituals of Women of Colour Working on Farms in the Western Cape. *Gender, Place and Culture: A Journal of Feminist Geography* 11(3): 437–443.

McClusky, L. 2001. *"Here, Our Culture Is Hard": Stories of Domestic Violence from a Mayan Community in Belize*. Austin: University of Texas Press.

McC. Netting, R. 1993. *Smallholders, Householders: Farm Families and the Ecology of Intensive, Sustainable Agriculture*. Stanford: Stanford University Press.

Medina, A. 1987. Los que tienen el don de ver: Los sistemas de cargos y los hombres de conocimiento en los Altos de Chiapas. In *Historia de la religión en Mesoamérica y áreas afines*, Vol. 1: *Coloquio*, 153–175. Mexico City: Universidad Nacional Autónoma de México, Instituto de Investigaciones Antropológicas.

Merchant, C. 1980. *The Death of Nature: Women, Ecology, and the Scientific Revolution*. New York: Harper and Row.

———. 1990. The Realm of Social Relations: Production, Reproduction, and Gender in Environmental Transformations. In *The Earth as Transformed by Human Action: Global and Regional Changes in the Biosphere over the Past 300 Years*, edited by B. L. Turner, 673–684. Cambridge: Cambridge University Press.

Mier Merelo, A. M. 2000. Del mito a la realidad. In *Tierra, agua, y maíz: Realidad y utopia*, 89–97. Colección Memoria Colectiva. Cuernavaca, Mexico: UNICEDES, Universidad Autónoma del Estado de Morelos.

Mintz, S. W. 1985. *Sweetness and Power: The Place of Sugar in Modern History*. New York: Viking Penguin.

———. 1996. *Tasting Food, Tasting Freedom: Excursions into Eating, Culture, and the Past.* Boston: Beacon Press.

———. 1999. La comida como un campo de combate ideológico. Paper presented at VIII Congreso de Antropología, Homenaje a la Xeración Nós, Santiago de Compostela, September 20–24.

Mohanty, C. 1984. Under Western Eyes: Feminist Scholarship and Colonial Discourses. *Boundary* 2(12): 333–358.

Monk, J. 1984. Approaches to the Study of Women and the Landscape. *Environmental Review* 8(1): 23–33.

———. 1992. Gender in the Landscape: Expressions of Power and Meaning. In *Inventing Places: Studies in Cultural Geography*, edited by K. J. Anderson and F. Gale, 123–138. New York: Wiley and Longman Cheshire.

Monk, J., and S. Hanson. 1982. On Not Excluding Half of the Human in Human Geography. *Professional Geographer* 34: 11–23.

Morayta Mendoza, M. 2000. *Reelaboración cultural e identidad en Ocotepec, Morelos.* Cuernavaca: Centro Instituto Nacional de Antropología e Historia, Morelos.

Museo Nacional de Culturas Populares. 1981. *El maíz, fundamento de la cultura popular.* Under the direction of Guillermo Bonfíl Batalla. Mexico City: SEP.

Naples, N., with C. Sachs. 2000. Standpoint Epistemology and the Uses of Self-Reflection in Feminist Ethnography: Lessons for Rural Sociology. *Rural Sociology* 65(2): 194–214.

Nast, H. J. 1994. Opening Remarks on "Women in the Field." *Professional Geographer* 46(1): 54–66.

Neurath, J. 2000. Tukipa Ceremonial Centers in the Community of Tuapurie (Santa Catarina Cuexcomatitlan): Cargo Systems, Landscape, and Cosmovision (North American Indians, Mexico, Huichol). *Journal of the Southwest* 42(1) (Spring): 81–110.

Norwood, V., and J. Monk. 1987. *The Desert Is No Lady: Southwestern Landscapes in Women's Writing and Art.* New Haven: Yale University Press.

Novo, S. 1883. *Cocina mexicana.* Mexico City: Editorial Porrúa.

Nuijten, M. 2003. Family Property and the Limits of Intervention: The Article 27 Reforms and the PROCEDE Programme in Mexico. *Development and Change* 34(3): 475–497.

Oberhauser, A. 1995. Gender and Household Economic Strategies in Rural Appalachia. *Gender, Place and Culture: A Journal of Feminist Geography* 2: 51–70.

———. 1997. The Home as "Field": Households and Homework in Rural Appalachia. In *Thresholds in Feminist Geography*, edited by J. P. Jones III, H. J. Nast, and S. M. Roberts, 165–182. New York: Rowman and Littlefield.

Ochoa, E. 2000. *Feeding Mexico: The Political Uses of Food since 1910.* Wilmington, DE: Scholarly Resources.

Oriak Villegas, M. 1997. *Tetecala ayer y hoy.* Tetecala, Morelos: n.p.

Orta Hernández, M. 1991. Análisis de una mayordomía en el medio urbano: Xochimilco, D.F. (Mayordomía del Niñopan). Master's thesis in social anthropology,
Escuela Nacional de Antropología e Historia. Mexico City, Dirección General
de Culturas Populares.

Ortner, S. 1974. Is Female to Male as Nature Is to Culture? In *Woman, Culture,
and Society,* edited by M. Zimbalist Rosaldo and L. Lamphere, 67–89. Stanford:
Stanford University Press.

———. 1995. Resistance and the Problem of Ethnographic Refusal. In *Recapturing
Anthropology: Working in the Present,* edited by R. G. Fox, 163–190. Santa Fe:
School of American Research Press.

Padilla Pineda, M. 2000. *Ciclo festivo y orden ceremonial: El sistema de cargos religiosos en San Pedro Ocumicho.* Zamora, Michoacán: El Colegio de Michoacán.

Peake, L., and G. Valentine. 2003. Editorial. *Gender, Place and Culture* 10(2):
107–109.

Pérez San Vicente, G. 2000. *Repertorio de tamales.* Cocina Indígena y Popular, 15.
Mexico City: Dirección General de Culturas Populares del Consejo Nacional
para la Cultura y las Artes.

Pilcher, J. M. 1998. *¡Que Vivan los Tamales! Food and the Making of Mexican Identity.* Albuquerque: University of New Mexico Press.

Pratt, G. 2000. Feminist Geographies. In *The Dictionary of Human Geography,*
edited by R. J. Johnson, D. Gregory, G. Pratt, and M. Watts, 259–262. 4th ed.
Oxford, UK: Blackwell.

Rangel Montoya, M. 2000. Monografía de Tetecala. Tetecala, Morelos, Presidencia
Municipal, Gobierno Municipal de Tetecala.

Redfield, R. 1930. *Tepoztlán, a Mexican Village: A Study of Folk Life.* Chicago: University of Chicago Press.

Reinhardt, N. 1988. *Our Daily Bread: The Peasant Question and Family Farming in
the Colombian Andes.* Berkeley: University of California Press.

Richardson, M. 1982. Being-in-the-Market versus Being-in-the Plaza: Material Culture and the Construction of Social Reality in Spanish America. *American Eth-
nologist* 9(2): 421–436.

———, ed. 1984. Place: Experience and Symbol. *Geoscience and Man* (LSU) 24: 1–3.

———. 1990. *Cry Lonesome and Other Accounts of the Anthropologist's Project.* Albany: State University of New York Press.

Rocheleau, D., B. Thomas-Slayter, and D. Edmunds. 1995. Gendered Resource Mapping: Focusing on Women's Spaces in the Landscape. *Cultural Survival Quar-
terly* 18(4) (Winter): 62–68.

Rocheleau, D., B. Thomas-Slayter, and E. Wangari, eds. 1996. *Feminist Political
Ecology: Global Issues and Local Experiences.* International Studies of Women
and Place. New York: Routledge.

Rojas, T. 1990. La agricultura en la época prehispánica. In *La agricultura en tierras mexicanas desde sus orígenes hasta nuestros días,* edited by T. Rojas. Mexico City: Grijalbo.

Rose, G. 1995. Geography and Gender, Cartographies and Corporealities. *Progress in Human Geography* 19(4): 305–320.

———. 1996. Geography as a Science of Observation: The Landscape, the Gaze and Masculinity. In *Human Geography: An Essential Anthology,* edited by J. Agnew, D. N. Livingstone, and A. Rogers, 341–350. Oxford and Cambridge: Blackwell.

———. 1997. Situating Knowledges: Positionality, Reflexivities and Other Tactics. *Progress in Human Geography* 21(3): 544–548.

Rosenbaum, B. 1993. *With Our Heads Bowed: The Dynamics of Gender in a Maya Community.* Studies on Culture and Society, Vol. 5. Institute for Mesoamerican Studies, University at Albany; State University of New York. Austin: University of Texas Press.

Rueda Hurtado, R. 1998. *Antecedentes históricos de la tenencia de la tierra en Morelos.* Mexico City: Editorial Praxis and Instituto Estatal de Documentación de Morelos.

———. 2001. *Sistema urbano de Cuernavaca.* Mexico City: Editorial Praxis.

Sack, R. 1986. *Human Territoriality: Its Theory and History.* Cambridge: Cambridge University Press.

Sarmiento Silva, S. 1997. *Morelos: Sociedad, economía y cultura.* Mexico City: UNAM.

Sauer, C. 1952. *Agricultural Origins and Dispersals.* New York: American Geographical Society.

Schroeder, K. 1990. Señora Camino's Kitchen: Cuisine as Strategy in the Sierra de Piura. M.A. thesis, Department of Geography, University of Texas at Austin.

Scott, J. C. 1985. *Weapons of the Weak: Everyday Forms of Peasant Resistance.* New Haven: Yale University Press.

———. 1990. *Domination and the Arts of Resistance.* New Haven: Yale University Press.

Seager, J. 1987. The Home as Landscape: Shaping an Ideal. Paper presented at the Annual Conference of the Association of American Geographers, Portland, Oregon, April 21–26.

———. 1992. Women Deserve Spatial Consideration: A Survey of the State of Geography. In *The Knowledge Explosion: Generations of Feminist Scholarship,* edited by C. Kramarae and D. Spender, 213–224. New York: Teachers College Press.

Seamon, D., and R. Mugerauer, eds. 1985. *Dwelling, Place and Environment.* Dordrecht: Martinus Nijhoff Publishers.

Secretaría de Industria y Comercio. 1971. *IX Censo General de Población 1970: Distrito Federal.* Mexico City: Secretaría de Industria y Comercio.

Sepúlveda y Herrera, M. T. 1974. *Los cargos políticos y religiosos en la región del Lago de Pátzcuaro.* Mexico City: Instituto Nacional de Antropología.

Simoons, F. 1994. *Eat Not This Flesh: Food Avoidances from Prehistory to the Present.* 2nd ed. Madison: University of Wisconsin Press.

Simpson, L. B. 1967 [1941]. *Many Mexicos.* Berkeley and Los Angeles: University of California Press.

Spain, D. 1992. *Gendered Spaces.* Chapel Hill: University of North Carolina Press.

Sparke, P. 1995. *As Long as It's Pink: The Sexual Politics of Taste.* London: Pandora.

Spradley, J. P. 1979. *The Ethnographic Interview.* New York: Holt, Rinehart and Winston.

Stea, D. 1995. House and Home: Identity, Dichotomy, or Dialectic? (With special reference to Mexico). In *The Home: Words, Interpretation, Meanings and Environments,* edited by D. N. Benjamin, 181–201. Brookfield, VT: Avebury.

Stephen, L. 1991. *Zapotec Women.* Texas Press Source Books in Anthropology, No. 16. Austin: University of Texas Press.

Sundberg, J. 1999. Conservation Encounters: NGOs, Local People, and Changing Cultural Landscapes. Ph.D. dissertation, Department of Geography, University of Texas at Austin.

———. 2003. Masculinist Epistemologies and the Politics of Fieldwork in Latin Americanist Geography. *Professional Geographer* 55(2): 180–190.

Torres Cerdán, R. 2000. *Las flores en la cocina mexicana.* Cocina Indígena y Popular, 22. Mexico City: Dirección General de Culturas Populares/CONACULTA.

Torres Lima, P. A., ed. 2000. *Procesos metropolitanos y agricultura urbana.* Mexico City: Universidad Autónoma Metropolitana, Unidad Xochimilco.

Vayda, A. P. 1983. Progressive Contextualization: Methods and Research in Human Ecology. *Human Ecology* 11(3): 265–281.

Velázquez Gutiérrez, M. 2000. Social Sustainability: Gender and Household Relations in Two Forestry Communities in Quintana Roo, Mexico. Ph.D. dissertation, Institute of Latin American Studies, University of London.

Villa Rojas, A. 1947. Kinship and Nagualism in a Tzeltal Community, Southeastern Mexico. *American Anthropologist* 49: 578–587.

von Mentz de Boege, B. 1995. *Ocotepec: Su historia y sus costumbres, relatado por Pedro Rosales Aguilar.* Cuernavaca, Morelos: PUBLI JVS.

Warman, A. 1976. *. . . y venimos a contradecir: Los campesinos de Morelos y el Estado Nacional.* Mexico City: Secretaría de Educación Pública (SEP) and Centro de Investigaciones y Estudios Superiores en Antropología Social. 2nd ed. 1988.

Wasserfall, R. R. 1997. Reflexivity, Feminism, and Difference. In *Reflexivity and Voice,* edited by R. Hertz, 150–168. Newbury Park, CA: Sage.

Watanabe, J. 1992. *Maya Saints and Souls in a Changing World.* Austin: University of Texas Press.

Weismantel, M. 1989a. The Children Cry for Bread: Hegemony and Transformation of Consumption. In *The Social Economy of Consumption,* edited by B. Orlove and H. Rutz, 105–124. Society for Economic Anthropology Publications VI. Lantham, MD: University Press of America.

———. 1989b. Cooking Houses and Sleeping Houses: The Zumbaqua Household as Constituted Process. In *The Household Economy: Reconsidering the Domestic Mode of Production,* edited by R. R. Wilk, 55–72. Boulder: Westview Press.

———. 1991. Maize Beer and Andean Social Transformations: Drunken Indians, Bread Babies and Chosen Women. *Modern Language Notes* 106: 861–879.

———. 1998 [1988]. *Food, Gender and Poverty in the Ecuadorian Andes.* Long Grove, IL: Waveland Press.

———. 1999. Tasty Meals and Bitter Gifts: Consumption and Production in the Ecuadorian Andes. In *Changing Food Habits: Case Studies from Africa, South America, and Europe,* edited by C. Lenz, 135–154. Food in History and Culture, Vol. 2. Amsterdam: Harwood Academic Publishers.

West, R. C., J. P. Augelli, et al. 1989. *Middle America: Its Lands and Peoples.* Englewood Cliffs, NJ: Prentice-Hall.

Westmacott, R. 1992. *African-American Gardens and Yards in the Rural South.* Knoxville: University of Tennessee Press.

WinklerPrins, A. 2002. House-Lot Gardens in Santarém, Pará, Brazil: Linking Rural with Urban. *Urban Ecosystems* 6(1–2): 43–65.

Woolf, V. 1989 [1929]. *A Room of One's Own.* Orlando, FL: Harcourt Brace Jovanovich, Publishers.

Index

abuelitas (grandmothers): and butchering of pigs, 68, 235; Christie's relationships with, 70; complaints by, against young women, 77; daily responsibilities of, 71; and fiestas, 87, 197–198; and food preparation, xxi, 14–15, 71, 76, 79, 81–82, 106, 152, 188, 198–205; as *mayordomas* of Niñopa celebrations, 70, 72–73; and mole recipe, 14–15, 70; as term of respect, 70, 253, 269n9; on traditional food, 204–205; traditional ways of, 180; in women's collective work parties, 76–77, 79, 81–82

abuelos (grandfathers), 125, 128, 131, 134, 206–208, 210

Adelita, Doña, 95–98, 116

agriculture: bean cultivation, 10, 156, 161–162; Doña Eustoquia on, 172–173, 272n17; and Esmeralda's family, 156, 157, 163; irrigation for, xxiii; pesticides and fertilizer in, xxiii, 190; in Tetecala, xxiii–xxiv; workers leaving, 190, 200, 204, 217, 274n12, 274n25; in Xochimilco, 241; young people's return to, 163, 204, 274n12, 274n25. See also *chinampa* hydroponic farming system; *ejidos/ejidatarios*; milpas and corn cultivation

agua de jamaica, 70, 141, 183, 269n10

agua loca (crazy water)/*agua brava* (wild water), 100, 122, 139

aguas frescas, 122, 141–142, 240

Agustín, Don, 59–63, 65

alcohol drinking: *agua loca* (crazy water)/*agua brava* (wild water), 100, 122, 139; beer, 37, 109, 122, 128, 129–130; deaths from, 258; excessive drinking and alcoholism, xxii, 76, 122, 174, 233; at fiestas, xxii, 44, 76, 121, 138; by men, 71, 74–75, 121, 122, 128, 169, 213; at Ocotepec fiestas, 109; rum, 74–75, 106, 109, 258; *tepache*, 128, 129, 131–132; tequila, 37, 71, 74, 89; by women, 106. *See also* pulque

almuerzo (brunch), 146, 169, 201

altars honoring the dead, 214–215, 222, 228, 250–251

Andrea, Doña, 140–145, 253

animals. *See* cattle; chickens; pigs

antojitos (traditional snacks), 184, 203, 235

Antonio, 59, 61, 64–65, 68–71

arroz. See rice (*arroz*)

atole (hot corn drink): *atole champurrado*, 80–81, 185, 256; for Candelaria celebration (Tetecala), 143; with chile, 200–201; Christie's drinking of, xvii, 37; for Day of the Dead, 215, 228; for dinner, 202, 203; ingredients for, 80–81, 159, 181, 184, 185, 200–201; for Niñopa celebrations (Xochimilco), 53, 79, 80–82, 237, 238; preparation of, 80–81

barbacoa (meat steamed in oil drums), 63, 80, 81, 137, 160, 184, 235, 257

barrios, 11, 44, 57–59, 92, 98–99, 188–189

beans: and blood sausage, 120; *coatatapas*, 204; cooking of, 116, 157, 159, 161, 196, 229; *frijoles adobados* as meal when person dies, 181, 250; *frijoles de olla*, 228–229; *frijoles lavados* (washed beans), 196–197; *guisado y frijoles* (stew and beans), 217; *ollas* for making, 108, 111–112; planting of, 10, 156, 161–162; and *quinceaños* fiesta, 137; and Santa Cruz celebration (Ocotepec), 126, 128; as staple, 259; for tamales, 116–117;

tacos, xxi, 71, 114, 235
tamales: with avocado leaf, 205; baking
powder in, 261; with "belly buttons,"
117, 118, 261; Christie's participation in
making, 21, 115–117, 145–150, 163; and
emotions of cooks, 106, 149–150, 216,
241; for fiestas, 4, 53, 58, 115–119, 123,
143, 145–150; fish tamales, 144, 183–
184; kitchen secrets for cooking, 150;
lard in, 261; meat tamales, 199; men's
preparation of, as laughable, 118–119,
235; for one-year anniversary of man's
death, xvii; pineapple tamales, 159;
preparation of, xxii, 115–119, 144–150,
157, 158, 159, 163, 199, 216; recipes for,
149–150, 199; from San Pedro, 60; sign
of the cross made during preparation of, 118, 199, 241; *tamales de elote*,
146–147, 149, 157; *tamales de frijol*
(bean tamales), 60, 116–118, 198, 199,
256, 261; *tamales de haba*, 119; *tamales
nejos*, 149–150
tamarind and tamarind water, 76, 79,
97–98, 114, 119–120, 132, 141
tea, 166, 185–186, 200
teachers, 71, 190, 195, 206, 218, 273n11
television, 81, 82, 174–175, 192, 238, 250
Teodora, Doña: on food and food
preparation, 199–205; food preparation by, at fiesta, 179, 198–199, 238;
household of, 197; marriage of, 79,
199–200, 203–204, 269n12, 274n24;
on offerings for the dead, 205, 274n26;
pregnancy of, and connotation of fat,
203, 242–243, 274n23; on water supply
for Xochimilco, 200
tepache (drink), 128, 129, 131–132
Tepoztlán, 6, 55, 112–113, 224
Tetecala: agriculture in, xxiii–xxiv, 9–10;
belonging in, 8, 141, 209; changes in,
xi, 148–149, 157, 160–162; description and history of, xxiii, 5–14; Día
de la Candelaria in, 11, 43, 44, 45, 80,
135–136, 139, 140–145; Días de los
Muertos (Days of the Dead) in, 135;
Doña Eustoquia in, 171–178; drug trade
in, 144; economic restructuring in,

xxiii–xxiv, 9; Esmeralda and her family
in, 156–171; fiestas in, 43–44, 135–150;
fireworks in, 139; funding for fiestas
in, 142, 145; geographic location of,
5, 6, 10; *gigantonas* for parades in, 19,
100, 138–140; indigenous language not
spoken in, 43–44; Jehovah's Witnesses
in, 44; market in, 155–156, 163, 176;
meaning of name, 11; mestizos in, 135,
143; *misceláneas* (mini-marts) in, 135,
140; neighboring town of, 11; plaza
in, 135; population of, 13, 161, 272n15;
private celebrations in, 45; *quinceaños*
in, 136–138; social organization of, 44;
and St. Francis of Assisi celebration,
135, 138; tourist attraction in, 10; tractor-tire hearth in, xxiv
theft, 67, 161, 221–222, 272n15
tías (aunts), xxii, 208, 253, 269n9
tlapiques (fish tamales), 144, 183–184
tlicuil (hearth), 255–256. See also *clecuil*
(firewood hearth)
tomatoes, xxiii, 76, 128, 194, 195, 201–202,
204
tortillas: blue tortillas, 271n8; for breakfast, 180–181; Christie's participation
in making, 21, 163; *comal* (griddle) for,
xxii, xxiv, 108, 164, 180, 200, 216; Doña
Dolores's cooking of, xxii; Esmeralda's
cooking of, 155, 159–160, 271n1; for
fiestas, 47–48, 54, 102–105; handmade
tortillas for dinner, 270n4; metate for,
xxii, 160, 256–257; *nixtamal* for, 176,
177, 228–229; photograph of cooking
of, 104; for *quinceaños*, 137; sale of
home-cooked tortillas, 216; Señora
Rosa's dislike for making, 182; various
uses of, 222. See also *tortillerías*
tortillerías: complaints about, 162, 217,
229, 236, 272n13; and fiestas, 48, 84,
116, 270n4; *nixtamal* used by, 109;
purchases from, 107, 108, 160, 217,
256, 271n1; reheating of tortillas from,
270n4; rental space for, 111; Señora
Rosa's dislike of, 182
tourism, 10, 47, 87, 90, 92, 269–270n15.
See also fiestas; and specific fiestas